AF541740

Valley of Red Snow

Praise for the book

'It's easy to spot bias in other people, especially those with whom we disagree. But it's not so easy to recognize our own biases. Jitendra Dixit's book is a triumph because it has tried to encompass the voices of several stakeholders in the Kashmir Valley who are "birthing" the "New Kashmir".'

—Mahesh Bhatt, veteran film-maker

'The story of Kashmir has been told time and again by various people. This book is an attempt to objectively narrate the changes in Kashmir through extensive ground reports.'

—Lieutenant General D.S. Hooda,
former Army Commander, Northern Command

'Kashmir is changing for good and this book offers a broad idea of what the Kashmiri Pandits are expecting from "Naya Kashmir".'

—Ashoke Pandit, film-maker and activist

VALLEY OF RED SNOW

KASHMIR BEYOND 370

JITENDRA DIXIT

RUPA

First published by
Rupa Publications India Pvt. Ltd 2022
7/16, Ansari Road, Daryaganj
New Delhi 110002

Sales Centres:

Allahabad Bengaluru Chennai
Hyderabad Jaipur Kathmandu
Kolkata Mumbai

ISBN:978-93-5520-397-7

First impression 2022

10 9 8 7 6 5 4 3 2 1

Printed at Parksons Graphics Pvt. Ltd, Mumbai

To the resilient people of Kashmir, who have endured decades of violence and uncertainty, and to various security forces posted in the Valley, who discharge their duty under the shadow of death.

CONTENTS

PREFACE

'All war is a symptom of man's failure as a thinking animal.'

—John Steinbeck

If you had to personify Kashmir, it would be a tall, good-looking young man with his clothes torn and marks of injury all over his body. Some people offer to heal his injuries, but he is sceptical. In the past, those who have claimed to alleviate his pain have instead aggravated it. Some people claim to be his well-wishers but clash with each other. He is scared, confused, uncertain about his future and in the grip of pessimism. His income has diminished and he needs some peace to restore it.

Working on my journalistic assignments, I have toured Kashmir several times during the past decade and have been able to observe this region closely, one of the world's most conflict-ridden pieces of land. I can relate to Kashmir: I was born and brought up in the locality of Mumbai 400003, often called 'Bombay Number 3'. This area has seen extensive bloodshed in the form of gang wars, communal violence and a terrorist attack. Growing up in such an area piqued my interest in covering crime and conflicts. My journalism career began as a crime reporter covering deadly gang wars between Dawood Ibrahim, Chhota Rajan, Abu Salem and the likes. Just like the Kashmir of the 1990s, Bombay also saw daily bloodbaths.

When I talked to some of my friends and colleagues about writing a book on Kashmir, their concern was that it would not be easy to be objective on this topic. They were so right! When you delve into the goings-on in the Valley, you cannot escape taking sides. And there are not just two sides in this conflict; there are many, and every issue has multiple truths. I have chosen to adopt a purely journalistic approach in my writing. I have put forward my experiences, observations and research in this book, and it is up to you readers to draw inferences from them and judge how far I have succeeded in remaining objective in my narration. I have attempted to provide a space for all voices, although a few people whose views I wanted to include in this book were inaccessible despite my earnest efforts.

In my view, the story of Kashmir needs to be told again and again at different times by different people. It must be told by Kashmiris and non-Kashmiris, by journalists, by bureaucrats, by members of the armed forces, by people working for intelligence agencies. Every story brings out different facets of the complex problem of Kashmir. More voices mean more insights.

The purpose of this book is to present an unprejudiced, non-judgmental and comprehensive story of how Kashmir is changing after one of the biggest events in the history of independent India—the abrogation of Article 370 (of the Indian Constitution) and the bifurcation of Jammu and Kashmir. The book narrates the events that happened in the years preceding the historic event, the immediate situation in the Valley at the time of the abrogation and then goes on to present the voices of various stakeholders in the Valley, with intriguing case studies. The book chronicles some of the momentous events that happened in the Valley in the decade 2011–2021.

The book is written as a travelogue and memoir, supplemented by my interviews with numerous people. I have written this book in an unacademic format, intended for non-Kashmiri readers, Kashmir watchers and enthusiasts of political non-fiction.

Kashmir is always in flux and many developments might have happened while this book was being written and undergoing the lengthy process of getting published and reaching your hands. However, the publisher and I have made efforts to keep the book updated as much as possible.

Writing this book has changed me. It has helped me understand Kashmir better and do away with some stereotypes and myths. It has made me more humane and full of compassion towards the lovely people of Kashmir and also towards members of the army, paramilitary forces and Jammu & Kashmir Police who also are, in a way, victims of the conflict.

On one of my trips, I was driving through the mountains in Kashmir. The snow on the distant hills appeared to be pure white, but the chunks of snow we saw beside the road had turned blackish as a result of absorbing the carbon monoxide emitted by the vehicles passing through. I have heard that often the snow in Kashmir gets another colour—red! Hundreds of times the conflict between militants and the armed forces have coloured the snow with blood. I see Kashmir as the 'Valley of red snow'.

Kashmir is in captivity of its turbulent history. In my view, the real freedom for Kashmir would be to free itself from the baggage of the past—to eliminate or anaesthetize the conflicts, pain and aspirations of the bygone era and look at reality with a fresh perspective. But this is easier said than done. This seems challenging, since a new approach has to be adopted by all stakeholders of the Valley—the common people, the politicians, the security forces and the government—and therein lies the problem. Everybody needs to be on the same page, but the big question is how. I am an optimist and so I hope that someday a thought will prevail across all sections to bury the past and build a peaceful and progressive Kashmir.

Jitendra Dixit
Mumbai, March 2022

PS: The Covid-19 pandemic threw some challenges while this book was being written. It led to the cancellation of my tour to Kashmir in April 2020, as a nationwide lockdown was imposed. Later, in October 2020, I got infected with Covid-19 and was hospitalized. A chunk of this book has been written while in a hospital bed. I was reinfected in April 2021 when this book was about to get completed.

Section I

EVENTS PRECEDING THE ABROGATION OF ARTICLE 370

1

2014: RECORD-BREAKING ELECTIONS

'This finger once used to pull the trigger of an AK-47. Today it pressed the button of an EVM (Electronic Voting Machine),' said a rugged pheran-clad man while showing his index finger inked with blue to my camera. He was Irfan, one of the early voters at the polling booth located on a hillock near Doda town.

It was 25 November 2014, when the first phase of a total of five phases of Jammu and Kashmir (J&K) assembly elections were being conducted. Unlike other states of India, assembly elections were conducted every six years in the state. My assignment to cover the state elections commenced with Doda, which was going to poll that day, along with 14 other districts.

Although Doda district geographically comes under the Jammu region, it had been paralysed by militancy along with the neighbouring district of Kishtwar. It was the second-largest district in the erstwhile state and once saw the highest concentration of militants. The Doda Massacre, an episode in the blood-soaked history of militancy in J&K happened here. In April 2006, heavily armed militants dressed in combat uniforms raided hamlets populated by Hindus and shot dead 22 people, including women and children, and injured 11 others. No major incident has happened in Doda since, although it continues to be one of the most sensitive districts from a security perspective.

As a journalist covering elections in J&K for the first time, I found it strange to see former militants participating in the elections. I had a mixed feeling of fear, suspicion and concern for them. Did they really believe in the Indian democracy or was it just a mask they were wearing? Weren't they scared of reprisal from the militant organizations? Was their praise for the Indian democracy just for my camera or to keep themselves in the good books of the authorities?

EVM Mightier Than the Gun

Forty-one-year-old Irfan had given up militancy 10 years before the Doda Massacre. He was a section commander with the militant organization Al-Jihad from 1991 to 1996. In 1996, he withdrew himself from militancy, lured by the government's surrender policy. Two years later, Irfan married Farida Shehnaaz and is now father to two sons and a daughter. For my camera, he narrated his experience with militancy and why he got disillusioned with it.

'I came in contact with the terrorist organization through people who were organizing public protests on the streets for separation of Jammu and Kashmir. They convinced me that the gun is the only solution to safeguard our interests and self-respect. So I went with them and got training to handle firearms and explosives in Pakistan Occupied Kashmir (PoK). But during my life as a militant, I realized that we were not told the truth. I felt that I and the other youngsters were being used. We were also not treated respectfully by our leaders. At that time, the Indian government came up with a surrender policy. We were promised employment. I surrendered, but things didn't happen as expected. I was given Rs 1,500 per month for a year for survival, but no job was provided. Some of the ex-militants who held higher posts in the militant organization got some benefits,' said Irfan while showing me a photograph of his younger days, in which he is seen proudly holding a Kalashnikov.

After surrendering, 10 of Irfan's batchmates from Al-Jihad were killed by other militant organizations for betraying their cause. Irfan claims that, so far, six attempts to kill him also have been made. He said, 'Some of my other batchmates, after feeling cheated, went back to militancy again.'

Irfan has accepted his sufferings as his fate. Even after the surrender, Irfan's past continued to haunt him. 'In 2001,' said Irfan, 'when my first son was six months old, I was picked up again by the cops on suspicion of my association with Lashkar-e-Taiba (LeT). My wife, Shehnaaz, went to the office of then home minister to plead for his intervention in securing my release, but she was not allowed to meet him. I was released after spending two years behind bars. Today I am earning my livelihood by repairing wristwatches at a small shop in Doda. Apart from my wife and kids, I have old parents to look after. Even after so much suffering, I have faith in the Indian democracy and that is why, today, I pressed the button of the EVM with the same finger that was used to fire an AK-47.'

While covering the elections, I met many others like Irfan who were once fascinated by militancy but surrendered after a few years and were now participating in the elections.

In Doda, I met another former militant named Ahmed, who is now working as a journalist and contributes articles to a local Urdu daily. He joined militancy in 1989 and surrendered in 1996.

'What led you towards militancy?' I asked.

'The general environment after 1987 state assembly elections,' said Ahmed, 'became very hostile towards the Indian government. We were convinced that the elections were rigged. Several protests were being organized, and such protests also facilitated militant groups to recruit their members. They took advantage of people's anger. Being young blood, I, too, got swayed by the circumstances and became a militant.'

'So what made you kick the gun?'

'We were taken to PoK for weapons training. We were asked to attend speeches and sermons by people invited by ISI (Inter-Service Intelligence) to brainwash us for their mission. Once we had an interaction with Prime Minister Nawaz Sharif also. ISI decided everything. They finalized the locations of attacks. Their attitude towards us was very condescending. They tried to dominate us, but they had to face resentment also. They were trying to treat us like slaves, and once we were even on the verge of a violent clash with them.'

Ahmed's life has not been peaceful even after he quit militancy; he has been under the suspicion of security agencies. On my camera,

Ahmed expressed his faith in the Indian democracy. 'I made a mistake of falling into Pakistan's trap,' he said.

But these former militants were not just voters, some of them were contestants too. One of them was Ashfaque Rana, contesting from Surankot seat of Poonch district as a candidate of Panther's Party. Explaining his motive to join militancy, Rana said, 'I had joined militancy in 1989 when there was widespread resentment against the 1987 election results. One of the first leaders to quit mainstream politics and join militancy was Yasin Malik, who was associated with a separatist militant organization named Jammu Kashmir Liberation Front (JKLF). Influenced by the thoughts of Malik, I decided to join the JKLF. I was a a young man of 25 then. I took training and vowed to participate in a violent struggle against the Indian government for securing the separation of Jammu and Kashmir. However, very shortly, I realized that the agenda of the separatist militant organization was very hollow and Pakistan was using the youths of Jammu and Kashmir to pursue its purpose. This made me disillusioned with militancy and so I surrendered.'

Now 45 years old, Ashfaque Rana has completed his postgraduation. 'I have full faith in the Indian democracy. India is a country that gives true freedom to the followers of all religions. I am happy that JKLF also has quit militancy and has come to the table for discussions,' he said.

Participation of surrendered militants in Kashmir's democratic process is not new. In the mid-nineties, such ex-militants became a force in themselves and helped in facilitating the electoral process. Some of them floated their own political parties too. Awami League of Kukka Parray and Awami Conference of Hilal Haider were such parties. Many former militants, like Irfan, Ahmed and Ashfaque, chose to lead a normal life after quitting militancy, while several others collaborated with the establishment to fight insurgency. Such people are known as *ikhwans*.

State of J&K before Elections

In 2012, I visited J&K on a tour arranged by the Konkan Railway to showcase the tallest railway bridge in the world over the Chenab River. Once completed, the bridge would connect Kashmir with the rest of India through railway tracks. Such news of development appeared to be an aberration, since the state had often been in the news for reports of violence, destruction and devastation. I interviewed many villagers residing near the project, and they appeared to be happy because the Konkan Railway was also building several approach roads passing through their villages, thus making life easier for people residing in those tough hilly terrains.

Militancy in Kashmir had also reduced considerably, if not completely, since 2008, and many districts were declared 'militancy free'. The situation was much different from what it was during the nineties and the first decade of the twenty-first century, when militancy was at its peak.

In October 2010, the Government of India set up a group of three interlocutors to review the situation in Kashmir. Their 2012 report made some important recommendations: stone-pelters and political prisoners against whom no serious charges have been framed should be released; the Armed Forces Special Powers Act (AFSPA) and Jammu and Kashmir Public Safety Act (PSA) should be reviewed; a policy for the return of Kashmiri Pandits must be formulated; restrictions on mobile phone networks and internet should be reviewed; an effective system should be set up to monitor that funds provided for central government schemes are properly utilized; and the state government should be allowed a say in the appointment of the governor.[1] This report seemed to suggest that the Government of India was considering options other than a militaristic approach or soft militaristic-cum-political approach to deal with the Kashmir conundrum.

Message from the LoC: 'T' for Terror and 'T' for Turnout

Old villagers cutting dry grass on the field, toddlers playing along the street, little children going to school, women heading home with groceries, grazing cows and sheep—Pakistani bullets spare no one, no discrimination, no hesitation. You may get killed or injured or lose your loved ones, neighbours or pet animals. Welcome to Sabjiyan!

Sabjiyan is a small cluster of houses adjacent to the Line of Control (LoC) near Pakistan Occupied Kashmir (PoK) in the Poonch district of J&K, a place where the Jammu region ends and Kashmir Valley begins. The area has been known as one of the points of infiltration. Adjacent to this village is a hill on top of which the Pakistan Army has built a post. Being at a dominant height, Pakistani soldiers get a bird's-eye view of the village below. They can see the movements of the villagers and shoot them whenever they want to distract the Indian security forces while making infiltration bids.

The second phase of the elections was being held in the constituencies close to the LoC. After covering the voting day at Doda town, I reached this village in Poonch district.

While visiting this area, I could sense the danger and the fear besieging the life of people living there. 'One moment everything seems normal and by the next moment, there could be a spray of bullets from the top and you are dead,' said Darshan Bhati, a journalist of *The Tribune* who accompanied me to Sabjiyan. 'Bullets may come anytime, whether it is broad daylight or the dark of the night,' he said. Just a few weeks before my visit, there was indiscriminate firing from Pakistani soldiers. I met Ashfaque Ali, an old man residing in Sabjiyan. One afternoon, around 2 p.m., while he was cutting dry grass on a field, Pakistanis started firing. There was chaos all over. Everybody started running to dodge the bullets. Ashfaque also tried to escape, but a bullet hit his right arm. Hours later, he was taken to a government hospital in Poonch. He had lost a lot of blood due to the injury, but he was able to survive. A nine-year-old girl was not as fortunate as Ashfaque. She was unable to escape and got killed.

Apart from civilian casualties, there have been numerous incidents where members of security forces were killed. Not very far away from Sabjiyan is a village named Jhallas, which is just opposite the LoC, from where Pakistani army posts are visible. There, I met a postman named Pashorilal alias Mitthu. This 40-year-old man's body was full of marks due to injuries from splinters. There were several in the village like him who survived in spite of being hit by Pakistani bullets and splinters and bore similar marks on their bodies. There were numerous houses in this village whose walls facing PoK had marks of bullets and splinters. Since 1 October 2014, there had been several instances of ceasefire violations by Pakistanis, in which eight people were killed and 94 injured, including 13 security personnel.

Such villages along the 725 kilometre-long LoC have had a long history of losing lives to Pakistani bullets. Many have migrated to safer areas. In 2003, there was a ceasefire agreement between the Indian and Pakistani governments wherein it was mutually decided that security forces of both countries would keep their artillery a few kilometres away from the LoC. This came as a great relief for these villagers, and they were able to sleep fearlessly. However, normalcy across the LoC was short-lived. Ceasefire violations started again.

If you look at the map of J&K, you will notice that except in the eastern direction, Poonch town is surrounded by PoK. At most locations, Pakistani forces are at dominant heights, while Indian forces have the advantage in some. Paresh Kumar, a resident of Poonch, said, 'Pakistanis start firing on our villages from their positions at a height. Indian soldiers also retaliate by firing from those posts where they are at an advantage.'

In these conditions, the record turnout of 70 per cent of voters in the first phase didn't go down well with the militant organizations.[2] They attempted to disrupt the next phase in the bordering areas. An infiltration attempt was made at Arnia near Jammu, which was foiled by the Indian security forces, and the terrorists allegedly intending to enter were eliminated in an encounter. The turnout of the second phase also saw around 71 per cent of voters.[3] Long queues were seen especially outside polling centres of villages that directly fell within the range of rogue Pakistani bullets. Uri, too, saw a large turnout in the third phase of the elections.

Mission 44+ and Article 370

The polling phases were preceded by high-voltage and aggressive campaigning by all the participating political parties. Four major political parties were contesting elections independently this time, unlike in the past when they allied with each other. Mission 44+ was the title of the Bharatiya Janata Party's (BJP) electoral campaign—44 was the number required to form a government in the assembly of 87 members. All parties aspired to attain this figure on their own so that they wouldn't have to form a post-poll alliance to form the government.

One word that could define the BJP's mood during the elections is 'sanguinity'. The party was on cloud nine due to recent electoral victories that year. In the Centre, the BJP returned to power with a good number of seats after 10 years, and it had won in the Maharashtra and Haryana assembly elections too. The BJP had never been in power in J&K. Its best-ever performance was in 2008, when it managed to win 11 seats. The hike in the number of seats was largely attributed to the 'Amarnath Land Row', which created a rift based on religion between Hindu and Muslim communities. However, this time, the BJP intended to make history. The slogan for the party's campaign in the state was 'Mission 44+'. The BJP leadership's confidence was boosted with the induction of stalwarts from the rival parties, such as Lal Singh, a Congressman and former Member of Parliament (MP), the National Conference (NC) leader Ajat Shatru Singh's son and Indian National Congress (Congress) leader Karan Singh.

The Modi Factor

The biggest source of optimism for the BJP in J&K elections came from the 'Modi Factor'. All the victories, whether in parliamentary elections or state assembly elections that year, were attributed to the

'Modi Wave'. Veteran journalist Rajdeep Sardesai described Modi's performance in the Lok Sabha results saying, 'Never before in the history of Indian elections has one leader exercised such complete dominance over voter mind space.'[4] Prime Minister Narendra Modi had aggressively campaigned in those elections and he had similar plans for J&K elections. Kashmir, with its complex politics, was not new for Modi. As a party functionary, he had worked in the state for almost a year and played a role in expanding the party. In 1992, when the BJP leader Murli Manohar Joshi had undertaken a rath yatra to hoist a flag at Srinagar's Lal Chowk, the role of Modi was pivotal in organizing the event.[5] During the 1990s, Modi played a key role in enrolling Muslims into the party. The rigging of the 1987 assembly elections led to the aggravation of militancy in the state and the Congress was seen as the culprit. Modi attempted to capitalize on the anti-Congress sentiments and augment membership numbers of the BJP in Kashmir. In 1998, when the BJP came to power in the Centre, Modi was made party incharge of J&K.[6]

For the 2014 elections, Modi toured four times in different parts of the state. I attended his first rally at Kishtwar in the Jammu region on 22 November. Although it was late November, the afternoon heat corresponded with the political climate of the state. Thousands of people who came in from neighbouring hamlets and towns eagerly awaited the PM's address. As soon as the air force helicopters' sound was heard, BJP workers began chanting 'Modi! Modi! Modi!' Few minutes after the engine switched off, Modi appeared on stage.

'People wonder why Modi has so much affection for Kashmir,' he began in his usual style of addressing himself in the third person. 'I have great affection for Kashmir. The work which Atal Bihari Vajpayee initiated, I have to complete that. Jamhuriyat, Insaniyat, Kashmiriyat—these words of Atalji have found space in the hearts of Kashmiri youth. Now it is possible to realize their dreams. In the last 10 years, Kashmir has been brought to what condition. I want to talk about development.'

After talking about his plans for the development of the state, Modi focused his speech on the BJP's political opponents.

'Who destroyed the state? To whom have you handed over this state? Will only two families rule this Kashmir? Do the youth of this place shine? Other families don't have the strength? Why have you mortgaged this state to these two families?' he asked the crowd. Although he didn't name them, it was obvious that Modi was referring to the families of Farooq Abdullah and Mufti Mohammad Sayeed, who have been ruling the state for decades.

Furthering his verbal attack on them, he continued, 'Both families are hand in glove. They have a tacit understanding and loot people turn by turn.'

He ended his speech by saying that he wanted to rebuild Kashmir, whose beauty would once again attract the world and film-makers would once again commence their shoots in the Valley.

Modi concluded his election campaign with a rally at Srinagar's Sher-e-Kashmir Stadium. In almost in all his rallies, Modi had referred to the Kutch district of Gujarat. He spoke about how Kutch was seen as a desert where people were reluctant to go due to its harsh topography and how he, as the chief minister (CM) of Gujarat, had transformed it into the fastest developing district of India. Modi said that he would bring the kind of development in Kashmir that had been witnessed in Kutch. He reiterated his slogan of '*Sabka Saath, Sabka Vikas*' and assured everyone that there would be no discrimination against anybody if his party came to power.

This rally was significant not for what Modi said but for the fact that after the outbreak of militancy in Kashmir, he was the first PM to address such a gathering in the heart of Srinagar. It was Modi's volition to address a rally in Srinagar that the BJP proudly propagated. Srinagar witnessed unprecedented security arrangements that day.

Omar Abdullah, then chief minister of the state, tweeted that Sajad Lone, a leader of People's Conference, had sent 80 vehicle-loads of supporters from Kupwara to help his 'big brother' make up the numbers.[7] This was a sardonic comment on Lone, who called Modi his elder brother a few days earlier. Lone denied Omar's charge that he helped Modi.

In the elections, the BJP had fielded over 70 candidates, out of which 32 were Muslims, chosen with tact to shrug off BJP's communal image. Out of the 32 Muslim candidates, 25 were in Kashmir Valley, six in Jammu and one in Ladakh. Four Kashmiri Pandits and a Sikh were also given tickets in the Valley.[8]

One of the most-discussed names during the elections was of Dr Hina Bhat, a young dentist who contested as a BJP candidate from Srinagar's Amirakadal constituency. She came into the limelight because of the juxtaposition—a Kashmiri Muslim woman fielded by a Hindu nationalist party. She was the BJP's lone Muslim face in Srinagar. Before getting her candidature, Bhat was the vice president of the party's women's wing in the state.

'There is no plan of the BJP to scrap 370. Till now Modi ji has just said there would be discussion and debate on the issue,' she told me during an interview in December 2014.

Though the abrogation of Article 370 was one of the prime issues for the BJP since its formation, one significant change was noticed during the campaign: the party completely eschewed mentioning the issue of abrogation. Considering the dynamics of politics in J&K and the sensitivities of voters in the state, the BJP thought it prudent to avoid mentioning Article 370 in its election manifesto. Hardly a year ago, in December 2013, Modi had led to an uproar when he said that there must be a debate on Article 370.[9] His statement ruffled separatists and political parties, like the People's Democratic Party (PDP) and the NC, who derided him. Neither Modi nor any of BJP's other senior leaders spoke about Article 370 during the campaign, although it was very much on the party's agenda till a few months ago during the Lok Sabha polls.

BJP's Opponents

Article 370, though missing from the BJP manifesto, was very much present in those of its political rivals, the NC and PDP—they vowed to ensure that the Article not be scrapped.

The manifesto of the NC released on 27 November read, 'This Article is the foundation on which the relationship of J&K with the rest of India is based. Article 370 cannot be abrogated. It cannot be tampered with.'[10] The manifesto also reiterated the demand to revoke the AFSPA and said that the state machinery was capable of dealing with any disturbance after its revocation.

The next day, the PDP also released its election manifesto, which read, 'The special status enshrined in Article 370 is required to empower the people of J&K and help deal with issues of identity, borders and governance.'[11] The manifesto also encompassed issues of corruption, economy and effective governance.

The manifesto of the Congress, released by senior party leaders Ghulam Nabi Azad and Saifuddin Soz, was silent on Article 370 like its rival, the BJP. The manifesto promised equitable development in three regions of the state—Jammu, Kashmir and Ladakh—and two regional councils, decentralization and facilitation of smooth cross-LoC travel.

One of the biggest faces during the electoral campaign was Omar Abdullah, who was incumbent as CM at the time of the elections. He is one of the early politicians from J&K who is very active on social media and frequently uses Twitter to articulate his views and target his opponents.

His first big success in state politics came in 2008, when the NC fought for the legislative assembly elections under his leadership. Although the party failed to secure a majority in the house, the NC emerged as the single-largest party, winning 28 seats. He brokered an alliance with the Congress, which had won 17 seats and was a coalition partner in the previous government.[12] His father and former CM, Farooq Abdullah, refused to accept the chief ministership and said, 'The job requires energy of a young man.' On his recommendation, the party nominated Omar as the CM candidate.[13]

Apart from anti-incumbency, which was aggravated due to the devastating floods two months before the polls, Omar Abdullah had to face multiple enemies. He had to fight friend turned foe, the Congress, the growing clout of the PDP and the ambitious BJP. Knowing that his return as CM was not easy, Omar indefatigably campaigned throughout the state. He was seen as the only crowd-pulling face from the NC.

Another regional party, the PDP, had high hopes for this election. After 11 years, the party was striving to see its leader on the CM's chair. The last CM from the PDP was Mufti Mohammad Sayeed. He became CM after the 2002 assembly elections, when the PDP and Congress agreed on sharing the CM's chair for three years each. Sayeed got the first chance and, in 2005, vacated the chair for Ghulam Nabi Azad of the Congress. The spirit of the PDP was also buoyed by constant electoral advancements since the party was founded in 1999.[14] The PDP made a stunning performance in the 2014 Lok Sabha elections, in which it won three out of six seats in the state, all from the Kashmir Valley. This electoral victory just a few months before the assembly elections was a big confidence booster for the party.[15] The most important faces during the electoral campaign of the PDP were the father–daughter duo, octogenarian Mufti Mohammad Sayeed and Mehbooba Mufti.

During his election rallies, Sayeed urged the crowd to 'change the fate as well as the history of Jammu and Kashmir.' In one of the public meetings, he compared himself with Modi and said, 'What Narendra Modi has done for Gujarat, my party has done for Jammu and Kashmir.' He promised that, if voted to power, his party would protect the 'ijjat' (honour) of the people and reminded them that when he was in the government in 2002, the arrests of young people by special security forces were stopped.[16]

Sayeed's daughter, Mehbooba Mufti, fiercely attacked the BJP and Modi in her rallies. Responding to Modi's charge of nepotism, she alleged that 'it seems the Prime Minister (Modi) has serious gaps in his knowledge about Jammu and Kashmir.'[17] She claimed that J&K and the rest of the country were aware of her integrity and credentials. Referring to her father's three-year tenure as the state's CM, Mehbooba said, 'The three years that Mufti Mohammad Sayeed-led coalition served the state are still remembered as a reference point for good governance and political maturity which changed the scenario not just in Jammu and Kashmir but in the entire region.'[18]

The Congress, which had been in power in the state for the past

12 years, first by aligning with the PDP and then with the NC, was fighting the elections independently. The prime face of the Congress party in the campaign was Ghulam Nabi Azad. He was a member of the Rajya Sabha and Leader of Opposition in the house. He had kept out of state politics since he resigned as the CM in 2008. However, the Congress realized that it had no credible or crowd-pulling face in the state except for him and the state Congress chief Saifuddin Soz.

Born in Bhalesa village of Doda district in the Jammu region, Azad was seen as having acceptability in the Valley too. He spearheaded the Congress campaign in the 2002 assembly elections.[19] In alliance with the PDP, the Congress was able to chair its first chief minister after a gap of 34 years in 2005.[20] Azad had held many key portfolios in P.V. Narsimha Rao's and Manmohan Singh's cabinets, which included ministries like Law, Justice, Parliamentary Affairs, Civil Aviation and so on.[21]

I met Azad in a village near Doda town where he was campaigning in an open jeep. While I interviewed him, he waved to the crowd of party workers gathered beside the road. He told me that if the Congress returned to power, it would make the Chenab Valley a modern and progressive region. 'It will be a model region of the state,' he said.[22] In his public speech, Azad stressed that the Congress party stood for '*Khushaal Jammu and Kashmir*' (Happy J&K) and aimed at the all-round development of the state.

The faction of the state Congress headed by Saifuddin Soz presented a different picture from Azad's optimism. While Soz said to journalists, 'You will be surprised to see the performance of Congress in the Valley,'[23] his earlier statements before the campaign began indicated that the party was lacking confidence. The Congress fought the 2002 and 2008 elections aiming to form the government on its own, but Soz candidly said that the next government would be a coalition and no government would be formed without support from the Congress. This talk of 'coalition' suggested that the Congress had already conceded defeat. However, Soz now claimed that the Congress would emerge as the single-largest party.

The Congress president, Sonia Gandhi, and vice president, Rahul

Gandhi, were the star campaigners for the party from the central leadership. In her rallies, Sonia Gandhi urged voters to maintain the 'secular character of the state' by voting for the Congress. In a rally at Anantnag, she said, 'I know we could not fulfill all the pro-people programmes like the food security bill and land compensation bill because of coalition compulsions during the last six years. But we have remained in the forefront of helping the people of Kashmir in times of need.'[24]

Like his mother, Rahul Gandhi, too, in his rallies, emphasized that coalition politics didn't allow his party to deliver. He lauded the Congress-led UPA government for creating an atmosphere of peace in Kashmir. Gandhi said that his party was serious about implementing its programme of connectivity in the state, which would help Kashmiris reach markets outside J&K.[25]

A relatively smaller but much talked about player in the fray was Sajad Lone's People's Conference. Sajad is the son of the party's founder Abdul Ghani Lone, who was assassinated during an election rally in 2002. People's Conference was seen as an ally of the BJP. After meeting Modi a month before the elections, he said, 'The PM is a great human being. I was pleasantly surprised to see his down-to-earth personality, his vision about bringing in investments into the state.'[26] His party was contesting in 12 seats, and he was a candidate from the Handwara seat. The BJP didn't field a candidate against him.[27]

Motivations for Voters

Late Syed Ali Shah Geelani, who was then an octogenarian, had earned the sobriquet of 'Hartal Man of Kashmir' due to his frequent calling of strikes and boycott of various elections. Geelani led the hardline wing of the Hurriyat Conference and had been calling for the boycott of elections since 1996. True to his image, on 29 October, he gave a call to boycott the assembly elections too. But this time his call didn't seem to have much effect.

What made voters both in Jammu and Kashmir Valley come

out to vote in such large numbers? I posed this question to several political commentators and journalists. Veteran journalist Bashir Manzar told me, 'The trend was improving since 2002. Till 2002, there was a monopoly of the NC in the state political parties and the Congress was a national party. The PDP triggered a competition. Apart from that, the militant movement slowed down, which facilitated the strengthening of the ground network of mainstream political parties. Relations between India and Pakistan were relatively better. There were talks between Manmohan–Musharaf and Vajpayee–Musharaf.'

Talking specifically about the 2014 polls, Manzar said, 'An anti-establishment factor was also there. People had high hopes from Omar Abdullah, which were not fulfilled. For the first time after 1947, Mufti Mohammad Sayeed had raised the bar of governance (during his term as CM of the state in 2002–2005), which the NC–Congress alliance was not able to attain.'

I spoke to Anuradha Bhasin, editor of *Kashmir Times*, who concurred with the views of Manzar. 'High turnout during 2014 elections was linked with the peace process. People were fed up with gun culture. There was a hope for dialogue,' she said.

As per Bhasin, while assessing high turnout, one must be clear that what pulled out the voters were daily issues and it was not related to the conflict. 'A Hindu government coming at the Centre raised alarm bells for the Muslim majority in Kashmir. One of the prime motivations for voters in the Valley was to keep the BJP out,' she said.

My colleague Asif Qureshi, who heads the Srinagar bureau of ABP Network, told me that the devastating floods that happened a few weeks before the elections contributed to the anti-incumbency factor and rallied people to come out to vote. Apart from the floods, Asif said that the PDP came up with a strong narrative of keeping the BJP out of power. 'After every election, there is an attempt to come up with a narrative that faith in democracy has been restored. I would say that the 2014 elections were largely influenced only by local issues related to administration. Militants also didn't disrupt them, which led to its success,' he said.

A Fractured Mandate

I was visiting Kashmir for the first time in winter. I got an opportunity to travel through the famous Mughal Road while reaching Srinagar from Poonch. It is an 84-kilometre-long ancient route and was widely used during the Mughal era. The scenic road is also one of the routes that connect the Jammu region to the Kashmir Valley. I was enthralled to see the snow-laced mountains of Pir Panjal and halted for a few minutes at Peer ki Gali, the highest point on the road at 11,450 feet, to click some pictures. The road is often shut during winters due to heavy snowfall, when manoeuvring vehicles becomes hazardous. However, fortunately for me, Mughal Road was still drivable when I was travelling in the region. I reached Srinagar a day before the counting date, on 23 December. The hotel I checked into was bang opposite the Dal Lake. Those were some of the extreme cold days of the season, which Kashmiris call *Chilai Kalan*.

The next morning, the temperature was -2 degree Celsius. The frozen water of Dal was an antithesis of the hot political climate in Kashmir. Everyone was keen to know what had been stored in the EVMs. Most of the political pundits had predicted a hung assembly. There were more securitymen at the Sher-e-Kashmir International Convention Complex (SKICC) than the polling staff, the party representatives and the media.

Like in Srinagar, most of the counting centres were in district headquarters. Out of a total 87 assembly seats, 46 were in Kashmir Valley, 37 in the Jammu region and four in Ladakh. Journalists were not allowed in the counting hall, but arrangements had been made for them at a separate media centre. Only the candidates and one of their agents were given access to observe the counting process. The total number of candidates across the state was 821, and over 10,000 polling booths were set up for over 77 lakh voters to exercise their democratic right.

The counting of votes began shortly after 8 a.m., and by 10.30

a.m., the trends were getting clear. It was turning out to be a hung assembly, as predicted. The 'star' at the counting centre was Hina Bhat, and all the news channels were struggling to get her live or do a one-on-one interview with her. She obliged everybody. By the time I got my share of her time, it became obvious that she was going to lose. Bhat was trailing on number three, and the PDP's candidate Altaf Bukhari was heading towards victory. At that time, the trend indicated that the BJP was emerging as the single-largest party with 31 seats.

'Although your party is leading on 31 seats, still Mission 44+ doesn't seem to be accomplished?' I asked her.

'The counting is still on. Just wait and see what happens. The counting has just started. Results are yet to come,' she answered with a confident smile.

'But, so far, the seats where the BJP is leading are from the Jammu region. The BJP seems to have become just a party of Jammu...'

'It is not at all like that. I am saying it again. Just wait for the results. When all results have come, we are going to form the government,' she replied, a bit irritated by my question.

'The trends indicate that there will be a hung assembly. In such a scenario, is the BJP open for alliance with other parties for government formation?'

'Let us see who gets what, then my party will decide,' she said and quickly switched to another TV channel reporter who was waiting for me to finish.

The conclusion of the counting by evening brought bad news for Hina Bhat but good news for her party. Altaf Bukhari of the PDP (who later founded another party) won the Amirakadal seat from which Bhat had contested. However, as the counting progressed, the BJP slid down to being the second-largest party and the PDP, with 28 seats, became the single-largest party in the state. Although the BJP failed to accomplish its Mission 44+, it secured 25 seats, which was the highest number of seats the party had won since it started contesting elections in the state. NC was on number three, with 15 seats, and the Congress got the lowest number, with 12 seats. Others won seven seats, including two seats of Sajad Lone's People's Conference.[28] So, no one party could form the government without an alliance.

Journalists approached Omar Abdullah and asked for his reaction to the results, which signalled that he had to leave the CM's chair. Omar had contested from two seats, viz. Sonwar and Beerwah. He won from Beerwah but lost the Sonwar seat to PDP's Ashraf Mir.[29] 'There was anti-incumbency against the NC. We also had to suffer due to the floods. I knew that Sonwar seat was not easy to win. So far no offer for the alliance has come and nor we are looking for any such offer. Let us digest the results. We are ready to play the role of a good opposition for the next six years,' he said.[30] Later, Abdullah gave me a detailed, one-on-one interview at his Gupkar Road residence.

'Are you open to supporting the PDP for government formation? What is your stand on the current scenario of a hung assembly?' I asked him.

'I don't have any stand. It is not my responsibility to form the government. I have 15 MLAs (Member of Legislative Assembly) of my own and some independent MLAs whom we have helped. I think they, too, will be with us. In such a scenario, first responsibility is of the PDP and the BJP. They should see if they are capable of forming the government or not. Currently, I am not talking to anybody nor knocking on anybody's door. If we have to sit in the opposition for six years, we will do that happily.'

'But are you open to supporting the PDP?' I asked.

'Many things are possible in politics. If Lalu and Nitish can come together, this, too, could be possible, but I will not knock on anybody's door. Let us see what happens,' he said, taking a deep breath.

'Okay. Your party has dropped to number three in these elections. What is the cause of this downfall?'

'I haven't spoken to my candidates yet. I will speak to them and find out, but there is no one reason. Different areas have different reasons. In Jammu, we had to face the Modi wave but still we won two seats there. In south Kashmir, we snatched two–three seats from the PDP, but in north Kashmir, we lost due to Sajad Lone.'

'Do you regret that you didn't fight the election in alliance with the Congress?'

'No regrets at all. We allied with Congress for parliamentary elections and were cheated. They didn't transfer votes to us. But it is good. The people who backstabbed us themselves have lost. I am satisfied that they are not standing anywhere today.'

'Do you see any such possibility where, to stop the BJP, the other three parties could come together?'

'No. I will not cook any such khichri. PDP has said that the BJP is not untouchable. This might be an idea of the Congress, but I am not interested.'

The PDP leader Mehbooba Mufti, in a press conference, thanked the people of the state for making her party number one in the elections. However, her words indicated that she was not in a hurry to form the government. 'We will not cobble together a government by hook or crook. It will take time to explore possibilities and the formation of the government to meet the people's expectations and good governance. It will be difficult to say when it will materialize,' she said.[31]

For the BJP, it was a day of double delight. The party got full majority in the Jharkhand assembly elections, which were conducted along with J&K. In a press conference at Delhi, an elated party president Amit Shah said, 'In Jammu and Kashmir, we have bettered our position to emerge as a relevant political force. In real terms, the abhiyan of Congress 'Mukt Bharat Abhiyan' is moving ahead.'[32]

The Congress was the worst performer among the big four parties but was hopeful that the PDP would invite it for an alliance. Since the Congress had allied with the PDP in the past, the leaders believed that the party would get one more chance to be back in power. Ghulam Nabi Azad said, 'Call has to be taken by the PDP whether they have to go with secular forces or communal forces. BJP and Congress can never go together. They (the PDP) know what is good for them.'[33]

Shocking Alliance of Nemeses

On 24 December, Omar Abdullah resigned as the CM, but the governor asked him to continue till the next government was formed.[34] The days following election results led me and other journalists to shuttle between the offices of various political parties or residences of their leaders. The next big news to come was who allies with whom to form the government. There was uncertainty that led to speculations. Would the BJP go with the NC? Since Omar Abdullah had been part of the National Democratic Alliance (NDA) in the past, considering the stalemate, it would not be problematic for both parties to come together again. Omar Abdullah had been a minister in Atal Bihari Vajpayee's cabinet, it was argued. Some felt that the BJP and the NC had no choice but to ally, since the ideologies and agendas of the PDP and the BJP were poles apart, and there was no possibility of them coming together. Another set of political commentators predicted that there could be a NC+PDP+Congress alliance to keep the BJP away from power.[35]

Amidst such talks, unexpectedly, unofficial parleys between the PDP and the BJP began. Both the BJP and the PDP hinted that an alliance could be possible if controversial issues were kept aside. The talks gained momentum by the second week of January; however, due to tough bargaining from both sides, no decision could be reached. Meanwhile, on 9 January 2015, President's Rule was imposed in the state, as no party or group of parties was able to form a government.

What stalled the talks between the two parties were issues like Article 370, AFSPA, resuming of talks with Pakistan and rotation of the CM's chair. The BJP wanted the chair to be rotated between the two parties for three–three years, but that wasn't acceptable to the PDP. The BJP also wanted to induct Sajad Lone into the cabinet—which portfolio he should be given was another issue of contention.

Finally, after a series of parleys between top leaders of both parties stretching upto three months, the stalemate ended on 24 February 2015. After meeting BJP party president Amit Shah for around 45 minutes in Delhi, Mehbooba Mufti made a formal announcement that her party was ready to form a government in alliance with the BJP. 'We have reached a consensus. Keeping in mind the development and aspirations of the people of Jammu and Kashmir, we have formulated an agenda of alliance between the BJP and the PDP,' Mehbooba told journalists.[36] Amit Shah said, 'I am happy that all obstacles in government formation have almost been removed.'[37] A picture of Amit Shah presenting a shawl to Mehbooba Mufti was released, depicting bonhomie between the two parties.

A week after the formal announcement, a common minimum programme (CMP) of the alliance was released. The CMP was projected as a roadmap to transform the state and indicated that peace would be pursued through dialogue.

An important highlight of the CMP was a resolve to follow the policy of '*Insaniyat, Kashmiriat, Jamhooriyat*'. The slogan was used by the earlier NDA government in the Centre led by Vajpayee. The CMP said that the government would facilitate and initiate dialogue with all the internal stakeholders irrespective of their political ideologies. This implied talks with the separatist All Parties Hurriyat Conference (APHC) also.

It was acknowledged that to meet the economic and political objectives of the state, there was a need to create an environment of peace, certainty and stability. The controversial AFSPA also found a place in the CMP. It was decided that the disturbed areas would be de-notified and would be considered by the central government for a review of enforcement of the AFSPA.

Other significant highlights of the CMP included settlement plans for PoK and West Pakistan refugees, and the promise of a smart, corruption-free and transparent government.

Both the parties agreed to maintain status quo on the issue of Article 370. It was also decided that the CM would be from the PDP and would continue for a complete term of six years, but there would be a deputy CM from the BJP.

Finally, on 1 March 2015, Mufti Mohammad Sayeed took oath as CM of J&K for the second time in his political career, after a gap of 12 years. A total of 25 MLAs were sworn in as ministers in the ceremony—13 MLAs, including Sayeed, were sworn in from the PDP, whereas 12 MLAs were from the BJP quota. Sajad Lone was sworn in from the BJP's list.[38]

Dr Nirmal Singh of the BJP was announced as deputy CM of the state. Dr Singh came from an RSS (Rashtriya Swayamsevak Sangh) background and had served as a pracharak[39] for its student's wing, Akhil Bhartiya Vidyarthi Parishad (ABVP). He played a key role in strengthening the BJP in Jammu region.

Two people who were the architects of the government were Haseeb Drabu, economist and senior leader of the PDP, and Ram Madhav of the BJP. Drabu enjoyed a good rapport with Madhav and held several negotiation meetings with him, leading up to the formation of the government. There were around 15 negotiation meetings between Drabu and Madhav.[40]

The formation of the PDP–BJP government is seen as a landmark development in the political history of modern India. It was the first time a Hindu nationalist government attained power in J&K. Many political pundits were flabbergasted to see a hardliner party joining hands with a party with a soft corner for separatists and in favour of talks with Pakistan over the Kashmir issue. The two parties had fiercely targeted each other during the election campaign, but all that was forgotten. The alliance once again enunciated that when it comes to achieving power, ideologies become redundant and the number game takes over. In realpolitik, if ideology doesn't become the facilitator in accomplishing that end, then it is not a constraint either.

Why Did the RSS Accept the Alliance?

How did the RSS approve an alliance of the BJP with a party that is against the abrogation of Article 370 and has a soft corner for separatists? It was seen as a paradox that an RSS pracharak, Ram Madhav, was playing a crucial role in cementing the alliance on behalf of the BJP.

The information available in the public domain tells us that the RSS reluctantly agreed to the alliance with the PDP, knowing that it would be short-lived. However, the consent of the RSS for the alliance signifies an attempt to modify or broaden certain fundamental policies of the organization. The RSS took the alliance as an opportunity to get India's only Muslim majority state close to the Indian union and project its inclusive image before upwardly mobile social groups. By this, the RSS intended to mitigate the alienation of Kashmiri Muslims. Since the 1970s, the RSS has been running programmes with the objective of cultural integration of Muslims, Christians and others who do not follow Hinduism as a religion. The RSS had its presence in Kashmir through its Muslim Rashtriya Manch (MRM) unit. A Kashmiri pracharak had been assigned the task of persuading Muslims to refrain from eating beef, practise yoga and accept Lord Rama as a cultural icon.[41]

One of the justifications for the coalition was the expansion of the definition of the word 'Hindu', which was not limited to a member of a particular religious community. The RSS wanted to make 'Hindu' synonymous with 'citizen of India'. This enlarged definition was distinct from the past notion based on cultural nationalism and territorial nationalism, and applied to all people living in India regardless of their religious beliefs.[42]

Bitterness and Break-up

There was no honeymoon period for the alliance government. Problems began cropping up within hours of Mufti Mohammad Sayeed's swearing-in as the CM. Sajad Lone was given charge of the Science and Technology and the Animal Husbandry ministries, which he was not willing to hold. His close aides circulated that he was eyeing more powerful ministries like Tourism or Forest.

The first sign of discord between the PDP and the BJP appeared just a week later. The cause was the release of separatist leader Masarat Alam from jail on 7 March. Alam, a functionary of the APHC, was accused of instigating stone-pelting and causing the death of several youngsters in 2010. He was incarcerated under the stringent PSA. He was released when CM Sayeed ordered the release of political prisoners, and this led to a furore amongst right-wing groups. Demonstrations were held in Jammu. The release of a separatist leader by a government of which the BJP was a part didn't match with its patriotic-nationalistic image. The pressure compelled the BJP to react. Home Minister Rajnath Singh sought an explanation from the J&K government over Alam's release. After being questioned by the Opposition, on 9 March, PM Modi said in his speech at the Parliament that the decision to release Alam was taken without the Centre's consent. 'I also lend my voice to the outrage on the release of the separatist... this is not one party's outrage, it is the nation's outrage,' he said.[43]

The alliance government faced a major setback when Mufti Mohammed Sayeed died due to multi-organ failure on 7 January 2016. During his two years as CM, contentious issues were sorted out amicably by the two parties. After his death, the reins of power came into the hands of his daughter Mehbooba Mufti. She took around three months to decide on succeeding her father on the CM's chair, possibly in an effort to extract certain concessions from the Centre. However, the BJP wasn't willing to deviate from the CMP finalized with her father. Mehbooba was an MP from the Anantanag Lok Sabha constituency at the time of her swearing-in as CM on 5 April. The death of Mufti Mohammad Sayeed and the ascendancy of Mehbooba Mufti was seen as one of the major causes for the bitterness between the two alliance partners.

After becoming the CM, Mehbooba took many controversial decisions unilaterally, such as her decision to pardon 4,500 first-time stone-pelters,[44] providing grants to religious organizations like Ahle-Hadees and refusing to relocate the Bakarwal community, which irked the BJP. Just three months later, in July 2016, the young militant Burhan Wani was killed in an encounter by security forces. This led to widespread violence in the Valley and also led to the emergence of a new breed of stone-pelters who were more dangerous and organized than the ones in the past. Mehbooba's sympathetic attitude towards such stone-pelters pinched the BJP.

Attacks by militants on security forces also increased after

Wani's death, and a large number of youngsters joined militancy. Although incidents of violence were on the rise in the Valley, Mehbooba Mufti was seen as adopting a soft approach towards the insurgents. In May 2018, she urged the Centre to announce a unilateral ceasefire, saying that it was necessary for the peaceful passing of the Amarnath Yatra and Ramzan Eid. Mehbooba believed that such a reconciliatory approach would help in bringing peace and ordered the release of 115 non-serious offenders. Heeding her request, a ceasefire was implemented by the security forces. Cordoning of suspicious localities and search operations were suspended with a view that people should not be inconvenienced. However, the central government claimed that the implementation of a ceasefire turned out to be counterproductive. During Ramzan, 22 cases of grenade attack and 23 cases of indiscriminate firing by the insurgents were reported. There were also seven cases of attacks on civilians.[45]

While there were talks of extending the ceasefire, respected Kashmiri journalist Shujaat Bukhari was killed on 14 June 2018, which was the eve of Eid. Shortly after Bukhari's killing, PM Modi chaired a meeting in which Home Minister Rajnath Singh, National Security Adviser Ajit Doval and then Indian Army chief Bipin Rawat were present.[46] It was decided that the ceasefire would not be continued.

A senior BJP functionary told me that the situation in Kashmir was getting worse and it was damaging the prospects of the BJP for the next Lok Sabha elections. There was a general opinion in the party that the experiment of aligning with the PDP had failed and it would be imprudent to continue in the government. The BJP could no longer be seen as a party sharing power with somebody who had a soft corner for separatists, militants and stone-pelters, and opposed the abrogation of Article 370. There was a feeling among the BJP functionaries that Mehbooba Mufti was giving unfair importance to the Kashmir region and other regions of the state, like Jammu, were being ignored, where the BJP had a stronghold.

Earlier that year, in January, the rape and murder of a girl from the nomadic Bakarwal community in Kathua rocked the state. The case took a political and communal twist. The Kathua case was another matter of discord between the two parties.

In March, in a statement at a Delhi event, Finance Minister Haseeb Drabu, stating that Kashmir was a social issue and not a political one, created an outrage not only within the PDP, to which he belonged, but also in other parties like the NC. Although Drabu claimed that he was misquoted, Mehbooba had made up her mind to drop her late father's confidante and architect of the PDP–BJP alliance from her cabinet. A few months later, Drabu resigned from the party.[47]

Drabu had a good rapport with the BJP leaders, especially with Ram Madhav. He was a good communicator and negotiator, and intervened whenever issues went out of hand. After he was sacked, there was no leader in the PDP with such skills.

Amidst talks of the coalition falling apart, Ram Madhav told the media that there was no rift between the two parties and removal of Drabu from the cabinet was an internal matter of the PDP.[48]

However, the RSS–BJP camp was increasingly feeling that the alliance with the PDP was turning out to be a miscalculation. The RSS was getting inputs from its information-gathering network that the Hindu population of Jammu was unhappy with the coalition government and so continuing in the government would be detrimental for the prospects of the BJP in J&K.

Three months later, on 19 June, Ram Madhav announced that the BJP had pulled out of the alliance. Justifying the break-up, he said, 'Terrorism, violence and radicalization have risen and fundamental rights and freedom of speech are in danger in the Valley.'[49] According to Madhav, keeping the larger national interest in mind and to solve the situation in Kashmir, it was decided to hand over the reins of the state to the governor.

After withdrawal from the government, Ram Madhav, in an interview, said, 'Had he (Mufti Mohammad Sayeed) lived longer, probably we would have succeeded in taking it forward.'[50]

Following the development, the PDP also called a meeting of its senior leaders. Shortly thereafter, Mehbooba Mufti went to

Governor N.N. Vohra and tendered her resignation. 'The alliance had a bigger motive. I have submitted my resignation to the Governor and told him that we are not looking for any other alliance,' she said.[51] Omar Abdullah requested the governor to take the reins of the state, as no party had the mandate to rule the state, but he urged that fresh elections should be organized soon. As no party or alliance approached the governor to stake a claim for the government formation, the state went under Governor's Rule, a concept unique to J&K, which was followed by the President's Rule six months later, under the provisions of Article 356 of the Indian Constitution.

A few months later, in an interview with a private news channel, PM Modi justified his party's decision to ally with the PDP and withdraw from the alliance four years later. He called the alliance 'an experiment' and said, 'The Kashmir mandate was a fractured one. No single party could have formed the government. We waited for a long time in the hope that the PDP and NC would ally, but they could not see eye-to-eye.'[52]

I later spoke to Haseeb Drabu, who has quit politics after leaving the PDP. Drabu resides mostly in Mumbai, does consultancy work for some corporates and is the director of a few companies. In Drabu's view, Mufti Mohammad Sayeed's death was the prime cause of the failure of the coalition government. 'Mufti Sayeed was a man with clear thoughts. He knew to run the government he has to keep Jammu in confidence. Since the BJP was in majority in Jammu region, he understood the need for an alliance, although nobody supported him for that.'

As per Drabu, Mehbooba was neither convinced nor in favour of the alliance. There were fights over petty issues. 'The BJP also felt that they have committed a mistake by allying with a party having an image of being a soft separatist,' he said.

Here, the words of P.C. Alexander, the former governor of Maharashtra, on coalition governments seem to be prophetic. In his book *Perils of Democracy* he wrote, 'Post-election coalitions formed mainly for enjoying power, as it happened in some of the states in the late 60s, had proved to be disastrous and disgraceful experiments in administration. If political parties which share common ideals come together based on agreed programmes and contest elections as partners in an electoral alliance, there will be justification for sharing power. On the other hand, if post-election coalitions are patched up merely to enable some political parties to have a share of power, they will both lack legitimacy and the competence to provide good government.'[53]

2

POSTER BOYS

'Jitendra, I don't think we will be able to return alive to Mumbai! We will be killed any moment. Please help us if you can.' This frantic SOS call was from Anil Tiwari, a friend who was working as executive editor of the Shiv Sena's Hindi mouthpiece, *Dopahar Ka Saamana*. It was around 8 p.m., on 8 July 2016, and I had just returned home from a coverage of heavy rains in Mumbai, when Tiwari hurriedly narrated his ordeal in a terrified voice.

Tiwari had gone for a pilgrimage to the Amarnath shrine in Kashmir with his extended family. That afternoon, they booked a minibus from Jammu and headed towards Pahalgam, from where their yatra would commence. As the bus approached Jawahar Tunnel, the cops asked the minibus to stop for checking. At that time, the driver, Raju, got a message on WhatsApp that an encounter had taken place between security forces and militants, and a few militants had been reportedly killed. Raju showed Tiwari pictures of the slain militants. Since encounters between militants and security forces were usual in the Valley, they took it as a routine confrontation, and their bus moved ahead, unaware of what was in store for them.

The Jammu–Srinagar Highway was secured by thousands of armed security personnel. The highway is heavily guarded throughout the year, considering the history of militant attacks on Amarnath pilgrims. As Tiwari's bus passed through Anantnag town around 7 p.m., he noticed an ominous silence. Shops were shut and there were small groups of people standing beside the road with grim expressions on their faces. From a tri-junction, the bus diverted towards Pahalgam. After a couple of kilometres, all of sudden, a big stone crashed on the windshield and broke it. As Tiwari tried to comprehend what was happening, he saw a car, around 200 metres ahead of the bus, being attacked with stones. Four to five stick-wielding youngsters surrounded the car and started hitting it with rods and sticks. 'I don't know what happened to the occupants of the car, as my driver immediately took a U-turn. They might have been lynched or grievously hurt,' said Tiwari.

Although Tiwari's bus sped back, he had no idea about where he could take shelter. A few more stones struck the bus. The driver asked all passengers to shut the glass windows and block them with some luggage so that stones couldn't enter the bus. Women and children, who were busy chattering or singing religious songs a few minutes ago, were now screaming and crying in fear. Tiwari recollected that he had seen an army camp a few kilometres after the bus turned towards Pahalgam. Assuming that the army would help the distressed pilgrims, he asked Raju to take him to the camp. At the camp, Tiwari narrated his ordeal to the sentry deployed at the gate and pleaded for help. After speaking to his superior, the sentry said that the pilgrims couldn't be taken inside the camp, as there was no permission for that. Soon many other damaged buses and cars reached the camp as well. Raju pointed out to Tiwari that all the vehicles whose number plate indicated registration in Jammu were being targeted. Around seven to eight people had been injured from the stone-pelting, and only they were allowed to enter the camp for first aid. An officer came out to speak to the stranded pilgrims. After Tiwari argued with him, he allowed the women and children inside the camp but asked the others to sit in their vehicles. The officer warned them that militants could throw grenades at them. As Tiwari was talking to the officer, he saw several cars and SUVs (sport utility vehicles) carrying youngsters who shouted *'Allahu Akbar'* while passing in front of the camp's gate. This added to the fear of the pilgrims.

The army officer advised Tiwari to go to the police station and seek help. At this, somebody told him that the police station, too, had been attacked and couldn't be of any help. After an hour, the women and children were asked to come out of the camp. It was around 2 a.m. by then. The officer informed them that some arrangements had been made at Qazigund by the army and everyone should head there. Tiwari feared that they would be attacked again en route to Qazigund and requested an escort by the army, but the officer said that he had no orders for the same. He told Tiwari that it was a safe time to travel since the agitators might have gone to sleep. Nobody had eaten anything after having lunch at Ramban that afternoon. Their dinner was planned at Pahalgam, but in that scenario, it appeared impossible to move in that direction. Tiwari decided to take a risk and head back to Jammu.

As the bus returned to the Srinagar–Jammu Highway, a few more stones struck the bus, although there were not many people on the road. The road was covered with stones. At several places, tree trunks had been placed in the middle of the road to block it. Tiwari and Raju had to get down and clear them to move forward. The women and children were continuously crying. Everybody thought they were going to die that night. Tiwari tried to alleviate their fear by saying, '*Amarnath Baba Raksha Karenge*' (Lord Amarnath will rescue us), although he was in the grip of trepidation himself. He tried to tweet some central ministers for help but internet services had been shut by then.

When they had planned for that tour, there were no reports of such violence or attacks on the pilgrims. This sudden violence was perplexing everyone. Tiwari was unaware that what he was experiencing was the commencement of the second big wave of militancy in Kashmir and a long period of disturbances in the Valley. Thousands of other pilgrims and tourists were stranded that night, scared or injured due to violent protests in different parts of the Valley. Hours later, Tiwari realized that the mayhem was a repercussion of the same encounter whose photographs the driver had shared with him last afternoon—the encounter of Burhan Wani at Kokernag, about 25 kilometres away from Tiwari's location.

At around 3 p.m. that afternoon, a special operations group (SOG) comprising personnel of Jammu & Kashmir Police and Rashtriya

Rifles surrounded and sealed all exit points from Bamdoora village in the Kokernag area of south Kashmir, 80 kilometres from Srinagar. The SOG had specific intelligence that a militant named Sartaz Shaikh, belonging to Hizbul Mujahideen, had gone there to meet his maternal uncle along with two accomplices. The trio was hiding in a house surrounded by apple orchards. Soon the team reached their hideout. Around 4.30 p.m., the encounter began when Burhan, Sartaz and their accomplice, named Pervez Ahmad, attempted to escape after allegedly firing on the team. They were killed in the retaliatory fire. Two security personnel received bullet wounds in the gunfight and four Kalashnikovs allegedly snatched from members of the armed forces were recovered. The crack team was jubilant after they ascertained the identity of the slain militants. The biggest name among them was Burhan Wani, on whose head there was a cash reward and who appeared on the list of most wanted militants in the Valley.

A Foodie, Cricket Lover and Militant

Before he joined Hizbul Mujahideen aged 15, Burhan Wani was no different from many other Kashmiri teenagers of his age. He was a handsome lad who liked playing cricket, wore fashionable clothes, relished chicken dishes, used hair gel to keep his hair stylish, hung out with friends and loved to ride a motorcycle. Burhan resided with his father, Muzaffar Wani, in Dadasara village of the Tral area in the Pulwama district. Burhan was not too keen on religion and didn't attend prayers regularly. He was also not concerned with the separatist movement.

In 2010, anti-government demonstrations were being organized throughout the Valley, when three youngsters were killed by the army in an encounter at Macchil. The encounter was alleged to be fake, and six army personnel were found guilty. There was an atmosphere of severe hostility between the agitators and the government forces. At many locations, violent clashes took place. Checking of vehicles and frisking of people by the security forces was happening all around. Burhan was out on a motorcycle ride with his brother Khalid and other friends when he was accosted by the cops. Allegedly, an argument ensued between them. Burhan's elder brother was assaulted and insulted. That incident had left a deep impact on Burhan's mind and he vowed to take revenge for the humiliation meted out to his brother. Hence, he turned towards militancy and, by the age of 21, rose to become a commander of the militant organization Hizbul Mujahideen, even though he never crossed the LoC for training in PoK. This story suggests that Burhan's initial motivation towards militancy was not the separatist sentiment or Pakistani propaganda but a desire to settle the score with the armed forces over a personal incident. Burhan's background brings to the fore a reality of human life that even a minor adverse experience can have a life-changing impact on somebody.

New-age Militant

What made Burhan the poster boy of militancy? How was he different from other militants? Why a young man in his early twenties had become such a threat to armed forces that a cash award was announced on his head? I needed answers to these questions.

Burhan Wani's ascendance was facilitated by social media. In 2015, Burhan had posted a picture on Facebook holding an AK-47 rifle in his hands and posing to the camera, accompanied by 10 of his associates, against a picturesque backdrop of the mountains. He also circulated a video playing cricket with his accomplices. His pictures and videos gave an impression that they were made by young college students having fun, except that they were carrying guns. Burhan used social media extensively to appeal to youngsters of the Valley to join their so-called 'resistance movement'. His posts soon started getting viral.

Many Kashmiri authors and journalists have noted that although Burhan joined militancy, he had a moderate approach that is said to have resonated with the people of the Valley. This is attributed to one of his videos, where he said that although security forces were harassing his family, he would not retaliate against them. In another video, he welcomed the return of Kashmiri Pandits to the Valley and also supported the Amarnath Yatra.[1] Some doubt if he had even fired a single shot from the weapon he was seen holding. Militancy was on the decline when Burhan surfaced with his videos and pictures on social media. In Gowhar Geelani's view, Burhan gave a fresh push to militancy and became the new young face of the 'resistance movement'. Geelani writes that Burhan led Kashmiris to think beyond Pakistan and believe that Kashmiris could rise against the Indian forces on their own. Another reason for Burhan's popularity was that people were getting disenchanted with the Hurriyat Conference due to its inability to deliver.[2] Veteran journalist Shujaat Bukhari wrote, 'Due to romanticism, the life of Burhan Wani infused among the youth, more and more youths started joining militancy.'[3]

Aftermath of the Encounter

The news of Burhan's killing had spread like wildfire through social media in various parts of the Valley by the time the authorities shut down internet and mobile phone services. The reaction was visible immediately after the operation concluded around 6 p.m. and continued at least for the next six months in various forms of violence. A mob began a protest at the encounter site, and the house where Burhan was killed was burnt down. The Hurriyat Conference announced a bandh to protest against the killing. The next day, at Burhan's native village in Tral, an unprecedented number of people, estimated between 1 to 2.5 lakh, attended his funeral. Pro-Pakistani slogans were raised at the time of his burial and his body was wrapped in a Pakistani flag.[4] Militant attacks and incidents of stone-pelting increased. Within four days of Burhan's encounter, 30 civilians and one policeman were killed. Incidents of torching of police posts, army camps and bunkers became frequent.[5] Subsequently, 90 civilians were killed in the clashes between protestors and security forces; 1,500 people, including young children, were injured; 1,100 received pellet injuries in their eyes; 2,300 FIRs were registered and 7,000 people were arrested.[6]

Shujaat Bukhari explains that there was a steep rise in the number of local militants after the encounter. Earlier, the ratio of foreign to local militants was 70:30, but in the years after the killing of Burhan, the ratio was reversed. In 2013, there were just 16 local militants, which rose to 88 by 2016.[7]

Political Response

Omar Abdullah of the National Conference shot out a series of tweets a day after Burhan's encounter. In his first tweet, Abdullah wrote, 'Aftr many yrs I hear slogans for "Azadi" resonate from the mosque in my uptown Srinagar locality. Kashmir's disaffected got a new icon y'day.'[8] In the next tweet, he feared that Burhan's killing would lead to the recruitment of more terrorists. 'Mark my words—Burhan's ability to recruit into militancy from the grave will far outstrip anything he could have done on social media,' he tweeted.[9]

Then CM Mehbooba Mufti reacted, 'Had I known about him [Wani], I would have given him a second chance in the wake of ongoing economic activity, improving situation and booming tourism.'[10] She said she was unaware of the encounter before it took place so didn't get the time to make advance security arrangements like Omar Abdullah as CM did when Afzal Guru, convicted of attacking the Parliament, was hanged. She stressed that there was a need to restart the peace process with Pakistan that had been initiated by former PM Atal Bihari Vajpayee. Mehbooba also opposed the use of pellet guns.[11] In later days, she was seen visiting families of slain insurgents, which prompted the right-wingers to call her a 'soft separatist'.[12]

The encounter of Burhan Wani and the events that followed sowed the seeds of disharmony between the incumbent coalition partners—the PDP and the BJP.

3

THE SEMINAL ATTACK AT PULWAMA

I am a hodophile and my job as a journalist complements my wanderlust. From Arunachal Pradesh to Rann of Kutch and from Kanyakumari to Kashmir, I have been fortunate enough to travel the length and breadth of the country. Some locations have been visited either as a solivagant or as a journalist to cover major news events like elections, natural calamities, conflicts or tragedies.

My superiors in office are acquainted with my wanderlust, and this is the reason why they find it appropriate to depute me for various major national and international news events. Hence, when the terrorist attack on a Central Reserve Police Force (CRPF) convoy at Pulwama happened on 14 February 2019, I was deputed for the coverage.

My brief was to do a reconstructive story of the route from the CRPF camp in Jammu to Pulwama in Kashmir Valley, where the attack had happened. I asked cameraman Sachin Shinde if he was willing to come with me. He agreed readily. Our tickets were booked, and we flew to Jammu, from where we had to travel by road till Pulwama in Kashmir to recreate the unfortunate CRPF convoy's journey.

Kashmir is one of those places in India that I have visited again and again. The first time I visited the Valley was in October 2007. I came as a tourist and visited all the tourist locations. I returned to Mumbai with an everlasting memory and a desire to visit the Valley again.

My visits to J&K after 2007 were professional ones, like the Konkan Railway media tour and the Vidhan Sabha elections in 2014. Although I have been to Kashmir repeatedly, I had never been there to cover violent conflicts, for which the state has remained in the news since the late eighties. This was the first time I was visiting Kashmir in the aftermath of an incident that led to a strong emotional response across India and when the state was in the grip of heavy tension.

Dilemma of a Reporter

All forms of mass media in India were full of news related to the Pulwama attack—images of coffins covered with the tricolour reaching villages, grieving relatives and funerals with gun salutes. The anchors called for a strong retaliation; the relatives and friends of the deceased sought revenge; the politicians dug up the past and accused each other of being lax over the issue of national security; some guests at the TV studios demanded a war while the pacifists asked for restraint. Jingoism was in the air.

The slain CRPF personnel hailed from 16 different states of India. My channel decided to send a camera team to the homes of each deceased soldier. The presence of a large media contingent at the homes of the dead is said to rob the relatives of their privacy in grief. However, another point of view is that this gives the family of the deceased the impression that their martyrdom is being recognized and valued.

Too much grief can get you so conditioned to it that you lose your sensitivity. I don't find that happening in my case. Being a reporter of crime and conflicts, and having covered scores of natural and man-made tragedies, I have widely reported stories of death and have seen grieving relatives who are unable to comprehend what has happened. I have often struggled to balance my job and my emotions. The worst part of a television journalist's job on such occasions is to get a sound bite of the closest relative of the deceased. Generally, the questions are like: When did you meet him last? When did you speak to him last? What kind of a person was he? What are his memories with you? In my view, the majority of field television journalists are sensitive people and care for the sentiments of others and would rather not do this. However, the nature of their jobs and the cut-throat competition makes them appear selfish, insensitive and often foolish. Thankfully, I was not assigned to visit the homes of the deceased soldiers but instead tasked with narrating the sequence of events that led to the attack.

The attack led to outrage across India, and anti-Kashmiri riots broke out in Jammu. Kashmiri students in different parts of the country were being attacked. Two Kashmiri shawl vendors were beaten up in Delhi while they were travelling to Haryana in a train. Dehradun, the capital city of Uttarakhand, had lost two soldiers in a recent militant attack and saw the most incidents of anti-Kashmiri violence. Members of right-wing organizations hunted for Kashmiri students in educational institutions, alleging that some students were sharing provocative posts on social media. The Kashmiri dean of a college in Dehradun was suspended when he rescued a Kashmiri girl from the clutches of a violent mob. The dean later claimed that he volunteered to get suspended so that tempers could be calmed.[1] News of anti-Kashmiri violence came from West Bengal too. A group of 200 rioters barged into the home of a shawl trader and beat him up and his friends. He was targeted for his four-month-old Facebook post in which he had written, 'I hate Indian Army.' The backlash against Kashmiris led thousands of them, mostly students, traders or different professionals, to rush back to their homes in the Valley.

Jammu vs Kashmir

On landing at the Jammu airport around 1 p.m., we realized that a curfew had been imposed in the city and no vehicles were being allowed to ply. The taxi stand was empty. A day after the Pulwama attack, Jammu Chambers of Commerce and Industries had called for a bandh. All shops and establishments were shut. Anti-Pakistan protests were organized in various parts of the city by right-wing organizations like Bajrang Dal, Shiv Sena and Dogra Front. The protests began with chanting slogans against Pakistan and burning its national flag but turned violent when some youths holding tricolours passed through Gujjar Nagar, an area dominated by Muslims, on motocycles, pelting stones and burning vehicles. It was alleged that some miscreants had thrown bricks and stones at the protestors, which triggered the violence. Soon the violence spread in other parts of the city too.[2] Over two dozen people were injured in the riots.

The Jammu & Kashmir Police imposed a curfew in Jammu to contain the violence. Two army columns were summoned to conduct a flag march and maintain peace. Internet was shut down as a precautionary measure.[3] However, protestors defied the curfew and came out on the road in huge numbers in some areas. When the crowd did not disperse after being warned, the police resorted to lathicharge and used tear gas to clear the protestors.[4]

These riots were not just knee-jerk reactions by right-wing organizations after the Pulwama attack but also a violent expression of hate that many people from two regions of the erstwhile state, viz. Jammu and Kashmir, have historically nurtured against each other. The state of J&K was divided into three administrative regions—Jammu, Kashmir Valley and Ladakh.[5] Out of the total of 22 districts, 10 belonged to Jammu and an equal number to Kashmir, while the two districts of Leh and Kargil fell in the Ladakh region. It was the only state in India where Muslims were a majority—68.31 per cent of the total population. They were in majority in 17 out of 22 districts, whereas Hindus had a total population of 28 per cent and were in majority only in four districts.[6]

The hate and distrust between the people of the two regions have predominantly communal aspects. Unlike Kashmir, Jammu city and some adjoining districts have a majority of Hindus. Many people who migrated after Partition have settled in Jammu. Some are erstwhile residents of PoK. Kashmiri Pandits, too, have made Jammu their home after the exodus in the late eighties and early nineties. These people have cultivated a sense of hatred towards Kashmiri Muslims in general due to their past bitter experiences and see them as responsible for their plight. The hostility between the two regions exists in spite of the symbiotic relationship between them. The supplies for Kashmir come from the traders of Jammu. There have been several initiatives of inter-state dialogue to end the hostility between the people of the two regions. Slain veteran journalist Shujaat Bukhari was one of the faces who made efforts to sort out misunderstandings between the people of the two regions of the state.

We required a car to travel from Jammu to Pulwama. I tried my Jammu counterpart Ajay Bachloo's mobile number but it wasn't reachable. We were stuck. How were we going to move ahead if no vehicle was available? The airport became deserted after an hour, as all the passengers who landed with us had left in the cars that had come to pick them up. Most of them were residents of Jammu and had called their relatives or chauffeurs to pick them up. After several attempts, my call got connected to Bachloo, who sounded overworked. However, he managed to reach the airport in 15 minutes. I told him about my situation, but he expressed his inability to fetch a car, considering the tension in the city. 'No taxi driver will take the risk. I can give my car to you, but then I will become handicapped here. There are so many incidents of violence happening in the city and I will not be able to move around if I don't have a car,' he explained.

After scratching his head for a moment, Bachloo called up a taxi driver who he thought could help and spoke to him in the Dogri language for few minutes. The driver agreed to transport us in his Innova but on two conditions—he demanded triple of the regular fare and, secondly, he would drop us only till Banihal and not till Pulwama. Banihal was 160 kilometres away from Jammu and took four hours to reach. The driver informed us that he could not go further. Just a day before, many vehicles with registration numbers of Srinagar (JK-01)[7] and other districts of Kashmir Valley like Anantnag (JK-03), Baramulla (JK-05) and Kupwara (JK-09) had been burnt down by rioters in Jammu, and the driver feared that in retaliation, rioters in the Kashmir Valley would be torching any car with a Jammu registration (JK-02). Banihal was a town close to the periphery of Jammu and Kashmir, and drivers of both the regions felt safe travelling only up to that point.

I informed my editor, Rajnish Ahuja, about the situation. He suggested that I take the taxi to Banihal. The next morning, reporter Adarsh Singh, who was already in Srinagar with a car, would travel back to Banihal and pick us up for the further journey. The editor also gave me a deadline of 3 p.m. the next day to complete my shoot and file the script, as the story was slated to be aired that evening at 8 p.m. I told Bachloo to call the taxi.

While we were waiting for the taxi to come, I asked Bachloo, 'Historically, the regions of Jammu and Kashmir have been at loggerheads, but what are the reasons for hostility between the two even today?' 'Broadly speaking,' said Bachloo, 'the people of Jammu feel that they are not being treated fairly. They feel like a neglected child. Most of the financial aid from the Centre goes to the Kashmir Valley. Any major project in Kashmir gets more attention than Jammu. For example, take the case of Gondola. This project was conceived simultaneously for both Jammu and Gulmarg in Kashmir. When the Gondola in Gulmarg started running in phase two, the work on Jammu one was yet to commence.'

He said the politics of the state was also dominated by Kashmir. 'You are from Mumbai, but you still might be knowing Mufti Mohammad Sayeed, Mehbooba Mufti, Omar Abdullah and a few others, who all come from the Kashmir region. But, tell me, how many politicians do you know of from the Jammu region? Except for one or two names like Jitendra Singh and Nirmal Singh, who came in the limelight after the PDP–BJP government was formed, you might not know anybody else.'

'Visit any of the government offices here,' Bachloo continued, 'You will see that most of the employees are Kashmiris. People of Jammu feel that they don't get fair employment opportunities.' He said that in the two and half years of rule of the government in which the BJP also shared power, they failed to deliver for Jammu and no big project was initiated. 'Jammu has good potential to be developed as a tourist destination, but nothing has been done in that regard. Some major projects should have been taken up to attract tourists to Jammu,' said Bachloo.

The nationalist sentiment also divides the people of Jammu from the people of Kashmir. 'The perception is that Kashmiris support separatists and Pakistan, which is abhorred by Jammu's people. Even Muslims of Jammu don't like Kashmiris due to this. When the exodus happened from the Kashmir Valley, not only Pandits but Sikhs and Muslims also moved to Jammu. These were the Muslims who wanted to keep their children away from militancy and politics. They wanted them to get a good education and grow. Many such Kashmiri Muslim families are staying in Jammu today.'

Our taxi then arrived at the gate of the airport, so our discussion ended.

It was around 2.30 p.m. I hugged Ajay Bachloo and he left for a shoot, asking me to call him up in case there was any trouble during the journey. We headed towards the CRPF camp that was located a few kilometres away from the airport. While passing through various roads of Jammu city, we could sense the tension in the air. There were cops at every nook and corner. We weren't stopped because we had stuck a printout with the words 'PRESS, ABP NEWS' on the windshield. The army vehicles were patrolling the riot-affected areas. In about 15 minutes, we reached the gate of the CRPF camp.

Villain Weather

The CRPF, with a strength of 246 battalions and over 3 lakh personnel, is one of the paramilitary forces deployed in J&K to counter insurgency. It was set up in 1949, two years after India attained freedom.[8] Apart from maintaining regular law and order and fighting militancy, the role of the CRPF becomes vital during various local, state and national elections. The camp where we reached acted as a transit facility for the CRPF. The personnel who returned from leave or were transferred from some other locations to be deputed in the Valley assembled there and were transported to different locations as per their posting.

The week preceding 14 February 2019, the day of the attack,

saw very heavy snowfall on NH-44, also known as Jammu–Srinagar Highway. NH-44 is one of the two major roads that connect the Jammu region with the Kashmir Valley. The other highway, Mughal Road, connects Shopian in Kashmir with Rajouri in the Jammu region, but it is shut mostly through the winter due to snowfall. As both the roads connecting Jammu and Srinagar were closed, the soldiers arriving at the Jammu transit camp got stuck there, leading to a gathering of around 6,000 soldiers, a number far above the capacity of the camp. It was necessary to clear the rush of incoming personnel from the transit camp and send them to their respective locations of duty.

After seven days, on 13 February, when information came that the highway had been cleared of snow and could be used, it was decided to send as many personnel as possible to Srinagar, as the weather was unpredictable in the Valley. A total of 2,547 CRPF personnel were ordered to embark on 78 buses and head towards Srinagar. The convoy of grey buses, which left the transit camp at around 3 a.m., formed a line so long that the last bus was 14 kilometres behind the leading bus.

I did an opening piece to camera (PTC)[9] of my story at the gate of the transit camp, describing the circumstances preceding the departure of the convoy.

Hellish Highway

Very soon our car touched NH-44. At the entry point, I did another PTC describing the significance of the highway. Soon we reached the Chenani–Nashri Tunnel smoothly. After we crossed the tunnel, the road condition deteriorated.

It was around 4 p.m., and we were feeling hungry by now, as the last we had eaten was around noon on the flight. I asked the driver, Ramanlal, to stop at some roadside eatery so that we could have some snacks and chai. Ramanlal stopped his car at a place named Peetha.

'Sir. This eatery is very famous for rajma-chawal. Those who have tasted rajma here once always stop to eat whenever they pass through this highway,' said Ramanlal enthusiastically. 'Ramanlal, I think rajma-chawal at this hour will be too heavy. Lunch time is over,' I said, smiling.

'Then also you must try, Sir,' Ramanlal insisted and ordered a plate for himself.

The aroma coming from the eatery's kitchen tempted Sachin and he suggested that we should order one plate and divide it between the two of us. We ordered one plate and shared it. The taste indeed appealed to our palate. We ordered one more serving. After filling ourselves, we ordered chai. Once we were done, we set off. Due to bumps and potholes on the road, we felt that we were on a camel ride. It was appalling to see that the most vital road of the state, which connected two capitals, was used by thousands of national and international tourists, transported soldiers and was an important route of supplies for the Valley, was in such an awful state.

As we were discussing the bad road conditions, an elderly Sikh man in a pick-up truck coming from the opposite direction waved at us to stop after looking at the registration number of our car. He shouted in Punjabi at Ramanlal, '*Gaddi pyari nahi hai tenu? Pata nahi odhar ki ho riya hai? O teri gaddi Sadh denge.*' (Don't you love your car? Don't you know what is happening that side? They will burn down your car.) I got worried at this, thinking that now Ramanlal would get scared and decline to take us further. However, he thanked the elderly man for his concern and moved ahead, saying, '*Ji pata hai. Udhar haalaat bahut kharaab hain. Ye media waale hain. Inhe Banihal tak chhodkar wapas lautunga.*' (Yes, I know that situation there is very bad. These are media people. I will return after dropping them at Banihal.)

Lonely Soldier and His Enemies

Dusk was setting in. One of the descriptions in my report of NH-44 was that it was the most militarized highway in the country. I needed to substantiate that with the help of visuals of armed soldiers from the CRPF and Rashtriya Rifles, who were posted at intervals of every 300- or 400-metre stretch beside the highway. At many places, single guards stood holding a rifle in areas that appeared completely deserted. The passing vehicles were the only signs of human presence. Mobile phone networks were not available. I told Sachin to get some shots quickly of such soldiers keeping a watch on the highway before the sunlight completely disappeared.

Spotting a uniformed soldier standing beneath a tree beside the road at some height, Sachin told Ramanlal to stop the car. As Ramanlal applied sudden brakes, the car stopped with a loud screeching sound and Sachin rushed out with his camera towards the guard. The guard, who had been relaxed, got into alert mode after noticing the halt of the car and a stranger rushing towards him. He swiftly lifted his rifle, put his finger on the trigger and pointed it towards Sachin. I rushed out and waved my microphone with the channel's logo on it and shouted, '*Hum media waale hain. Aap chinta matt kijiye*' (We are media people. Don't worry.) I realized my mistake. We should have stopped our car a few metres away from him and then walked up to him. We could have taken the required visuals after talking to him. This mistake could have proved fatal for us. We could have been mistaken for the militants and been killed.

The soldiers guarding the highway live in the shadow of death. Terrorist organizations like Hizbul Mujahideen, Lashkar-e-Taiba and Jaish-e-Mohammed have a good network of overground workers (OGWs) in the areas adjacent to highways, and the attacks by them have led to numerous casualties in the previous years.[10] Just 3 years ago, in June 2016, at a place known as Frestbal on that highway, eight CRPF personnel had been killed and 20 grievously injured in an attack by militants. In the same month, three Border Security Force (BSF) men had been killed and seven injured when militants belonging to Hizbul Mujahideen fired at a bus carrying personnel from Jammu to Srinagar.[11]

In such a scenario, when death doesn't give a soldier time to think and retaliate, the knee-jerk response of the soldier could have killed us.

After seeing my microphone, the soldier lowered his rifle. I walked up to him and informed him that I was a journalist working on a report that focused on the martyrdom of his colleagues. After getting convinced about our credentials, he allowed us to take his shots.

It was dark by the time we finished taking shots of that soldier. Around 9 p.m., we reached Banihal town, which appeared to be deserted. Ramanlal took his fare and dropped us at the first hotel in his sight beside the road. Sachin asked him to wait till we checked into the hotel, but Ramanlal said it would be better for him to return immediately, as many Muslims stayed in Banihal and he didn't want to take a risk. The six-hour-long journey from Jammu had tortured our bodies and minds. We were exhausted. I felt sorry for Ramanlal who had to drive back on the same road without any rest. I allowed him to go, handing him a couple of extra bucks as a tip.

Cold Night at Banihal

As we came out of the car, we were overwhelmed by the cold. The temperature was 3 degrees Celsius and would dip further as the night progressed. We wanted to get into the hotel room as soon as possible. We could see the reception of the hotel through the locked grill gate in the jaundiced light of a zero-watt bulb, but nobody was manning it. Sachin shouted, '*Koi hai kya*?' (Is anybody there?) However, even after calling out three to four times, no response came. Sachin angrily picked up the luggage and began moving. Both of us had our bags of clothes apart from the camera bag, a tripod that weighed around 10 kilograms and a LiveU unit of 5 kilograms, which we use to uplink the footage. The cold, the exertion of travel and now the burden of carrying this heavy luggage had made our condition distressful. We regretted allowing Ramanlal to leave. We walked for around 200 metres and reached another hotel. A teenage boy sitting at the reception said that the hotel had just five rooms and all were full. He suggested we try our luck at the Tourism Department's rest house, which was few yards away at the northern end of the town.

We couldn't afford disappointment in our next attempt. If that failed, there was no option but to spend that cold night on the roadside.

Both Sachin and I were shivering mildly now. As I reached the gate of the rest house, Sachin lit a cigarette and felt a bit relieved from the cold. At the reception, I saw a man wearing a traditional Kashmiri pheran updating a register. I enquired about the room and he said that just one room was left and it would cost us Rs. 800 for the night. We checked in immediately after furnishing the required documents. The rest house was in the shape of a large hut, in which there were four to five rooms in a line. There was a small ground just outside the room that was also used as a parking area.

The receptionist led us to our room. Looking at our clothes, he remarked, 'Sir, your warm clothes from Bombay are not going to help you here. People from Delhi and other north Indian cities don't face many problems because they experience weather that is colder than Bombay. I have resided in Bombay for few years, so I know.'

The room was a perfect setting for a horror movie. The plaster was peeling from the walls and cobwebs hung in the corners. A large window beside the bed had a view of the parking area outside. The attendant told us to be careful while using the geyser, as the wire didn't have the sockets to get it plugged for an electricity connection. Pointing to a button beside the bed, he asked us to press it in case anything was required.

It was sad to find the tourist resort of a state whose main source of revenue was tourism in such a condition. The J&K government was spending crores of money on publicity to bring tourists back to the state. I remember meeting Mehbooba Mufti at JW Mariott in Mumbai when she was CM of the state and had come to the city to urge film-makers to shoot in the Valley. In an interaction with me, she had said that her state was safe for tourists and people from Mumbai should visit Kashmir. 'Given a chance, I would like to choose Salman Khan to promote tourism there,' she said.[12]

In normal circumstances, we would have never checked into such a room, but that night we were glad to find shelter from the unbearable cold. Sachin was feeling better after puffing two cigarettes in quick succession, but the discomfort due to cold was evident on my face. At this, Sachin smiled and took out a half bottle of Captain Morgan from his bag. 'I knew that we might need it, so I pushed it inside the bag before leaving.' He knew it was my favourite brand. I took two servings undiluted. The spirit gave some warmth and I felt better. Shortly after, we went to a Punjabi eatery across the road, which was the only place open at that time. A few Sikh truck drivers were having their dinner. The hot food added to the relief that we had gotten from the spirit. Before going to sleep, I spoke to my colleague Adarsh Singh, who confirmed that he would reach Banihal from Srinagar by 8 a.m. to pick us up.

Fearful Morning

At 6.30 a.m., I was woken up by some commotion outside my room. I pulled the curtain aside and saw around 100 people gathered in the parking area. Most of them were wearing skullcaps and had a beard. They were talking loudly and sounded very angry. I wondered why so many Muslims had gathered there so early in the morning and why they were so agitated. Sachin also got up and suspected that we might get attacked because we were Hindus. As we were thinking about what to do, somebody knocked forcefully at the door of our room. As I opened the door, two people pushed themselves inside and rudely took away two chairs kept in the corner without bothering to ask us. This enraged Sachin, but I asked him to remain calm.

The chairs were meant for the two elderly men towards whom the crowd was being respectful. As they sat in the middle of the ground, the crowd surrounded them. They were talking loudly in Urdu. 'They are burning vehicles of our people in Jammu. We must also retaliate in the kind,' suggested an angry youngster. Others in the crowd supported him. However, the elderly people sitting on the chairs disagreed. One of them said, 'It is true that whatever is happening in Jammu is not right and we must condemn it. But our Banihal has been peaceful so far. Resorting to violence, stone-pelting or burning vehicles will put us all in trouble.'

'So how are we going to express our anger?' someone in the crowd shouted.

'We must organize a bandh to protest against the violence. The whole town must be closed,' the old man opined.

'Yes, and we must not allow any vehicle to pass through Banihal. The highway must be shut down,' somebody else suggested.

'No, I don't support this,' the elderly man replied.

As the crowd and two elderly men debated on how to organize the protest, we thought it prudent to get ready and checkout from the rest house. Even one or two furious men could charge up the crowd. I got a call from Adarsh, who informed me that he had left Srinagar and was on his way to pick us up. I was worried that if the protestors began blocking the road, then it would be difficult for Adarsh to reach us. Within an hour, we checked out with our luggage and went to the eatery across the road for breakfast. By 8.30 a.m., Adarsh picked us up. He came in a car with a Kashmiri registration. Adarsh, his cameraman Mohit Castley and driver Ghulam had left around 5.30 a.m. and had to face many obstacles on the way. At some places, road-opening parties (ROPs) had not cleared the vehicular movement and there were long queues of vehicles. Before allowing regular traffic on the road, the ROPs ensure that there are no natural or manmade hazards on the road. However, he displayed his identity as a TV journalist at various closure points to the army officers and they cooperated by giving him priority of movement once the clearance was given for civilian traffic.

Long Wait at Jawahar Tunnel

As we came out of Banihal town, a breathtaking view greeted us. The highway now passed through the snow-clad mountains of Pir Panjal. That was our first tryst with snow during the journey. The view of sunrays reflecting off the white hills was spectacular. We were mesmerized by the beauty of the location and had forgotten the tension that dominated our minds a few minutes ago. Kashmir Valley, with its natural magnificence, was near.

After negotiating sharp curves and the gradient, we reached the entrance of the Jawahar Tunnel, which is also known as the Banihal Tunnel. Approximately 3 kilometres long, this tunnel is an important link between the Jammu region and the Kashmir Valley. There was a long queue of about 50 vehicles at the entrance. Only one lane of the tunnel was being used for both up and down traffic. A CRPF convoy was about to pass, and the tunnel was closed for civilian traffic due to heightened security measures post the Pulwama incident. I got concerned because a delay in completing the shoot meant missing the 3 p.m. deadline. I pleaded my case with the army officer in charge of the entry point. He told me that my vehicle would be the first to enter the tunnel once the CRPF convoy passed, but that would take around 45 minutes. He asked our car to be positioned at the beginning of the queue. We didn't have any option other than to wait. I did a PTC at the entrance of the tunnel, describing its importance for the Valley. Sachin got engrossed with army jawans and was delighted when he was told that the same convoy of buses that was attacked on 14 January was coming back from Srinagar. The visuals of the same convoy would add weight to our report. This time the convoy was transporting the personnel who had completed their duty in Srinagar and were either going on leave or to a different posting.

After a short while, the convoy arrived, and it took over 15 minutes for its last bus to get out of the tunnel. After taking the shots, we hurriedly got into our car. The officer kept his word and allowed us first entry. Thanking him, we drove ahead. As we exited the tunnel, our driver, Ghulam, announced that we were finally in the Kashmir Valley. We had reached Qazigund. Generally, the convoys coming from Jammu are escorted by armoured vehicles after reaching Qazigund for their further journey towards Srinagar. However, on 14 February, the ill-fated convoy hadn't gotten the cover of armoured vehicles, as the preceding bad weather and the large number of CRPF men travelling together had messed up the security arrangements. I did a PTC there against the backdrop of an armoured vehicle.

The further journey was very stressful. Due to the movement of the convoy, the traffic towards Jammu had been halted, and it led to over a 15-kilometre-long traffic jam of trucks and pickup vans on the highway. As a result, we covered a distance of 48 kilometres from Qazigund to Lethpora in three hours. My blood pressure was shooting up at the thought of the deadline.

An Attack that Altered India's Political Discourse

Finally, we reached Lethpora of Pulwama district, where the CRPF bus had been blown up. Driving a Maruti Eeco car, 22-year-old Adil Dar from the terrorist group Jaish-e-Mohammed had gotten inside the moving convoy and rammed a bus full of CRPF personnel of the 76th Battalion. It had led to such a big blast that the sound could be heard more than 5 kilometres away. Parts of the bus and the mangled bodies of CRPF personnel had scattered all around the highway, and a crater had formed at the site. Flames and black smoke had engulfed the surroundings. The cops didn't allow us to go near the spot, so we had to take shots from a distance.[13] The initial investigation conducted by the National Investigation Agency (NIA) suggested that over 200 kilograms of explosives, ammonium nitrate and RDX had been used for the blast. I did a closing PTC at ground zero and completed shooting my story. This attack was going to impact, even alter, the political discourse of India in the days to come.

Next, we had to reach Srinagar from where, using the hotel Wi-Fi internet, we had to send the footage to our Noida office. It was 3.30 p.m. and I had missed the deadline. I hurriedly began typing the script on my mobile phone, while Ghulam sped up the car towards the hotel, considering the urgency.

Retribution

Hours after the attack, a strongly worded statement was released by India's External Affairs ministry, which said, 'This heinous and despicable act has been perpetrated by Jaish-e-Mohammed, a Pakistan-based and supported terrorist organization proscribed by the United Nations and other countries. This terror group is led by the international terrorist Masood Azhar, who has been given full freedom by Government of Pakistan to operate and expand his terror infrastructure in territories under the control of Pakistan and to carry out attacks in India and elsewhere with impunity.'[14] The statement stressed that India was committed to taking all necessary measures to safeguard national security.

On 26 February, 12 days after the Pulwama attack, warplanes of the Indian Air Force struck Balakot in Pakistan. Twelve Mirage 2000 jets dropped 1,000-kilogram bombs during an operation conducted for 19 minutes before dawn.[15] The targets were alleged terrorist camps 80 kilometres away from the LoC in Pakistan's Khyber Pakhtunkhwa province. The NDA government claimed that the airstrikes demolished the biggest terrorist camps of Jaish-e-Mohammad and eliminated a 'very large number' of terrorists and their trainers. The government claimed that they were pre-emptive strikes, since more terrorist attacks were supposedly being planned at the camps. Then External Affairs Minister Sushma Swaraj said that the objective of the airstrikes was the destruction of terrorist camps and that India didn't want further escalation.[16] It was for the first time since the 1971 war that Indian warplanes had attacked Pakistani soil.[17]

As the news of the airstrike broke on TV, celebrations began in various parts of India. Crackers were burst, sweets were distributed and processions with Indian flags were paraded on the streets.[18] India had avenged the martyrdom of its soldiers and had given a befitting reply to Pakistan. However, the Pakistan government contested Indian claims. The Pakistan Army organized a tour of foreign journalists and diplomats to the area where the Indian Air Force claimed to have launched the strikes. The journalists who participated in the tour said that several restrictions had been imposed upon them. The journalists reported that they saw a medium-sized crater, perhaps caused by the dropping of a bomb by an Indian warplane, as well as a few fallen trees and a damaged house. The Pakistan Army's spokesperson Major General Asif Ghafoor said that no harm had been done by Indian warplanes and the allegation that terror camps were being run in the vicinity was false.[19] However, international news agency Reuters reported that its reporters made three attempts in nine days following the attack to reach the religious school on a hillock that the Indian government claimed was a terrorist camp of Jaish-e-Mohammed but were blocked by the Pakistani military.[20] Whether any actual damage was done during the airstrike remains a contentious issue, with claims and counterclaims from both sides.

On 27 February, however, Wing Commander Abhinandan Varthaman, who was chasing an intruding Pakistani aeroplane in his MiG-21, crossed into Pakistani territory and was taken prisoner by the Pakistan Army. It was feared that in the prevailing tension between the two countries, he would be tortured and killed. However, after 60 hours in the enemy's captivity, he was handed back to India after Pakistani Prime Minister Imran Khan announced in the Parliament that he was being released as a 'peace gesture'. BJP party president Amit Shah claimed that this was a 'diplomatic victory' for India.[21]

Replicating the UP Formula

In the days following the 26 February airstrikes, all the news platforms were full of content related to nationalism, national security, diplomacy, terrorism, the valour of Abhinandan Varthaman and so on. All this was happening at a time when the nation's parliamentary elections were hardly three months away in May. The BJP decided to capitalize on the widespread emotions and public sentiments during its electoral campaign, as it had done earlier, in 2017, during the Uttar Pradesh Vidhan Sabha elections immediately following the Indian Army's surgical strike in Pakistan in retaliation to the Uri attack.[22]

The BJP began showcasing the airstrikes as its achievement to claim power at the Centre once again.

Modi made national security a primary theme of his election

campaign. Although the Opposition attempted to highlight unemployment and other issues, they took a secondary place. On 18 April 2019, in a public meeting at Amreli, a coastal town in Gujarat, he said, 'But Pakistan did not know what Modi is like. It suspected that India could attack from the land or the sea route. But we did it from the air. And, for the first time, the world saw Pakistan weeping.' He said that India had virtually brought Pakistan to its knees.[23]

Unprecedented Electoral Victory

It was a historic day for the BJP on 23 May 2019. The results made the BJP the single-largest party in the Lok Sabha with 303 seats and the National Democratic Alliance (NDA), which the party was leading, got 353 seats. The party's vote share rose by 6 per cent from 31.34 per cent in 2014 to 37.4 per cent in 2019.[24] Such an electoral victory was rare for any political party in the past three decades. The biggest face of the Opposition, Rahul Gandhi from the Congress, was defeated from the Amethi seat, which had been known as the party's bastion for decades.

The pains of demonetisation, the hasty implementation of the Goods and Services Tax, the bad shape of the economy and the farm crisis—all the issues raked up by opposition parties failed to connect with a large number of electorates. The Balakot airstrike was counted as one of the primary factors for BJP's victory, among others, such as the Ujjwala scheme, which allocated cooking gas connections to households below the poverty line.[25]

Such a startling victory for the BJP had many implications. A strong and stable government was at the Centre now, so the BJP had achieved the power to implement many policies and programmes which were on its agenda. Achieving much more than the required number of seats for the majority implied that the BJP could no longer be blackmailed by smaller allies like Shiv Sena, which the party had to face during previous NDA governments. Protests by the allies to BJP initiatives also became irrelevant. Overall, Modi was sworn in as a more powerful PM than he had been in 2014. The landslide victory also empowered the Modi government to pursue the BJP's agenda on Kashmir.

Section II

ABROGATION OF ARTICLE 370 AND BIFURCATION OF JAMMU AND KASHMIR

4

AN UNFORGETTABLE AUGUST

As we were about to land at Sheikh ul-Alam International Airport of Srinagar, the captain made the highly unusual announcement that all window shades must be pulled down, considering the security measures due to the prevailing situation in Kashmir. Srinagar being a military airport, the passengers are generally instructed not to click photographs, but things were on a different level this time. I got an idea of what I was going to see in the Valley.

I expected driver Ghulam to pick me up from the airport as planned. I waited for around half an hour, but Ghulam didn't turn up. There was no way to contact him, as mobile phones and the internet were not working. The taxi stand was around 100 metres away from the terminal, but it was raining heavily. As I was about to approach another passenger for a lift, I heard somebody shouting, 'Dixit Sir!' I looked back. Ghulam was huffing and puffing as he walked towards me, half-drenched in the rain. 'Sorry, Sir. There were security checks at too many places while coming to the airport. Hence, I got late,' he said, picking up our luggage and leading us towards his Mahindra Xylo, the same MPV (Compact Multi-Purpose Vehicle) with a Kashmir registration that he used to pick us up at Banihal six months ago.

Ghulam, a tall Kashmiri man in his early 50s with a grey beard, was a sincere driver. An intelligent man, he had an interest in current affairs; he loved to read in his free time and had travelled to many parts of India. I felt relieved to see him.

Our stay was arranged at Hotel Sarovar Portico, located adjacent to the United Nations office near Dal Gate. It was also very close to Gupkar Road, which is one of the most high-profile avenues in the Valley, with the residences of former CMs Omar Abdullah and

Mehbooba Mufti and many other top politicians. Hari Niwas, the palace of Kashmir's last king Hari Singh and formerly the CM's official residence, is also not far.

En route to the hotel, I noticed that the security was much heavier than it had been during our visit to Srinagar six months ago. Checking of vehicles by the cops and frisking of its occupants was also more frequent this time. The roadside shops were shut and the shutters of some of them had been covered with anti-India graffiti. Such sights are common in south Kashmir, where words like 'We want freedom, 'India your game is over', 'Boycott elections', 'AK-47' and so on are painted on shop shutters and walls. However, counter-graffiti has also been seen of late, with messages like 'We want freedom from stone-pelters', 'I love Modi', 'India your game is good'.[1] Although the hotel was just 13 kilometres away from the airport and there was not much traffic on the road, it took us over an hour to reach, due to frequent stops for security checks. The Kashmir Valley was seeing a build-up of such an environment from around 10 days ago.

On 29 July, *Greater Kashmir* published an article saying that legislative assembly elections were likely to be conducted in October or November that year.[2] It was a welcome development, as the state had been under President's Rule for the past two years because the BJP had withdrawn support from CM Mehbooba Mufti's government in June 2017. However, on the very next day, a confidential police communication was leaked to the media—it sought details of the management committees of mosques in Srinagar to be submitted to the higher authorities. Due to their past experiences, the security establishments believed that mosques were sometimes used as places to incite and fuel protests. After the furore over the leaked communication, the senior superintendent of police (SSP) of Srinagar confirmed that he had authored the communication and the order was routine.[3] News of another police order asking for the passenger capacity of taxis and the fuel capacity of petrol pumps, and instructing the construction of security pickets and fresh bunkers in certain parts of the old city aggravated the tension.[4]

On 30 July, the annual Amarnath pilgrimage was suspended till 4 August, citing bad weather. However, an order from Shaleen Kabra, principal secretary (Home) of the J&K government on 2 August raised many eyebrows. It read, 'Keeping in view the latest intelligence inputs of the terror threats, with specific targeting of the Amarnath Yatra, and given the prevailing security situation in the Kashmir Valley, in the interest of safety and security of the tourists and Amarnath Yatris, it is advised that they may curtail their stay in the valley immediately and take necessary measures to return as soon as possible.'[5] Was such a big decision taken based on just intelligence input regarding a terrorist attack or was it just a 'pretext' for something else? Some were sceptical.

Every year, thousands of Hindus undertake a pilgrimage of the Amarnath Temple, which stretches upto five days. According to Hindu mythology, Lord Shiva enlightened his wife Parvati about life and eternity here. The devotees climb up around 12,756 feet to catch a glimpse of the Shivling formed naturally inside a cave every year between May and August. The cave is surrounded by snow-clad mountains, and the path leading to it often becomes hazardous in bad weather. Despite the natural hazards, the ban on the yatra by various militant organizations and repeated terror attacks, the number of pilgrims has been increasing, even crossing 6 lakhs in some years.[6] Elaborate security arrangements are always in place for this reason.

Former CM Omar Abdullah tweeted, 'Friends staying in hotels in Gulmarg are being forced to leave. State road transport Corpn buses are being deployed to bus people out from Pahalgam & Gulmarg. If there is a threat to the yatra why is Gulmarg being emptied?'[7]

The travel advisory to the tourists and the discontinuation of the Amarnath Yatra triggered a panic in the Valley—the J&K government asked the Indian Air Force to airlift Amarnath pilgrims from the Valley; the Ministry of Civil Aviation instructed civil airlines to keep a check on their surging fares due to a high number of tourists leaving the Valley; government hospital employees were directed not to leave their stations; students residing in the government hostels were asked to vacate immediately; the National Institute of Technology (NIT) suspended its classes and many schools and colleges were shut down. People rushed to stock groceries and other essentials.[8] Long queues were seen at petrol pumps and ATMs.[9] There was chaos at the airport and railway stations across the state, as pilgrims, tourists, students and labourers rushed to leave. All of a sudden, the presence of armed forces across the Valley increased, as 38,000 more troops were sent to the Valley.[10]

Afshan Anjum, my friend and former colleague who worked as sports editor for NDTV in Delhi, had relocated to Srinagar after quitting her job a year earlier. 'My gardener who used to cycle down to Srinagar from Shopian every day advised me to stock up supplies, as he felt that something very terrible was going to happen in Kashmir. During my year-long stay in Srinagar, it was for the first time I had seen so much trepidation on the faces of Kashmiris. I overheard the conversations of people in shops, markets and offices. They discussed that doomsday was about to come and soldiers would intrude into their homes and beat them up. They were speaking all this based on their experience,' said Afshan.

'The policemen,' continued Afshan, 'were pulling out tourists from their hotels. The daily-wage earners from Uttar Pradesh and Bihar were pushed into buses. I saw young boys and girls from Shamli and Bijnor, who worked for salons and beauty parlours, being forced to pack up and leave. Security forces were deployed in the parks.'

At one level, the public was panicking, fearing a prolonged shutdown. The political class, too, sensed the developments as preparation for the Centre's conspiracy. The leaders of political parties like the Congress, the National Conference and the PDP suspected that the Centre was going to tamper with Article 35A and Article 370 of the Indian Constitution, which gave special status to Kashmir. Satya Pal Malik, then governor of J&K, when asked about the prevailing tension and possibility of abrogation of Article 370, said, 'It is normal. Only rumour mongering is going on. It's a very routine thing here. If you sneeze at Lal Chowk, it becomes an explosion when it comes here. Unnecessary panic is being created by vested interests, especially some political parties.'[11]

Mehbooba Mufti, along with leaders of the PDP and a few smaller parties, met Governor Malik and asked him to dispel rumours that had created panic in the Valley. Malik told them to maintain calm and reiterated that there was no plan of the government to take away the special status of J&K. However, Mufti wasn't convinced by the governor's words and said, 'New Delhi is preparing to rob people of Jammu & Kashmir of whatever little is left to protect their unique identity.'[12] Just four months ago, in April, she had given a very aggressive statement when, in its manifesto, the BJP had once again reiterated that it would abrogate Article 370. 'J&K is already on a heap of explosives and we saw a glimpse of it in Pulwama. If the BJP doesn't stop making such statements and give up such intentions, it will not only burn J&K but the entire region. So my warning to the BJP is to stop playing with fire. There is explosives in J&K. If you will light a spark, everything will go up in flames… there will be no Jammu or Kashmir or India left,' she warned.[13]

A day after Mufti's meeting with the governor, Omar Abdullah met the governor and addressed a press conference thereafter. Abdullah said that Malik had assured him that no announcement related to Article 370 or trifurcation of the state was going to be made. However, he also said, 'Governor isn't the final word on J&K. The final word on J&K is the Govt of India. Therefore, more than what Governor tells us publicly, I definitely would like to hear from Govt of India publicly that there is nothing people have to worry about.'[14]

Ghulam Nabi Azad, senior Congress leader from Kashmir, also issued a statement saying, 'The advisory issued by the government was worrisome and scared not only the people of J&K but also the entire nation. No government has ever asked tourists to go back. Such thing has never happened.'[15]

While the leaders of the NC, the PDP and the Congress were worried about what was going to come, a tweet from the official Twitter handle of the BJP's state unit added to the suspense, saying, 'BJP will unfurl tricolor on Independence Day in every Panchayat of the State: BJP State President Sh. @RavinderBJPJK.'[16]

Amidst the prevailing uncertainty, a tweet by veteran actor

Anupam Kher, who has been a supporter of PM Modi and whose wife Kirron Kher is a BJP MP, gave hints of what was coming up. He wrote, 'Kashmir Solution has begun.'[17]

The tension in the Valley also made separatist leaders uneasy. The Hurriyat Conference, a conglomeration of various social and political groups who believe that Kashmir is in India's occupation and demand separation, called a meeting of its members, which was presided by octogenarian Syed Ali Shah Geelani. In his address, Geelani said that the situation in Kashmir was chaotic and confusing. 'Increasing the forces' deployment, rumours of tampering with special provisions of state, suspension of (Amarnath) Yatra, evacuating tourists, students and yatris has created a war-like situation,' said Geelani. He also asked the youth of Kashmir to be ready for a 'long and tough' struggle.[18]

Gupkar Declaration

At 6 p.m. on 4 August, all parties barring the BJP decided to hold a joint meeting. As the police had instructed hotels in Srinagar not to allow political parties to hold a meeting on their premises, Mehbooba Mufti's residence was fixed as the venue. However, at the last moment, the venue was changed to Farooq Abdullah's house on Gupkar Road. The meeting was attended by leaders of the NC, the PDP, People's Movement (newly formed party by former IAS officer Shah Faesal). It was unanimously resolved that they would protect the autonomy of the state of J&K.[19] The resolution, later on, became famous as the 'Gupkar Declaration'. After the meeting, Mehbooba Mufti accused the Centre that it was creating a civil war-like situation. 'It is a very sinister design that is going on,' she said.[20]

Around 11 p.m., mobile internet service was shut down across the state. Shortly after, landline and cable television networks were also blocked. Although Kashmir is accustomed to the frequent shutdowns of the internet, restriction on landline telephone service was rare. Almost all forms of communication were made inaccessible to the general public. On the intervening nights of 4 and 5 August,

Section 144 of the Criminal Procedure Code was enforced, restricting any gathering of the public.[21] Although, technically, it was not a curfew, the ground situation reflected a curfew-like situation, with the barricading of several roads, heavy deployment of armed personnel and restriction of movement in certain areas. Riot control vehicles were kept on standby.

Next, a series of political detentions began. The first person to be detained was Omar Abdullah, who tweeted about it late at night, 'I believe I'm being placed under house arrest from midnight tonight & the process has already started for other mainstream leaders. No way of knowing if this is true but if it is then I'll see all of you on the other side of whatever is in store. Allah save us.'[22]

Soon cops landed at Mehbooba Mufti's residence and detained her. A few minutes after her detention, Mufti tweeted at 12.09 a.m. on 5 August 2019, 'How ironic that elected representatives like us who fought for peace are under house arrest. The world watches as people & their voices are being muzzled in J&K. The same Kashmir that chose a secular democratic India is facing oppression of unimaginable magnitude. Wake up India.'[23]

National Conference chief Farooq Abdullah was also not allowed to move out of his house, and his residence was cordoned off by the cops. He later alleged that the central government wanted to kill him and his son Omar.[24]

Congress leader Usman Majid and CPI (M) leader M.Y. Tarigami were also detained along with People's Conference chairman Sajad Lone.[25]

D-day

India woke up the next morning with newspapers full of what had happened during the night in Kashmir and TV channels screaming that the Kashmir solution was underway. All the changes clearly indicated that the Centre was going to take a very drastic step. It also implied that the advisory based on the likelihood of a terrorist attack on Amarnath Yatra was just an eyewash to camouflage the real intentions. The assurances given by Governor Satya Pal Malik to the political leaders and the media were just a part of the plan. It became clear, soon after daybreak, that the worst fears of Kashmiri politicians and many other sections of people were being realized.

On 5 August, when the list of business of the day for the Rajya Sabha was out, it listed that Home Minister Amit Shah would move two statutory resolutions and introduce a bill for consideration and passing.[26] All private news channels had switched on to the video feed of Rajya Sabha TV and had set up a panel of guests consisting of 'Kashmir experts' and spokespersons of various political parties.

Shah reached the Rajya Sabha after attending a cabinet meeting in the morning at the PM's residence, at which National Security Adviser (NSA) Ajit Doval was also present. The words of the resolution proposed by Amit Shah made everything clear. The first resolution read:

> In exercise of the powers conferred by Clause (3) of article 370 read with clause (1) of article 370 of the Constitution of India, the President, on the recommendation of the Parliament, is pleased to declare that, as from 5th of August, 2019, all clauses of the said article 370 shall cease to be operative except clause (1) thereof which shall read as under, namely:—
>
> All provisions of this Constitution, as amended from time to time, without any modifications or exceptions, shall apply to the State of Jammu and Kashmir notwithstanding anything contrary contained in article 152 or article 308 or any other article of this Constitution or any other provision of the Constitution of Jammu and Kashmir or any law, document, judgement, ordinance, order, bye-law, rule, regulation, notification, custom or usage having the force of law i`n the territory of India, or any other instrument, treaty or agreement as envisaged under article 363 or otherwise.

The second resolution pertained to the referring of Jammu and Kashmir Reorganization Bill by the President of India to the Rajya

Sabha and explained on what technical grounds the house was empowered to take up the bill.[27]

As Shah proposed the resolution in the house, it led to a huge uproar. Furious PDP members Nazir Ahmad Laway and Mir Mohammad Fayaz tore copies of the Constitution. Marshalls were asked to take them out.[28] Members of the Congress, the Trinomool Congress (TMC), the Dravida Munnetra Kazhagam (DMK), the Aam Aadmi Party (AAP) and the Nationalist Congress Party (NCP) shouted slogans in protest and squatted near the well.[29] It was shocking to see that members belonging to the Janata Dal (United) (JD), who are part of the BJP-led NDA, also walked out of the house to convey their disapproval. However, the resolutions were passed by voice votes. The first leg towards the abrogation was complete.[30]

Shah defended the move forcefully. He presented Article 370 as an evil law that didn't allow democracy to flourish in J&K and facilitated corruption. 'I want to tell the people of J&K what damage 370 & 35A did to the state. It's because of these sections that democracy was never fully implemented, corruption increased in the state, that no development could take place,' he asserted.[31] He alleged that due to the Constitution of J&K, many public welfare schemes of the Centre related to the health and education sector were not getting implemented in the state. 'Give us 5 years and we will make J&K the most developed state in India,' he announced confidently.[32]

Although Shah vowed to make J&K 'the most developed state of India', his further moves in the house implied that it was no longer going to remain a 'state'.[33]

Making History and Changing Geography

The move to abrogate Article 370 was officially kept concealed till 5 August. However, opposition parties had got a wind of it by observing the developments in Kashmir. The BJP was expected to move in that direction eventually, as the abrogation of Article 370 had been on the party's agenda for a long time. But what people were not prepared to hear was that apart from revoking the special status of J&K, the BJP-led government would also bifurcate the state and take away its statehood.

Amit Shah introduced the Jammu and Kashmir Reorganization Bill, 2019. The statement of the object read:

> The Ladakh division of the State of Jammu and Kashmir has a large area but is sparsely populated with a very difficult terrain. There has been a long pending demand of the people of Ladakh to give it the status of Union Territories to enable them to realise their aspirations. The Union Territory of Ladakh will be without Legislature.
>
> Further, keeping in view the prevailing internal security situation, fuelled by cross-border terrorism in the existing State of Jammu and Kashmir, a separate Union Territory for Jammu and Kashmir is being created. The Union Territory of Jammu and Kashmir will be with legislature.[34]

By 6.30 p.m., the bill was put to vote—125 voted in favour of the bill and 61 voted against it. The voting revealed the differences within the Opposition over the issue. While the NCP supported the move, the party was irked at how it was brought into the house and hence decided to abstain. The Bahujan Samaj Party (BSP), the Telugu Desam Party (TDP) and the AAP also supported the bill. It was opposed by the Congress, the Samajwadi Party, the Rashtriya Janata Dal (RJD), the DMK, the The Communist Party of India (Marxist) (CPI(M)), the Communist Party of India (CPI), the Muslim League, the Kerala Congress and the Marumalarchi Dravida Munnetra Kazhagam (MDMK). The bill was passed in the Rajya Sabha.[35]

Congress leader P. Chidambaram expressed his surprise over the introduction of the bill and asked Shah, 'Scrapping Article 370 was in your manifesto. But why give it a Union Territory status?'[36]

Ghulam Nabi Azad pointed out that a year-long consultation was done before a south Indian state was bifurcated into Telangana and Andhra Pradesh, but such an exercise was not undertaken in the case of J&K.[37]

'We are rectifying a historical blunder!'

The next day, 6 August, the resolutions and the bill were put before the Lok Sabha. The proceedings of the house began by observing silence for those who were killed in an atom bomb attack on Hiroshima city of Japan 74 years ago. Shortly after paying homage, the anger of opposition parties exploded in the house. Just before the voting, Samajwadi Party members, including its leader Mulayam Singh Yadav, walked out. The TMC and the NCP members also left the house. Like they did in the Rajya Sabha, members of JD(U), which was an ally of NDA, opposed the resolution and the bill in Lok Sabha also and left the house.[38]

At 7.10 p.m., the resolution to abrogate Article 370 was passed by the Lok Sabha with 351 members voting in support and 72 against it, while one member abstained.

About 35 minutes later, the Jammu and Kashmir Reorganization Bill, 2019, was also passed, with 70 members opposing the bill. Interestingly, the number of members who supported the bill was 370.[39]

During the debate on the bill, All India Majlis-E-Ittehadul Muslimeen (AIMIM) chief Asaduddin Owaisi criticized the move, dubbing it as the 'third historical mistake'. He said that the earlier two mistakes were the arrest of Sheikh Abdullah in 1953 when Jawaharlal Nehru was the PM and the second was the rigging of the 1987 state assembly elections in J&K. Owaisi remarked that it was dishonourable to replace a full-fledged state with two Union Territories.[40]

While replying to various charges by the leaders of opposition parties, Amit Shah said that only three families benefitted from Article 370 and not the people of Kashmir. He said that over 41,500 people had died in the state due to militancy during the three-decade-long militancy and the said article was to be blamed for it. 'This is not a historical blunder but we are rectifying the historical blunder,' Shah retorted.[41]

Former home minister and senior Congress leader P. Chidambaram dubbed it as the worst day in the constitutional history of India.[42]

The same day, in the evening, President Ramnath Kovind signed the resolution to abrogate the article and a declaration to that effect was published in *The Gazette of India* under the section 'EXTRAORDINARY'.[43] Three days later, on 9 August, he gave his assent to the Jammu and Kashmir Reorganization Act. With the President's approval, the legislative process of the abrogation of Article 370 and bifurcation of J&K was complete.

What Does the Change Imply?

What the world watched on television during those two days (5 and 6 August) was historic. Was it the culmination of events happening in the region in the past seven decades or was it the commencement of a new series of events? Would the situation of Kashmir mitigate or aggravate further? Would militancy end now? What would happen to the separatists? What would be the future of political discourse in Kashmir? How would the abrogation alter the life of Kashmiris? Would the Valley retain its charm? There were so many questions with no immediate answers. However, there are several de jure changes which the abrogation implies for the erstwhile state. But before understanding the implications of abrogating Article 370, it is pertinent to have a brief understanding of what the contentious article was all about and under what circumstances it came under effect.

In 1947, when British colonial rule ended in India, there were around 500 princely states in India. Kashmir was one of the largest among them. Although the majority of the population was Muslim, the state was ruled by a Hindu king, Maharaja Hari Singh. While he contemplated whether to join India or Pakistan or remain independent, Pakistani tribesmen, backed by the army of Pakistan, attacked Kashmir. At this juncture, Hari Singh deemed it prudent to join India and was supported by the leader of Kashmiri Muslims, Sheikh Abdullah (whose son Farooq Abdullah and grandson Omar Abdullah became chief ministers of Kashmir). Responding to Hari Singh's decision to join India, the Indian Army came to the rescue and dealt with the attackers. In 1949, the war ceased after the intervention of the UN. A Line of Control was created. India calls the other side of the LoC Pakistan Occupied Kashmir (PoK), while Pakistan calls it Azad Kashmir (or Independent Kashmir). However, de facto it is Pakistan that dominates the government in that part of Kashmir. In the undivided J&K state, India continued to keep 24 seats that fell under PoK, out of the 111 seats, vacant in the Vidhan Sabha.

When Hari Singh acceded to India, it was agreed that Kashmir would get autonomy. The central government of India would only control the defence, foreign affairs and telecommunications. It was also decided that the state would have its flag and a constitution. To offer constitutional sanctity to the above agreement, Article 370 was included in the Indian Constitution.[11] On 26 January 1950, along with the Constitution of India, a presidential order also came into force that detailed how Article 370 would be implemented. It specified the subjects on which the union government could make laws for J&K and on which subjects the law could be made in consultation with the state government. The presidential order also stipulated which provisions of the Indian Constitution were not applicable in J&K and the ones that were partly applicable or were applicable with certain modifications.

In 1952, another presidential order was issued that abolished monarchy from the state. The constituent assembly of the state had passed a resolution to abolish monarchy. The union government called a delegation of J&K leaders to Delhi and, after much discussion, an agreement was reached between the Centre and state leaders. This agreement is known as the 'Delhi Agreement' and, as per its provisions, the monarch was replaced by 'Sadr-e-Riyasat', who was to be elected by the legislative assembly. Karan Singh, the only son of Maharaja Hari Singh and the regent, became the first and only Sadr-e-Riyasat of J&K. In 1965, this post was replaced by the 'governor' appointed by the central government. Karan Singh became the first governor of the state as well.[45]

In 1954, a third presidential order was issued by President Rajendra Prasad on the advice of PM Jawaharlal Nehru. It was the most comprehensive order designed to implement the Delhi Agreement. It led to the inclusion of Article 35A in the Indian Constitution. This article gave powers to the state legislature to decide who the permanent residents of the state were. It gave privileges in the state government jobs, acquisition of property in the state, settling in the state and the right to scholarships and other forms of aid provided by the state government.[46]

Shujaat Bukhari, the slain veteran journalist from Kashmir, explained that the article helped the state to retain its distinct character in terms of residents. 'It actually protects a law that was passed by the Dogra monarch Maharaja Hari Singh during British rule to stop the influx of Punjabis into the state. The maharaja passed the law at the behest of Kashmiri Pandits who were powerful in the state at that time,' wrote Bukhari.[47]

The revocation of Article 370 has scores of implications. J&K would no longer have its separate constitution, flag and anthem. The citizens of J&K would not have dual citizenship. They would be just citizens of India. Since 1932, the Ranbir Penal Code (also known as J&K RPC) was the major criminal code in Kashmir. It was introduced by Dogra ruler Maharaja Ranbir Singh. This was replaced with the Indian Penal Code, which is enforced in other parts of India. Since the new Union Territory of J&K now completely comes under the purview of the Indian Constitution, it implies that its citizens are entitled to all the fundamental rights enshrined in it. All laws passed by the Parliament apply to the Union Territory. Any Indian citizen can now buy property in J&K and, subject to domicile laws, claim access to government jobs, scholarships and other benefits.[48]

Those who had been opposing the abrogation feared that it was being done to alter the demography of the state by settling people from other parts of India with the right to acquire property and vote in elections. In 2017, when Article 35A was challenged in the Supreme Court, Hurriyat Conference leader Mirwaiz Umar Farooq commented on the move by saying that it was aimed to reduce the 75 per cent Muslim majority of the state and change the basic character of the state. He suspected the litigation to be a part of a deliberate plan by the central government, led by the RSS.[49]

Those who had been opposing Article 370 claimed that it was just a temporary constitutional measure. However, this position was not upheld by the courts in numerous cases. In 2017, the High Court of Delhi rejected a plea that demanded the repeal of the article. Next year, the issue came up at the Supreme Court, which observed that although the head-note of Article 370 used the word 'temporary', it cannot be considered temporary. The apex court had also ruled, in 1969, that the article never ceased to be operative.[50]

Why was Ladakh Separated from J&K?

Along with the abrogation of Article 370, the separation of Ladakh from J&K was another major historic development. This hilly state surrounded by China in the east and Pakistan-administered Gilgit-Baltistan in the west is of strategic significance to India. Ladakh has two districts, Leh and Kargil, and the total population is 2,74,000.[51] Kargil has a majority of Shia Muslims who comprise 76.87 per cent of the population, whereas Buddhists are 14.29 per cent.[52] On the other hand, in Leh, the Buddhists are in majority with 66.40 per cent population and Muslims are 14.28 per cent.[53]

Ladakh has a history of Muslim–Buddhist conflict. In July and August 1989, there were violent riots, which began after the Ladakh Buddhist Association and Ladakh People's Movement organized protests in Leh against discrimination by the state government and to demand that the region be directly ruled by New Delhi. During one such protest, a brawl broke out between Muslim and Buddhist youths, and the demonstration turned violent. The police fired to control the violent mob, which led to the killing of three demonstrators. Thupsthan Chhewang, a member of Ladakh's former royal family and leader of the Buddhist Association, was arrested.[54] After the riots, Buddhist organizations called for a social and economic boycott of Muslims, which was lifted three years later.

Although no major clashes have happened after 1989, tension between the two communities has fluctuated due to cases where

Buddhist girls have converted and married Muslim men. The Buddhists felt that Buddhist girls were lured into wedlock based on lies to convert them to Islam. They were disappointed with the state machinery for not doing anything to end such conversions.[55]

What was the interest of the BJP in separating Ladakh from J&K, and making it a Union Territory? To understand this, let us take a brief look at the speech given by Jamyang Tsering Namgyal, the BJP's MP from Kargil, in Lok Sabha on 6 August. Namgyal's speech in Hindi went viral on social media and made him famous.

Namgyal began his speech by admonishing the opposition leaders who had spoken about Ladakh a day earlier. 'For the last seven decades Ladakh was never accepted and a statement was made in the house (Lok Sabha) that Ladakh is that piece of land where not even grass grows. Do people making such statements even know Ladakh? Do they understand the culture, language, lifestyle, food habits, climatic conditions, and difficult terrain of Ladakh or are they speaking just based on reading books?' he asked.

'Ladakh,' continued Namgyal, 'has struggled to become a Union Territory for the last 71 years. We wanted to become an inseparable part of India.' The first plea to this end was given on 4 May 1948, he said, but this was not done.'Under Kashmir, our development, our political aspirations, our language, our identity has been lost and Article 370 and the Congress is responsible for it.'

He continued by saying that becoming a UT has been in his political agenda, and he won with a record margin because all the people in Kargil and Leh wanted a UT, regardless of their religion.

Targeting the discriminatory attitude towards Ladakh in issues of development, jobs and education, he commented, 'Yesterday in Rajya Sabha's debate many people said that if Article 370 is gone then there will be no equality. I want to ask them when you took funds from the Government of India it was for all the three regions of Jammu, Kashmir and Ladakh but when the turn of development in Ladakh comes, you eat away Ladakh's fund in Kashmir. Is this your equality? There are two capitals in Jammu and Kashmir, a summer one and a winter one. In both places, there are civil secretariats. Check how many employees are from Ladakh in both of them. Jammu people fight and get some jobs, but you don't give even 10 jobs to Ladakh residents. Congress has not given a single higher education institute in Ladakh. Is this your equality? Very recently only Modi gave a university. You have recognized the Kashmiri language. You have recognized the Dogri language but to date, you have not recognized the Ladakhi language. Is this your equality?'

Namgyal accused major parties of Kashmir of creating a communal divide in Ladakh and said, 'You have misused Article 370 and attempted to finish Buddhists in J&K. This is your secularism. These families divided Ladakh in 1979. Buddhist majority was made Leh district and Muslim majority was made Kargil district. They made two brothers fight. Is this your secularism?'[56]

With the separation of Ladakh from J&K, the BJP looked at its further political consolidation in the region.

Amit Shah: Man of the Moment

If one has to give a face to these landmark events of Indian history then no doubt it would be that of Amit Shah, the man Friday of Narendra Modi. The way Shah did his homework, understood the technical and legal aspects, took advance measures in Kashmir, presented the bill in the Parliament and aggressively defended it while debating it with opposition leaders, once again proved why he became the most trusted man of PM Modi and one of the sharp-minded albeit controversial politicians of contemporary Indian politics.

Both Modi and Shah had joined the BJP almost together in the mid-eighties. Modi was a pracharak of the RSS, while Amit Shah entered politics through the ABVP. Shah's organizational and strategy-making skills led to his ascension in the party hierarchy, and he soon became one of the most powerful faces of the BJP in Gujarat. In the mid-nineties, Modi and Shah collaborated to dismantle the Congress in Gujarat.[57]

Shah had earned such clout for himself that, in 2014, when Modi shifted to national politics, his name was one of the probables for the CM's post. However, the criminal cases against him, like ordering fake encounters of alleged gangsters, for which he had to spend a few months in prison, were cited against him.[58] Instead, Modi made him responsible for the growth of the BJP across India, for strengthening his position as the PM and implementing the ideas of the party. Two months after Modi became the PM, Amit Shah was made national president of the BJP. Shah didn't disappoint the party. Under Shah's leadership, the BJP spread in various parts of the country. The BJP was able to form its government whether in alliance with regional partners or on its own in various states like Maharashtra, Haryana, Uttar Pradesh, Jharkhand and Assam. He also took the bold and shocking decision of allying with the ideologically opposed PDP in J&K. It is because of his tact that the party was able to form governments in states like Karnataka and Goa in spite of numbers not favouring the BJP. In 2019, the BJP returned to power with an overwhelming majority in the Lok Sabha. With these achievements, Shah is regarded as the most successful president of the BJP so far.

Shah was next given charge of the powerful Home portfolio, through which some historic decisions were to be implemented. Shah did his job diligently. Abrogation of Article 370 clubbed with the separation of Ladakh from J&K was the first such delivery by him. Later in the year, he got another controversial legislation, the Citizenship Amendment Act, passed. The BJP, during its election campaign, had widely used the slogan *'Modi Hai To Mumkin Hai'* (If Modi is there, then it is possible). Political commentators observe that it is Amit Shah who realizes all the dreams of Modi. It is due to this quality that he has acquired nicknames like 'Motabhai' (big brother), 'Sankatmochak' (troubleshooter) and 'Chanakya' (the advisor of historical Maurya ruler Chandragupta), and is said to be the potential successor of Modi.

Situation after the Abrogation

In the days following the abrogation, over 5,000 political workers, alleged stone-pelters and separatists were taken into custody.[59]

The high number of detentions led to a space crunch in prisons, and the administration had to hire private properties, such as the Sher-e-Kashmir International Convention Centre in Srinagar, to hold those taken into custody. Many were slapped with the PSA.[60]

Afshan Anjum, who was in Srinagar for about a week after the abrogation before flying to Delhi for Eid, recollects the systematic restrictions. 'If you are living in a particular area you could move around from one street to another if required; however, you couldn't move to somebody's house in a different area. With such restrictions people thought it better to keep themselves at their homes,' said Afshan.

Narrating her experience, Afshan said, 'Kashmir was shut and, for the first time, we felt what it means to keep yourself locked at home. For the first time, we experienced how to survive within the four walls of your house by eating just potatoes and rice. People were cut off not only with the mainstream but also with each other. A large population in Kashmir comprises elders whose children work in cities like Delhi, Mumbai or Dubai. There are many homes where the well-being of parents could be checked only by mediums like WhatsApp or telephone. Think about such youngsters who were not able to hear their old parents. Think about that old man who is a heart patient and couldn't call the neighbour or ambulance by a phone call.'

Kashmir was all over the news channels. Visuals of celebrations similar to those seen after the airstrikes six months ago were seen again. Some celebrated it as the victory of India and the defeat of Pakistan.

Although Kashmir was the top word on all communication mediums across India, no news was coming in from Kashmir. While all major national news channels had sent three to four reporters to Srinagar to cover the situation of Kashmir after the abrogation, the logistics was a big problem in the dissemination of news. There was no internet, landline telephone or mobile phone connection, and this constrained the task of the journalists. The media got some relief when the J&K administration opened a media centre at Hotel Sarovar Portico, where a mobile phone and computers with low-speed internet connection were provided. It was a few days later that TV journalists got an option of communication via satellite when their OB[61] vans reached Srinagar from Delhi after being stopped at several locations en route by security forces.

One of the initial visuals which came from Kashmir after the abrogation was of NSA Ajit Doval. Wearing a sleeveless jacket, Doval was seen eating and chatting with locals in Kashmir. The visuals were said to be from Shopian, which is dreaded as a hotbed of militancy. A few other visuals showed him praising and encouraging the members of the J&K Police and the CRPF.[62] Political commentators soon realized that such visuals were being released to convey that Kashmir was peaceful after the abrogation and security forces were equipped to tackle any disturbances. It would have been a matter of pride and achievement for the Centre to show that such a historic decision was being implemented without any protests. The potential 'troublemakers' were already in confinement.

5

BJP, RSS AND ARTICLE 370

'Everybody said that abrogation of Article 370 was our daydream. That impossible has become possible. Next impossible will also become possible,' said Indresh Kumar, a senior pracharak of the Sangh and advisor to Muslim Rashtriya Manch, which is informally seen as the Muslim wing of the RSS, when I asked him whether he considered the abrogation of Article 370 as a step towards the RSS doctrine of '*Akhand Bharat*'.

But why was it important for the BJP-led central government to revoke the special status of J&K? To understand this, a brief look at history is needed.

The abrogation of Article 370 was the zenith of an around seven-decade-old campaign led by the RSS. Established in 1925, the raison d'être of the RSS is to promote religio-cultural nationalism in India and abroad. The special status of Kashmir through the constitutional provisions conflicted with its ideologies. Hence, the RSS commenced a multidimensional campaign against Article 370, and its mission was accomplished in August 2019.

Campaign of Seven Decades

Broadly, there have been two discourses about Kashmir in India. One discourse is religio-cultural, which rejects the special Kashmiri identity and believes that Kashmir is essentially Indian and has been a centre of Vedic culture, Brahmanical and Buddhist learning, that it has been essentially a Hindu region, supported by myths, sages who resided here and the rulers. This is stressed upon by referring to Muslim invaders and claiming that all Kashmiris were predominantly

Hindus who were forced to convert. This view is in contrast to the secular narrative, which acknowledges that Kashmiris are Indians but stresses that they represent India's unique 'unity in diversity'. As per this narrative, Kashmir is an amalgam of various religious, ethnic and dynamic influences. The RSS subscribes to the former narrative that conforms with its religio-cultural ideology. A resolution passed by the RSS affirms, 'Kashmir is an integral part of Bharat naturally, morally, culturally and constitutionally.'[1]

Role In Convincing the Maharaja?

A book by Arun Bhatnagar, a former bureaucrat, claims that the RSS played a role in the accession of J&K into India. In 1947, when Maharaja Hari Singh was indecisive over the future of his state, then home minister Sardar Vallabhbhai Patel sought Madhavrao Golwalkar's help to convince the maharaja to sign an instrument of accession with India. Golwalkar was the second sarsanghchalak (head) of the RSS. Golwalkar met the maharaja in October 1947. The maharaja reportedly told Golwalkar that it was unviable for him to join India since his state was dependent on Pakistan—routes connecting Kashmir pass through Sialkot and Rawalpindi, and the air connectivity for the state was through Lahore. At this, Golwalkar reminded the maharaja that he was a Hindu king and if he decided to accede to Pakistan, then his subjects would have to suffer, and the transportation links with India could be established rapidly, so it would be in his interest to join India. After eight days, the maharaja signed an instrument of accession with India.[2]

The engagement of the RSS in Kashmir dates back to the pre-Independence era. In 1942, Golwalkar had sent a pracharak named Balraj Madhok to the princely state with a brief to set up shakhas (branches) of the organization in the Jammu area and organize Hindus to defend their interests in a Muslim-majority area. Madhok was successful in laying the foundation of the RSS in the state. In 1947, with the help of Pandit Premnath Dogra, he established a political outfit named Praja Parishad Party (PPP). The PPP set up its structure on the existing network of the RSS and got associated with a right-wing nationalist political party named Bhartiya Jana Sangh (BJS), which was the political arm of the RSS.[3]

Controversial Land Reforms by Sheikh Abdullah

After coming to power in 1949, Sheikh Abdullah started to execute his vision of 'New Kashmir', and a significant step towards the realization of that vision was land reforms. With the patronage of the maharaja, Hindus were a rich minority in the Valley.[4] Under the Big Land Abolition Act, 1950, passed during his dispensation, land ownership was limited to 22.75 acres. There was a perception that most of the land was occupied by Dogras and most of the tillers were Muslims. The policies of Abdullah were aimed at distributing land to those who were the actual tillers of the land. The issue took a communal colour, and Abdullah's policies were projected as anti-Hindu by the PPP.[5]

The PPP focused on the grievances of the Dogra community and opposed Abdullah's policies.[6] According to the RSS, during the tenure of Abdullah, after the accession of J&K, persecution of Hindus continued. Kashmiri Hindus, who were already being killed, their women raped, their temples destroyed, were gradually being driven out from the Valley due to Abdullah's policies, according to the RSS.

It was decided that the Vidhan Sabha would fix the amount of compensation for the landlords whose 'excess' land was taken away, but it was later decided that no compensation would be provided. This way, J&K became the only state in India where big land owners were not given any compensation. This led to an aggravation of unrest among Dogras and Kashmiri Pandits, who were already disgruntled due to the transfer of power from the maharaja. They felt the Abdullah government was snatching away their rights. More non-Muslims than Muslims were impacted by the land reforms. Kashmiri author and journalist Ashish Kaul counters the narrative that Kashmiri Pandits got a discriminatory advantage from the maharaja in the case of land holdings. Kaul's maternal family along with other Kashmiri Pandits were litigants in cases where their land was allegedly usurped. In Kaul's view, Sheikh Abdullah introduced the Land Reforms Act to grab land held by minority aboriginals. At that time, 95 per cent of the land custodians in the Kashmir Valley were Hindus. He explains that there were two types of land. One type of land was managed by Hindus on behalf of the maharaja and an annual tax was given to the kingdom. Another type of land was purchased and owned by Hindus for farming and making residential buildings. 'This land,' says Kaul, 'was not gifted to them. They used to pay a fixed yearly sum against the particular land allocated to them by Maharaja Hari Singh of Kashmir.' He says that, in contradiction to the popular theory, these custodians of land were from the low-income group and many of them tilled the land themselves.

Kaul explains that after several deliberations few concessions were given; however, there was a catch. As per the law, only the land that fell within 6 kilometres of the erstwhile owner's residence could be claimed. However, the land of many Pandits was outside this limit. So their land was sold at a paltry sum of Rs. 500 per kanal against the then prevalent rate of Rs. 1 lakh.[7]

Due to loss of power and property, this section of the population became reactionary and became a nemesis of Sheikh Abdullah. Religion became their unifying factor and led to their affinity with Praja Parishad.[8] The RSS, which had been banned by Sardar Patel after the assassination of M.K. Gandhi in 1948, was looking for an issue to revive itself. It got the same by propagating nationalism in a Muslim-majority state.[9]

Agitation Against the Delhi Agreement

In July 1952, Sheikh Abdullah signed the Delhi Agreement with the Indian government, which laid the framework of the Centre–state relationship. The agreement provided autonomy to the state within India. The RSS, the PPP and the BJS vehemently opposed the agreement.

In the same year, a resolution was passed by the working

committee of the BJS, declaring J&K as an integral part of India. The declaration emphasized that the provisions in the Indian Constitution about J&K were temporary and violated Indian sovereignty.[10] A decision was taken to launch an agitation by the end of the year, with the objective of abrogating Article 370.

The agitation was spearheaded by the PPP, with the support of the RSS and other Hindu organizations. One of the demands of the agitators was the separation of Jammu from Kashmir. Kashmir became one of the top agendas of the Sangh Parivar. The agitation spread to some areas of Punjab and Delhi. This was the first time that mass mobilization over the contentious issues about Kashmir had taken place.[11] The agitation turned violent in Jammu, resulting in the damage of government property. Then PM Jawaharlal Nehru asked then Intelligence Bureau Chief B.N. Malik to reach Kashmir to convince Praja Parishad to end its agitation and explain to them that the unification of Kashmir with India was complete. However, as the case was with the Security Council, the special status of Kashmir had to be maintained for few more years. A few years later, the privileges would lapse automatically and Kashmir would become just like any other state of India. Secondly, Malik was asked to speak to Sheikh Abdullah and dissuade him from making anti-Hindu speeches.[12]

Death of S.P. Mukherjee

Shyama Prasad Mukherjee, the founder of the BJS, became the biggest face of anti-Article 370 agitations. His statement '*Ek desh me do vidhan, do pradhan aur do nishan nahi chalenge*,' (One country can't have two constitutions, two prime ministers and two national emblems) is often quoted by members of the RSS and the BJP during discussions over the Kashmir issue. Mukherjee was a minister in Jawaharlal Nehru's cabinet but distanced himself in protest against the Nehru–Liaqat Pact of 1950. During his speech in the Parliament, Mukherjee pointed out the temporary nature of Article 370 and opposed the adoption of a separate flag for J&K. He took up the issue of appropriation of the Hindu Endowment Trust's property and funds. Mukherjee believed that the policies of the government were discriminatory towards the Jammu region and protested against making Urdu a compulsory language.[13]

At that time, the government made it mandatory for people coming to the state to get a permit from Kashmiri authorities to cross the border. As a part of his agitation, Mukherjee decided to cross the border and was arrested on 11 May 1953 while doing so. Around a month later, he died in custody. The RSS and its affiliates revere Mukherjee as a martyr. Mukherjee's death aggravated the bitterness between Nehru and Abdullah, which ultimately led to Abdullah's dismissal and arrest.

Mukherjee's death weakened the public campaign against Article 370, but the RSS and the BJS continued the agitation through various forums.

The Constitution of Jammu and Kashmir adopted in 1956 defined a 'permanent resident' as a person who was a state subject on 14 May 1954 or had been a resident of the state for at least 10 years, and rights to vote, hold public office and own property were limited to permanent residents. These provisions were vehemently opposed by the RSS and the BJS. The RSS believed that the provisions were discriminatory towards Hindus, undermined the scope of what it is to be an Indian and appeared to support Jinnah's two-nation theory.[14]

In 1960, Deendayal Upadhyay, organizational secretary of the BJS, wrote a critique of Article 370, 'So long as this article continues, normalcy in matters of constitutional arrangements vis-à-vis Bharat will not be restored.' Golwalkar concurred with Upadhyay and said that the only way to keep Kashmir was complete integration and the scrapping of Article 370. 'If the border area of NEFA (North-East Frontier Agency) can be centrally administered through the army then why not border areas of Kashmir?' he asked. Balraj Madhok of the RSS believed that the problem of Kashmir was basically religio-political and not socio-economic. 'Wrong diagnostics leads to the application of wrong remedies resulting in further worsening of the situation,' he said.[15]

Article 370: A Constant in BJP's Manifesto

The BJP has consistently pursued the ideologies and aspirations conceived by the RSS. This implies that Kashmir and Article 370 have been one of the top agendas of the party.

The BJP took the first electoral plunge in the 1984 Lok Sabha elections and, in its very first manifesto, suggested deleting Article 370. Although the party managed to win just two seats, the leadership was convinced that the emotions which 'Kashmir' and Article 370 evoked would take the party far. This was enunciated in subsequent election manifestos.

The next Lok Sabha elections happened in 1989, when militancy and violence permeated the Kashmir Valley, as was regularly reported in the news. It was also reflected in the BJP's election manifesto, which promised revocation of Article 370.

The dissolution of the 16-month-old Chandrashekhar-led central government called for Lok Sabha elections again in 1991. The exodus of Kashmiri Pandits from the Valley had begun, and the violence and displacement they faced got a place in the BJP's election manifesto. The manifesto promised to 'weed out Pakistani elements from the Valley' and reiterated its promise to remove Article 370.

In the 1996 election manifesto, too, 'Kashmir' was mentioned numerous times and three regional councils in Ladakh, Jammu and Kashmir were promised. The manifesto not only blamed the Congress rule for the mess in Kashmir but also promised to reclaim the territory occupied by Pakistan for around five decades. The Lok Sabha elections were conducted again in 1998, after the BJP-led National Democratic Alliance collapsed, and the BJP replicated its stand on Kashmir once again.

The election manifesto of the BJP in 1999 proved to be an exception, where, for the first time, there was no mention of Article 370. 'Article 370' was missing in 2004 as well, although the party's vision document repeated its 1996 promise of a three-way development of the state.

In the 2009 Lok Sabha elections, Article 370 reappeared in the

BJP's election manifesto. The manifesto read, 'Article 370 poses a psychological barrier for the full integration of the people of Jammu & Kashmir with the national mainstream. The BJP remains committed to the abrogation of this Article.'[16] The manifesto not only promised revocation of Article 370 but also assured resettling Kashmiri Pandits, providing rights to PoK refugees, initiating developmental projects and combating terrorism. In 2009, Kashmir found mention in the Congress manifesto also, which talked about how the Congress-led United Progressive Alliance (UPA) had disbursed funds for the development of the state.

Kashmir has been consistently mentioned in subsequent election manifestos of both the national parties. In 2014, the BJP manifesto said that the party remained committed to the abrogation of Article 370 and would discuss the issue with all stakeholders. In 2019, the party manifesto repeated the promise of abrogating the disputed article. Interestingly, it was in this year that the Congress, for the first time, enunciated its stand on the issue, dedicating a whole section to Kashmir in its manifesto. It read, 'We also acknowledge the unique history of the state and the unique circumstances under which the state acceded to India that led to the inclusion of Article 370 in the Constitution of India. Nothing will be done or allowed to change the constitutional position.'[17]

With the BJP finally delivering on the promise that it had made in the past four decades, Article 370 will now cease to feature in the party's future election manifestos, though, I believe, it will be surely mentioned in election campaigns as an achievement of the BJP-led government.

6

INDEPENDENCE DAY

Eid al-Adha, which fell on 12 August 2019, a week after the historic decision, was a different one for the people of the Valley. The restrictions imposed by the security forces and the curfews kept them locked inside their homes. For many families, Bakr Eid was meatless that year. It was for the first time in recent history that Eid prayers were not allowed at Eidgah or the historic Jamia Masjid but only at local mosques. The authorities had apprehensions that a large assembly of people could ignite a law and order problem. Later in the evening, the administration informed the media that Eid went off 'peacefully' and no major incidents were reported. The authorities maintained that the situation was very much better than the aftermath of Burhan Wani's encounter and only two people had been hospitalized with injuries due to a clash with security forces. After the prayers of Eid al-Fitr on 5 June, some clashes were reported in Srinagar, Sopore and Anantnag between stone-pelters and the security forces. In the Nowhatta area, some youngsters, with their faces covered with masks, were reported to have displayed banners in support of Jaish-e-Mohammed chief Masood Azhar and slain militant commander Zakir Musa.[1]

Just three days after Eid was 15 August, India's Independence Day, a date which has been keeping security forces in the Valley on their toes for the past three decades. National festivals like Republic Day and Independence Day have often been preceded by militant activities and tension. Security forces are on high alert to foil any attempt at sabotage. In 2016, a gunman attacked a police station in the Nowhatta area, leading to the death of one police officer and injuring 10 paramilitary personnel. Next year, in 2017, four security personnel were wounded when a militant hurled a grenade on a ROP of the CRPF. In 2018, too, separatist leaders like Syed Ali Shah Geelani, Mirwaiz Umar Farooq and Yasin Malik called for a complete shutdown and asked people to observe the date as 'Black Day'. The militant organization Hizbul Mujahideen, through letters, warned parents to keep away their children from schools on the date. Internet and mobile phone services were temporarily shut down, citing security concerns. Train services were discontinued. The Amarnath Yatra was suspended on 13 August.

Considering this history of volatility, Independence Day 2019 seemed to be a bigger challenge. It was a test for security forces to thwart any attempt of disruption or pre-empt any law and order situation. The eyes of the world were on Srinagar to see how India was celebrating a national event on a land where it had implemented a controversial and landmark decision. It required elaborate preparations not only in and around the Sher-e-Kashmir Cricket Stadium, where the celebrations were to be held, but also in Srinagar city and other sensitive areas of the Valley.

The brief for us journalists was to look out for any trouble and report the situation. There were three reporters from my news channel: Gyanendra Tiwari and Jainendra Kumar from Delhi and me. We decided that Jainendra Kumar and I would scout different parts of the city to capture the situation on our cameras, while Gyanendra Tiwari would be inside the stadium to cover the celebrations. Gyanendra had interviewed Governor Satya Pal Malik a couple of days ago, when he said, 'Independence Day celebrations will be better than it has been celebrated so far.'[2]

Sher-e-Kashmir Stadium

The Sher-e-Kashmir Stadium located in the Sonawar area in Srinagar is technically a playground for cricket but has been used for other purposes too. For many years, it was occupied by the CRPF. Mega political events have been held there, like in 2002, when the NC held a special session to elect a new president. Former PM Atal Bihari

Vajpayee addressed a rally at this stadium in 2003, as did Narendra Modi in 2015.

Although the stadium was just half a kilometre away from Hotel Sarovar Portico, journalists left as early as 6 a.m., anticipating strict security arrangements for the function that was to begin at 9 a.m. Gyanendra told me that it was a task to get inside the stadium with his camera equipment in spite of possessing the entry pass because of the multi-layered security arrangements. It took over 10 minutes for each media team to clear the security and get inside the stadium. The roads leading towards the stadium were blocked and a high number of security forces surrounded the stadium.

There was speculation before the event that Home Minister Amit Shah would also airdrop to participate in the celebrations. Considering that PM Modi and Amit Shah have a penchant for giving shocks and surprises and to create events that aid the BJP's growth, this was possible. In the past, the BJP had launched several movements over the unfurling of the Indian flag in Srinagar as an expression of its nationalist agenda. However, by the time the celebrations commenced in the stadium, it became clear that Shah was not coming.

There were around 500 spectators in the stadium, which was just about one-fourth of its total capacity. The spectators comprised mainly government servants and people from armed forces dressed in plain clothes. A few civilians were also allowed, who came from different states of India and chanted *'Bharat Mata ki Jai!'* from a corner. There were separate arrangements for the seating of media personnel. Most of the chairs were occupied by journalists from Delhi, as local newspapers were not functional due to curbs on travel, communication blockades and other logistical issues.

The celebrations began in the presence of Governor Satya Pal Malik and NSA Ajit Doval, who had been frequenting Kashmir to monitor the security situation. In previous years, Kashmiri politicians like Omar Abdullah, Farooq Abdullah and Mehbooba Mufti had attended the event with their supporters, but this year they were all under detention. In his speech, Malik praised the decision to revoke the state's special status and said that the move would bring prosperity and development to the region. He asserted that Kashmir would become a big hub of tourism and industry, as the historic decision had opened up new opportunities for development. Malik said that recruitment of militants had reduced and weekly stone-pelting incidents had ended.[3]

What Malik said resonated with PM Modi's Independence Day speech in New Delhi, in which he lambasted people who opposed the revocation of Article 370 and alleged that such people were playing politics.[4] He said that Article 370 encouraged corruption and nepotism.[5]

Gyanendra noticed that the celebrations lacked a Kashmiri flavour. There were no local schoolchildren, as the schools were shut. A dance troupe of about 50 young men and women in traditional attires were invited from Jammu to perform cultural dances of Jammu, Kashmir and Ladakh. There were dance performances by different units of the security forces also. Most of the songs played were in the Punjabi, Dogri and Ladakhi languages. A Kashmiri song was also played, but those who danced to it were non-Kashmiris. A symbolic presence of Kashmir was represented through the Jammu & Kashmir Police band that had a few Kashmiri officers. After the celebrations were over, a few TV channels assembled some spectators outside the stadium who enthusiastically chanted *'Vande Mataram'* and *'Bharat Mata ki Jai!'* in front of the cameras live-streaming the visuals.

Lal Chowk: Today's Questions, History's Answers

We got an idea of the security arrangements in the city as soon as our car moved out of the hotel gate. The street connecting Gupkar Road to Dal Gate was blocked by CRPF personnel. We had decided to visit Lal Chowk first but were told to take a detour. Since our driver was a Srinagar resident, he knew an alternate route that passed through narrow and arduous streets. Still, at several roundabouts, we were stopped and questioned by the security personnel. The distance from our hotel till Lal Chowk was just 3 kilometres but, due to diversions and multiple security checks, it took us over half an hour to cover the distance.

An evening earlier, BJP's Kapil Mishra had shared a picture that showed an Indian tricolour atop the clock tower at Lal Chowk. Jamyang Tsering Namgyal, BJP party leader from Ladakh, also tweeted the same picture. We decided to check if a flag had been hoisted at the clock tower. If it had, it was failure on our part for not being aware of such an event.

We reached near Lal Chowk, but the place was out of bounds for us. The area resembled a cantonment. Hundreds of J&K policemen and CRPF personnel had surrounded Lal Chowk and the clock tower was made inaccessible from a radius of over 300 metres. As we got down from our car at the main road adjacent to the clock tower, the CRPF men rushed towards us angrily, asking us to leave immediately. We informed them that we were journalists and would leave the place after taking a few shots, but they weren't in a mood to listen and didn't allow us to take out our camera. Realizing that there was no point in arguing with them, we decided to approach the clock tower from a different direction. Reportage on Srinagar would be incomplete without showing the situation at Lal Chowk. There were a few streets adjacent to Lal Chowk that led to the clock tower.

We reached close to the tower. Although we were several metres away from it, we could get a good shot. What Mishra and Namgyal had tweeted was not true. Later on, a fact-check by some news outlets revealed that both the leaders had become victims of photoshopping and had shared the image without ascertaining its veracity.[6] It was an embarrassment for the party and gave a gala time to the trolls.

Reporters from other TV channels also reached the location. Although there was equivalent security in this direction of the tower as well, the security personnel here were not as aggressive and intimidating as the ones posted towards the main road. They cooperated and asked us to quickly finish our shoot and leave the place.

I had visited Lal Chowk during my previous tours to Srinagar. One could experience the regular hustle-bustle of a marketplace with numerous shops selling consumer items ranging from dry fruits, saffron and clothes to utensils, stationery and electronics, except there were men in uniform also all around and one could see tin sheds and sandbags in some corners. I often bought walnut and rajma from the shops at Lal Chowk while returning to Mumbai. Lal Chowk used to be alive till 1 or 2 a.m. in the night when many shopkeepers downed their shutters after the last show of movies at Palladium Cinema, a cinema hall that was gutted by a fire in the nineties.

That day, I saw a different Lal Chowk. The cinema hall still existed but its screen was blank and CRPF personnel had replaced the patrons. Lal Chowk and the streets adjoining it were deserted, and the only human presence was in the form of solemn-faced men in uniform holding firearms. Why was Lal Chowk such an inaccessible place that day? The answer lies in the history of the place.

Lal Chowk has witnessed several landmark events in the history of Srinagar. While Dal Lake has been on Kashmir's tourist map due to its natural beauty, houseboats and shikaras, Lal Chowk is somewhat an antithesis of what Dal Lake stands for. Lal Chowk's history has been marred by political upheaval, violence, riots and protests. Lal Chowk means 'Red Square' in English, and the square stands for all the connotations of red: vibrance, danger, blood and communism. It is said that Lal Chowk was named after Moscow's Red Square by leftists who were inspired by the Russian Revolution and drew parallels between the rule of the Russian tzar and the reign of the maharaja in Kashmir.

The famous clock tower was built in 1980, but Lal Chowk had become a centre of historical and political importance much before that. In 1948, it was at this Lal Chowk that former PM Jawaharlal Nehru unfurled the national flag. Standing beside him, Sheikh Abdullah famously said, '*Man tu shudi, tu man shudi, ta kas na goyed, man degram, tu degri*.' It is a Persian verse that means, 'I become you and you become me, so no one can say we are separate.'[7] Five years later, under Nehru's regime, Abdullah was arrested for conspiring against India. In 1975, the Indira–Sheikh Accord, which was seen as another watershed event in Kashmiri history, was announced by Sheikh Abdullah at Lal Chowk.

In 1990, the Jammu Kashmir Liberation Front (JKLF) placed a colour TV set and challenged that whoever dared to raise the Indian flag could take it away as a reward. A unit of armed forces deployed in the Valley did that and took away the TV set, which was installed in their mess.[8]

In 1992, BJP leader Murli Manohar Joshi announced that he would unfurl the Indian flag at Lal Chowk in Srinagar, where his Ekta Yatra would culminate on Republic Day. It was a time when militancy was at its peak in the Valley. The government imposed a curfew in the city and Lal Chowk was cordoned off. Joshi arrived at Lal Chowk in a bulletproof car with a few supporters and unfurled the tricolour. Nobody had then imagined that the young bearded RSS pracharak, dressed in a black jacket, named Narendra, accompanying him would become the PM of India 22 years later and it would be under his tenure that Kashmir would see one of its biggest upheavals. There had been a few incidents of violence preceding the event.[9]

On 10 April 1993, a big fire engulfed Lal Chowk, allegedly caused by a violent clash between the locals and BSF personnel, which had ignited due to some altercation. The fire destroyed several homes, shops, office buildings, commercial complexes, schools and a shrine. Many people died, some due to the fire and others due to bullet wounds.

In the aftermath of Burhan Wani's encounter, the separatists gave a call to occupy Lal Chowk and the airport road. A curfew was imposed to deter them. Clashes between stone-pelters and the security forces were reported from different parts of the city.

Apart from political clashes, Lal Chowk has also endured the wrath of nature. The devastating floods of 2014 had impacted this locality and submerged the whole of Lal Chowk, causing huge financial losses.

Today, Lal Chowk has become an epicentre of political movements and resistance. Unfurling a flag at Lal Chowk is seen as a political statement. In the past, separatists have organized their own flag hoisting ceremonies and have unfurled different kinds of flags, including that of Pakistan. Since the nineties, the BSF or the CRPF camped at Lal Chowk and raised the Indian flag there on Republic Day, but the tradition was discontinued in 2009. But Lal Chowk is not just a place for nationalists and separatists to highlight their beliefs, it is also the venue for different kinds of protests. The chowk regularly witnesses protests by labour unions, students' associations, semi-political groups and non-governmental organizations.

Just a few minutes before I reached, a youngster with an Indian flag had managed to reach the square. However, before he could get close to the clock tower, a security personnel detained him and handed him over to the local police. I swiftly did a walkthrough of the place, briefly narrating the history of Lal Chowk, comparing how it used to look during 'normal' days (normal has a different description in Kashmir) and how it looked that day. After winding up my shoot, I headed downtown.

Tiranga Yatra

As we were crossing the tourist reception centre, we saw around 10 people standing outside a building near a taxi stand. They didn't appear to be Kashmiris. What were they were up to and how did they manage to come out in such a group when there were restrictions on movement imposed in the city? Out of curiosity, we stopped our car and approached them. Upon enquiring, they told us that they were BJP workers and had come from Haryana and Punjab. They wanted to take out a 'Tiranga March' from Lal Chowk to Sher-e-Kashmir Stadium. However, they were scared of the cops and didn't dare to take out the tricolour from a bag they were carrying. I couldn't help smiling after listening to them. In such a tense situation and with the ubiquitous presence of security forces, it appeared impossible for them to publicly display their patriotism. As they were pondering over what to do, a TV journalist and his cameraman reached there. He apparently ran a local TV channel from the place these guys had come from and had given them this idea. A BBC journalist who was passing by, too, stopped after seeing us.

I decided to wait for them to start their 'Tiranga Yatra' and see if they could manage to reach the stadium. It would become a part of my report describing the 'situation in Srinagar on Independence Day', I thought. However, the men appeared to be too scared to do anything, even though the journalist tried to convince them. When we decided to move on after waiting, the journalist pleaded with us to wait a little more. The crowd reluctantly agreed to take out the yatra a little later.

The tricolour was taken out and the crowd started walking towards the stadium, chanting *"Bharat Mata ki Jai"* and *'Vande Mataram'* slogans. We began taking their shots. As the march had moved hardly 200 metres, two police vans arrived swiftly. 'Today is a day of double celebration for us,' one of the participants gave us a sound bite. Before I could speak to more of them, the cops bundled them into their vans and sped off. The Tiranga Yatra ended there.

Downtown

The area surrounding our hotel and the stadium was trouble-free so far due to the presence of the UN office in the vicinity and due to it being in the proximity of the high-profile Gupkar Road. It was believed to be one of the highly secured areas in Srinagar, but many other localities were also vulnerable to violence. We decided to check on downtown Srinagar, which was one of the sensitive neighbourhoods and prone to violent protests. There were reports of violent clashes between agitators and security forces after the decision of the abrogation of Article 370 had been announced. There were incidents of stone-pelting on Eid also. However, the administration downplayed such incidents.

We drove through various areas like Nawakadal, Alamgiri Bazaar and Zainakadal. The main road was deserted and all the shops were shut. Nobody was seen on the road except the security personnel. Then, we moved inside the bylanes adjoining the main road. The scene in the inner lanes was a contrast to the main road. There were small groups of youngsters outside their houses and at corners of streets. I thought of getting down and speaking to them, but the driver warned us against doing so. 'If these youngsters come to know that we are from media, you can't imagine what they will do to us,' he said. He advised taking shots of the locality while the car was in motion in such a way that the camera was not visible from outside. Sachin was adept at doing so and got good footage.

From downtown, we moved towards Dal Lake. The promenade surrounding the lake was empty. A few shikara owners sat silently in a group near the entry gate where people get into the boats. Most of them were middle-aged or old men and looked depressed. I got down from my car and, after introducing myself, asked whether they would like to speak on camera on how the decisions of the preceding week had affected them and how they were surviving. Most of them politely refused to talk but a few younger ones among them belligerently asked us to leave, alleging that the media had caused major damage to their livelihood. The driver suggested that I should not argue with them and leave the place.

After moving half a kilometre ahead, we saw a man selling vegetables at the promenade, although there were no customers visible. Vegetables like carrots, radishes, collard greens, bitter gourd, brinjal, *nadru* (lotus root), tomato and so on are cultivated on plots built on the embankments. Floating gardens are found in different parts of Dal Lake, and many farmers earn their livelihood by cultivating vegetables in the fertile ecosystem of this waterbody. Through small boats, they transport their produce to the lake's market area, at the promenade or in vegetable markets of the city. I got down from my car and bought half a kilogram of bitter gourd to initiate a conversation with the man.

'*Sabji bik paa rahi hai?*' (Is vegetable getting sold?), I asked.

'*Haan thodi bik jaati hai lekin mushkil se gujara ho pa raha hai*' (Yes, some get sold, but it has become very difficult to survive).

'What do you think about the decision of abrogation of Article 370?'

'Was there any need to do all this? Politicians must come and see how their decisions affect poor people like us.'

'But these are just temporary measures. After some days, when the situation gets normalized, security measures will be relaxed.'

'I don't see that happening.'

He then asked me where I came from. After I told him that I was from Mumbai, he laughed and said, 'Take me along with you if there is any job for me.'

Noticing that in this short conversation the vegetable vendor became friendly with me, I revealed my identity as a TV journalist and asked whether he would like to express his views on my camera. He refused and warned, '*Sangbaazon ko agar pata chala aap yahan ho to aapke liye mushkil ho jayegi*' (If stone-pelters come to know that you are here, you will be in trouble).

Shankaracharya Temple

We decided to wind up our shoot at the Shankaracharya Temple. This temple dedicated to Lord Shiva is located on a hill opposite Dal Lake, at an elevation of 1,000 feet from the Valley. It provides a bird's-eye view of Srinagar city and Dal Lake, so we thought that doing a PTC from the hill would provide a good backdrop to finish our report. One can cover a major distance by road and then climb around 250 steps to reach the temple premises.

During this time of the year, Shankaracharya Temple is usually thronged by pilgrims who come to Srinagar after the Amarnath Yatra. But that day, the temple had a deserted look. Except for CRPF men and a few media personnel who had come from outside Kashmir, no devotees were seen in the temple premises.

After offering a quick prayer, I looked around for a vantage point from where we could take good shots. Looking down from the hill, Srinagar looked very soothing. The wide lake with numerous houseboats and shikaras in its centre offered a visual treat. However, the view from the top was deceptive or rather paradoxical when compared with what one experienced on the ground. From that height, Srinagar looked calm and beautiful, and there was a cool breeze blowing, but below, actually, there was tension, fear and acrimony in the air. I decided to describe this paradox in my closing comments of the story. However, Sachin said that the PTC couldn't be done from that location. The sunlight was in opposite direction, and if I attempted to do a PTC from there, my face would be underexposed, while the backdrop would be bright. We dropped the idea of doing a PTC from the hilltop and decided to do it on the promenade with the houseboats of Dal Lake in the background. To conceal our identity, we had removed the logo of our channel from the microphone.

7

MEDIA IN THE CROSSFIRE

As I was about to deliver my lines in front of the camera, a shout interrupted me.

'*Jooth kyon bolta hai*?' (Why are you lying?)

I saw that a youth in his twenties was rushing towards me on the promenade where I was going to shoot my concluding PTC. He was holding a stone in his right hand. I hadn't spoken a word till then and wondered why this man was accusing me of lying. Within seconds, he reached me and, aiming the stone close to my face, once again asked, '*Jooth kyon bolta hai*?' His eyes were full of rage and he was looking at me as if I had caused him some harm. Shortly, seven–eight more of his friends appeared out of nowhere and encircled me and cameraman Sachin. They all looked furious. We were trapped. There were no policemen visible, whom we could approach for help. We felt that we were going to be lynched by these angry youngsters.

There is no scope of escaping, but at least I should speak to them before getting beaten up, I contemplated.

'*Kya jhooth bola maine*?' (What did I lie about?), I asked.

'You people are telling that everything is normal in Kashmir huh…Is this not a lie? Your face is not going to be normal now. Show that on TV and tell that the situation in Kashmir is like my face. You liars coming from Delhi think that we are fools! Aren't you ashamed of yourself for telling lies? Nobody is happy, and nothing is normal. Why aren't you showing this reality?' the youngster yelled at me while breathing rapidly.

'Let them go back with broken bones and then let us see if they say that everything is normal on TV,' another youth suggested.

I attempted to convince them that I was not reporting in the way they assumed, but they didn't allow me to speak and continued showering expletives. Getting beaten up by those angry youngsters seemed imminent. Fortunately, our driver Ghulam, who had parked on the other side of the road a few metres away, noticed the commotion and rushed towards us. He spoke to them in Kashmiri and tried to defend us. Fortunately, after arguing with the driver for about five minutes, they went away, asking us to leave the place immediately. After they left, Ghulam informed us that he told the agitators that I was not like other journalists and reported everything neutrally. He also told them that we were not TV journalists but worked for digital platforms. That was true because the news network for which I was working had digital platforms also and the stories done by me were carried on them as well. We were rescued, but the incident gave us a first-hand experience of how thorny it was to report from Kashmir.

'Jooth Bolta Hai!'

I think that almost all the reporters who had gone to Kashmir from various parts of the country to cover the situation post the abrogation of Article 370 might have heard these words—'*Jooth bolta hai!*' This line had become like a slogan for those who were riled up by the media's portrayal of Kashmir and was used on every reporter.

The reason why the media was being targeted by the agitators was their belief that media personnel were acting as agents of the central government and under-reporting the ground situation. On one hand, Kashmir was boiling and there was the issue of excess security forces, but, on the other hand, the TV channels were falsely reporting that everything was normal in Kashmir, they complained. This belief generated hostility towards the media in their minds and they attacked any Indian news channel crew, barring employees of one or two brands and correspondents of foreign news organizations like the BBC.

I was one of the fortunate ones who escaped without getting

beaten up or losing my camera equipment. Many TV journalists had been thrashed brutally. A week earlier, a TV crew was waylaid by motorbike-borne youngsters near Rajbagh and was beaten up. Their camera was damaged. A senior TV journalist who was sitting in the backseat of another car was slapped and spat on his face. They snatched away the tripod of his camera and threw it down from a bridge. A news anchor who wished to do a live anchoring of her prime-time show from Gupkar Chowk had to be protected by CRPF personnel. Every evening, when we returned to the hotel after finishing the day's work, there was discussion in the media room over 'who got beaten up today'. Almost every reporter had some story of being roughed up by angry youngsters. It was risky to take out a camera from the bag in downtown Srinagar and several other areas. Mediapersons were the most hated lot after the men in uniform.

My colleague Gyanendra Tiwari, who had been in Kashmir since 2 August, recollected, 'Although strict security measures were implemented, the administration ensured that the supply of essential commodities was not interrupted. Milk, fruit, grocery, medicines and all other items of necessity were available. I reported this in my coverage. One day, when I was travelling towards some location in Srinagar, some youngsters waylaid my car. They thrashed me and my cameraman, accusing us of telling lies. My shirt got torn. They found out the hotel in which we were staying and pelted stones at the hotel building. The management of the hotel got scared and forced us to check out. We scoured many hotels, but nobody gave us a room, fearing rampage by stone-pelters. After facing numerous refusals, finally, one hotel checked us in. Although we got a shelter, the Kashmiri hotel staff, including the receptionist, waiters and watchmen, looked at us with hateful eyes. Their fierce gaze stung us.' However, Gyanendra befriended them soon by playing cricket with them and offering them cigarettes regularly.

One day Gyanendra went to do a story at Pulwama on the plight of saffron farmers. He had to hide his identity of being a journalist from a national news channel and pretended that he was a representative of some portal that covered agricultural issues. Veiling his identity helped Gyanendra.

Ashutosh Mishra of Aaj Tak was in Ladakh on 6 August. After covering the ground situation in Leh, he reached Kargil. 'The situation in Kargil,' said Ashutosh, 'was much different from Leh.' Leh was by and large peaceful, but Kargil was tense. There were protests on the streets. Ashutosh noticed that people were angry because they had not been consulted by the central government before taking such a decision that affected their identity. They were furious over the fact that their Kashmiri identity had been taken away, since Ladakh was separated from J&K and Kargil comes under Ladakh. The people took pride in that they helped the Indian Army during the Kargil War of 1999 but were riled up about the bifurcation of the state. Apart from the government, their target was the media. On the advice of a local contact, Ashutosh left Kargil and went to Srinagar.

At Srinagar, Ashutosh planned to shoot a ground report at Eidgah in downtown but was not allowed to shoot there by the security forces. As they were returning from the place, people surrounded them and pelted stones at their car, shouting abuses. Ashutosh and his cameraman faced a similar situation again when they went to do a ground report from a village at Awantipura. As they were about to leave the village, a crowd of villagers attacked them. They hit Ashutosh and pulled his collar. With great difficulty, he managed to escape from them by pretending to be an employee of some foreign news agency. Ashutosh said that most of the agitators were young, but some elders of the village intervened and rescued him from getting lynched. 'Since phone and internet were not available, I strived to come on the TV every two hours with some report so that my family members could know that I was alive and safe,' said Ashutosh.[1]

Ashok Raj, correspondent of Asian News International (ANI), was trapped in hostile situations multiple times. When he landed in Srinagar in the second week of August, Ashok was unaware of the tension prevailing on the ground. He decided to go to the downtown area and approach people about their views on the decisions. Some locals attacked his OB van there, and the windshield was broken by stone-pelting. Rushing out of that place was the only option to avoid getting lynched, he felt. Another incident happened when he was returning from Kupwara after covering a shoot of 'Operation Sadbhavana' arranged by the army. When he stopped at an eatery on the way, the locals got a whiff that he was a mediaperson. Five to six men surrounded him and abused him, saying that the media was showing the wrong picture of Kashmir and that he should leave Kashmir. Ashok hurriedly left the place before the crowd could get violent.[2]

'The militants consider us to be agents of Indian security forces and the police thinks that we are sympathizers of separatists. We get beaten up from both sides,' the Srinagar bureau chief of a national channel told me. He said TV reporters working for national news channels had to face hostility from the local people who were sympathetic towards separatists and were furious over Delhi-based channels' nationalist stance. He even received threats from militant groups conveying that his reportage was being monitored. 'Both sides wanted to control what was shown,' he said.[3]

My colleague Jainendra Kumar said that whenever he left the hotel for news gathering, there was always a threat of being stoned. 'Security,' said Jainendra, 'is the one word that describes our reporting experience in Kashmir'.

Interestingly, his experience was a bit different this one time. Once while doing a ground report, he was surrounded by people who complained that the media was just parroting the government's narrative. However, they spoke civilly and didn't harm him. 'I met many Kashmiri people who wanted to talk to us. They were not supportive of any of the narratives of the state or the separatists. These were people who were just concerned about Kashmir, who believed that even though nature had given so much to Kashmir, the state's tourism was still backwards compared to some other locations of the world. In a scenario that was bitterly divided between "this side" and "that side", these voices didn't get any space.'[4]

Who is Robert Thorpe?

History tells us that those who have expressed themselves through words have often paid with their blood in Kashmir. Near the place where I was accosted by angry youngsters below Shankaracharya Hill, a half-British and half-Kashmiri writer named Robert Thorpe was murdered in 1868. When he travelled to Kashmir for the first time, he was appalled by the condition of people living under the maharaja's rule. He wrote an account of the miserable lives of Kashmiris in his book *Cashmere Misgovernment.*

The way Thorpe highlighted the plight of the people angered the maharaja. One winter morning, when he was walking near Shankaracharya Hill, few men stabbed him with daggers. Thorpe was killed for what he wrote. His grave is at a Christian cemetery near Lal Chowk.[5]

Robert Thorpe was not the last person to sacrifice his life for writing about the plight of people in Kashmir. Even a hundred years after his murder, people are still being killed or tortured for expressing themselves. Thorpe was targeted by the ruler, but today journalists are being attacked by multiple parties.

Killing the Messenger

Since the early nineties, 19 mediapersons have been killed in J&K; some were pumped with bullets, while others were blown up in blasts. One of the landmark events of militancy in Kashmir and the first case of an attack on any mediaperson was of Lassa Kaul, director of the Doordarshan Kendra in Srinagar. One evening, in February 1990, he was shot dead by militants of the JKLF on the outskirts of Kashmir. Kaul was reportedly threatened by the militants to not air certain programmes, but he didn't take the threats seriously. After Kaul was killed, many employees of Doordarshan and Radio Kashmir resigned in fear. For the next few years, the broadcast for TV and radio was done from Jammu stations.[6] Many other killings followed.

On 10 August 2000, militants threw a hand grenade towards the entrance of the State Bank of India branch at Residency Road in Srinagar. This led to security forces and mediapersons reaching the spot. Fifteen minutes later, a powerful bomb kept in a car parked few feet away from the crowd was detonated, killing 31-year-old photojournalist Pradip Bhatia of *Hindustan Times*. Later on, the militant organization Hizbul Mujahideen claimed responsibility for the blast and apologized for the death of Bhatia, saying they had been targeting the security forces.[7]

The series of murders of journalists continued. In May 2002, Iqbal of the daily *Kashmir Images* was shot outside his office. A year later, in 2003, Parvez Sultan of News and Features Alliance (NAFA) was killed by unidentified gunmen in his office. Next year, in 2004, journalists Asiya Geelani and Abdul Majeed Bhat were killed in separate bomb blasts. In 2008, a cameraman named Javed Ahmed Mir was shot dead while covering a demonstration.[8]

Apart from assassinations of journalists, there have been several cases where they were assaulted, held hostage and their family members harassed.

Shujaat Bukhari Murder Case

'He was not a government's man. He was not an establishment's man. Nor was he in sympathy with the extremist elements...He was a voice for a just solution, however difficult that is going to be in Jammu and Kashmir.'[9] This is how veteran journalist N. Ram of The Hindu Group of Publications described Shujaat Bukhari during an interview with a TV channel.

Shujaat Bukhari is the last big name on the list of the journalists killed in the Valley. Based in Srinagar, he edited the broadsheet *Rising Kashmir*, which he founded in 2012. Bukhari had also worked for various English and Urdu newspapers and magazines. With his unbiased writing, he had earned a reputation of being an upright, fearless, balanced and well-informed journalist of the Valley. Bukhari pursued peace and a solution to the ongoing crisis in Kashmir. He believed in Track-II diplomacy between India and Pakistan to end the violence. Apart from journalism, Bukhari was involved in several projects aimed at making people outside J&K understand the complexities of the region and was a member of some literary and cultural organizations. To facilitate dialogue, he tried to bring all the stakeholders to a common platform. Bukhari worked to give the rest of India an understanding of Kashmir from all perspectives. For this purpose, he helped in setting up the Kashmir Initiative Group, whose members travelled across India and discussed Kashmir.[10]

Bukhari's journalism and activism didn't go down well with some people, and two attempts were made on his life. Once he was kidnapped by militants backed by Pakistan, and once by Indian militants. He was given police protection since 2006, after an unsuccessful attempt to kill him. This security cover proved to be futile on 14 June 2018. It was the eve of Eid al-Fitr, and Bukhari had been invited to an iftar party. At 7 p.m., when Bukhari came out of his office in Srinagar's Press Enclave area and was about to get inside his car, three motorcycle-borne assailants fired at him. Bukhari was killed, along with his two security guards.

Bukhari's murder led to a huge uproar, from politicians to journalists and foreign diplomats. For the first time in several decades, prominent newspapers of the Kashmir Valley kept their editorial page blank to protest against the murder. Separatist organizations called for a shutdown in the Valley. For the BJP, the killing of Bukhari was one of the reasons to withdraw from its alliance with the PDP, citing the breakdown of law and order in the Valley.

The motive behind the killing is still unclear, but his writings possibly irked some militant groups and their handlers in Pakistan. Just before he was killed, Bukhari had welcomed the ceasefire initiative of the government during Ramzan, as it would help end the cycle of violence in the Valley. An influential Kashmiri supporting a government initiative didn't go down well with the militants.

Just a few days before Bukhari was killed, he had approached the state government to enhance his security. Before the government could take any decision on his request, he was killed.[11]

Shockingly, LeT issued a statement and blamed Indian agencies for the murder.[12] However, the J&K Police said that Bukhari was killed by LeT itself. The conspiracy to kill Bukhari was hatched in Pakistan. The police claimed to have got breakthroughs in the case through CCTV footage and cellphone records of the suspects. Four people were identified as the killers.[13]

'Survival is the first challenge for any journalism venture in Kashmir,' Bukhari had said just three months before he was killed.[14]

Bukhari is survived by his wife and two children.

Media vs Police

In the days preceding and immediately following the abrogation of Article 370, three different sets of mediapersons were present in the Valley. All three had different experiences. We have seen the hostility Indian TV news channels' journalists faced. The second set, comprising foreign broadcasters or international news agencies, were allowed to work freely and allowed access to areas, including downtown, where Indian TV journalists were being chased away by the stone-pelters. The third lot were the local Kashmiri journalists who had literally become jobless due to the shutdown of communication mediums and restrictions on movement.

In the days following August 2019, there were several instances where Kashmiri journalists and the police were at loggerheads. In February 2020, the Kashmir Press Club (KPC) organized a meeting of all media associations of the Valley. After the meeting, a strongly worded statement was issued, saying that the government was not allowing the media to operate freely in the Valley after 5 August 2019. The KPC alleged that journalists were being intimidated, threatened and summoned for investigations that hampered their work. 'The government,' read the statement, 'should ensure freedom of speech and expression as guaranteed in the Constitution instead of muzzling the press.'[15]

Journalism in Kashmir has been like walking on a tightrope. Highlighting the views of militants or separatists leads to accusations of 'romanticizing' or 'glorifying' them. Publishing the official version puts them at risk of being branded as government agents by militants.

There have been cases where journalists have been booked under the Unlawful Activities Prevention Act (UAPA) and other laws for allegedly spreading misinformation. This led Amnesty International to issue a statement saying, 'Under international human rights law, any restrictions on the right to freedom of expression must be demonstrably necessary and proportionate. The media plays a crucial role in reporting human rights abuses and is essential to inform the public about the factual situation and measures taken by the governments in response to Covid-19. Yet time and again, UAPA, India's principal counter-terrorism law, has been abused to target journalists and human right defenders who criticize government policies.'[16]

I spoke to Anuradha Bhasin, editor of *Kashmir Times*, whose case is a much-discussed example of the hostility between the government and Kashmiri media. In October 2020, the office of *Kashmir Times* situated in the Press Enclave area of Srinagar was sealed by the authorities. She believes that this action was taken against her as vengeance for criticizing the government's policies and speaking up for the freedom of the press post-abrogation. The state department claimed that the proper procedure was followed. Bhasin also filed a plea in the Supreme Court pleading to remove the communication blockade and the impediments that journalists were facing since 5 August.

On 2 June 2020, the UT administration came up with a media policy that empowered government officials to decide what is 'fake news' and take action against journalists and news organizations. It was seen by the local journalists as another ploy by the government to keep a check on the content of the media. 'It is censorship. A bureaucrat has been given the right to decide what is fake news,' said Bhasin, reacting to the policy.

Mood in the Media Room

Apart from facing violent mobs on the streets, TV journalists from Delhi and other locations had another elephantine challenge to face. How should they communicate with the head office? Reporters were required to inform their head office about press briefings, arrange for somebody's live chat or send scripts of stories they had covered. But the communication blockade affected their work. A media room was eventually set up by the administration in Hotel Sarovar Portico.

The media centre was full of journalists throughout the day. It was the one room in the Valley from where the world got to know what was happening in Kashmir. A mobile phone was kept on a table in a corner, and the journalists had to line up for their turn to speak on it after logging their name and the number to be called. Everyone was allotted two minutes, and if anyone spoke even for a few seconds longer, others in the queue began screaming. My cameraman Sachin was about to have a physical scuffle with another journalist who had help up the phone for over five minutes. The four computers were mostly used by print journalists to file their stories, and there, too, the journalists had to wait for their turn. Often the connection went down and the wait got longer.

As soon as possible, most TV reporters arranged for OB vans, which allowed satellite communication. Whenever a reporter needed to talk to the office, he simply attached his camera to the OB van and stood in front of it. The office in Delhi was instructed to constantly check for any visual input coming from Srinagar. As the reporter appeared on screen and waved, the concerned producer in the head office spoke to him on the talk-back system of the OB van. TV reporters wrote their scripts in longhand and then filmed the pages, uplinking the footage to the head office via the OB van. The producer in Delhi then typed the script on the computer. It was a learning experience for us in circumstances without mobiles phones or internet.

Rohit Kansal's face was the most seen on TV and most quoted in the newspapers post the abrogation. One of the most high-profile bureaucrats in Srinagar, from the 1995 batch IAS, Kansal was appointed as the spokesperson of the administration. Kansal had earlier worked as the principal secretary in former CM Mehbooba Mufti's government and as principal secretary to ex-union minister Farooq Abdullah. He held briefings twice a day at 10 a.m. and 5 p.m. at Hotel Sarovar Portico to update the media about the situation in Kashmir and the government's security measures.

Soft-spoken Kansal did his job diligently, ensuring that everything looked peaceful and calm in Kashmir after the abrogation. In all his on-camera briefings, he insisted that curbs would be removed soon and there had not been many agitations and incidents of violence. He stressed that despite strict security measures, essential supplies had not been affected. Very often, he was accompanied by senior police and administrative officers. In such briefings, Kansal summarized happenings of the day and answered questions from the journalists. Whenever some uncomfortable questions were asked, his standard reply was, 'I can't answer that.' Often press notes were also handed over to the journalists, and Kansal's speech didn't give more than the contents of the press notes. After the daily briefings, he spent about an hour or so meeting reporters over coffee and sharing some 'off the record stuff' with them.

The number of journalists seen in the media room declined with the passing days. By the last week of August, the conference room, where once journalists struggled to stand, had many empty chairs during the media briefings. Kashmir-related content on TV gradually declined as the days passed.

8

URI: LIFE AT THE LOC

'We have to spend hours gathering the scattered pieces of our relatives' bodies.'

'We sleep in the night, unsure of seeing the sun the next morning.'

'Firing and shelling force us to stay away from our homes for days.'

These heart-rending voices are of the people who live at the border. Their life is constantly at the 'border' of life and death as well as the geographical border. 'Uncertainty' is another word that defines the life of the people who live near the Line of Control (LoC) or International Border (IB) in J&K. During my August 2019 visit, I caught a glimpse of the miserable life these people lead.

Independence Day had passed with no major untoward incident. Another story was needed to justify my presence in Kashmir. Staying in Srinagar was not going to yield much information. Many ideas were brewing in my mind, but movement restrictions and the hostile atmosphere weren't conducive to attempting such stories. Apart from covering the daily morning and evening briefings by Rohit Kansal, there wasn't much to be reported from Srinagar city. One evening, over tea, I asked a commandant of the CRPF, whom I had got acquainted with, about possibilities of doing stories outside Srinagar.

'Why don't you go to Uri? There have been frequent ceasefire violations at the LoC areas since this (abrogation of Article 370) happened. You must report the kind of life villagers are leading there and how our armed forces are dealing with the situation. The SHO (station house officer) there is my friend. He will help you,' he suggested.

After I expressed my eagerness to work on the story, the commandant called the SHO and told him about my visit. It was decided that the next morning I would meet him at the police station in Uri.

'How's the Josh?'

Uri is a town and a tehsil in the Baramulla district of north Kashmir and is inhabited by approximately 10,000 people. Around 102 kilometres away from Srinagar, the town is connected by a national highway. Uri was in the news when four alleged fidayeen (suicide bombers) of the Pakistan-based terrorist organization Jaish-e-Mohammed infiltrated a brigade headquarter of the Indian Army near the town on 18 September 2016 before dawn and killed 19 personnel of the Bihar and Dogra regiments before being shot. Eleven days later, India retaliated with a 'surgical strike', when commandos of the Indian Army allegedly crossed the LoC and destroyed 'launch pads' of the terrorists. As per the Indian government, many terrorists waiting to infiltrate into the country were eliminated. However, these claims were contested by the Pakistan government.

Three years later, a Hindi movie named *Uri: The Surgical Strike* was produced, based on the incident. A dialogue from the movie—'How's the Josh? High Sir!'—became popular across India. I had a brief appearance in the movie, where I was shown interviewing then Defence Minister Manohar Parrikar. Around a fortnight before coming to Kashmir, in the last week of July 2019, I shared the stage with Lieutenant General (Retired) D.S. Hooda at an event in Pune. He was the Northern Army commander during the surgical strike. I asked him how much truth had been depicted in the movie and how much of it was 'creative liberty'. 'You can say it was mostly creative liberty,' he replied with a smile.

As soon as we finished our breakfast at the hotel, driver Ghulam picked us up. Rizwan, an employee of the hotel, heard from Ghulam that we were going towards Uri and requested a lift till Baramulla. Rizwan hadn't gone to his village during Eid and was very excited to be going back home.

'Sir, try to finish your work quickly at Uri. We must reach Srinagar before sunset. The route becomes unsafe at night,' Ghulam cautioned us.

'Don't worry. We are not going to shoot a movie there but a small story for TV,' I said casually.

Soon, we got out of Srinagar and touched the highway. Seeing me mesmerized by the natural beauty of the road, Rizwan asked with a smile, 'Janab, are you coming to Kashmir for the first time?'

'No…no…I have come here before also many times…but it is for the first time that I am travelling on this road. It is very beautiful.'

'From Baramulla onwards, you will like it more,' he said.

'Kashmir is beautiful everywhere, but for people like us coming from Mumbai, it seems dangerous also. What do you think about Article 370? Has the right decision been taken?' I asked.

'Why are you asking me this, Sir?' Rizwan's cheerful face turned serious.

'I am eager to know about the views of Kashmiri youths like you on the issue,' I told him.

'You are a journalist, Janab. You travel to so many places and meet so many people. You might have got an idea of what people think,' he said.

'That's true…but they hate TV journalists and attack us when we approach them to ask their views. I haven't spoken to many Kashmiris after I reached here,' I said.

'Sir, we shouldn't discuss politics. I don't take any interest in such matters. I am just concerned with earning and feeding my family,' he said in an irritated voice.

'Okay...okay…I was not asking you all this on camera,' I said.

As the car reached a junction near Baramulla town, Rizwan got down. 'Thank you, Sir, for this help. Sorry I didn't answer your question. While returning, please drop into my home for kahwa. I will be happy to introduce you to my parents,' he said, avoiding eye contact with me and with a touch of guilt in his voice.

'That is not possible,' said Ghulam nervously. 'After completing work in Uri, our priority should be to reach Srinagar as soon as possible,' he said and drove ahead. I waved at Rizwan while trying to control my laughter over the driver's nervousness. Displeased at my laugh, he said, 'For his hospitality, we can't risk our safety.' Ghulam's otherwise cheerful face had been tense since he picked us up from the hotel.

After reaching the police station, we were told that the SHO who was supposed to help us in getting access to the villages near the LoC had gone to Srinagar on some urgent official call. There was no way to call him, since mobile phones were not working. A constable suggested that we should approach the district superintendent of police (DSP) who might help us. So after around 15 minutes at the police station, we reached the DSP's office. We found the DSP in a small lawn outside his office, with two-three cops queued before him with files in their hands. The DSP appeared to be in a bad mood and was reprimanding somebody on the phone. I began to lose hope, but I introduced myself and requested his help. He looked at me hatefully, and his eyes, red from sleep deprivation, appeared to say, 'Why the hell has this uninvited guest dropped in!' Having covered the crime beat in Mumbai, I could understand such behaviour—he was overworked and stressed. In the late nineties, I saw many officers of Mumbai Police with a similar appearance when the underworld gangs were wreaking havoc in the city. I didn't feel offended by the DSP's hateful gaze.

Although visibly irritated by my request, he asked me to sit and called for tea. After thinking for a while, he said, 'I can give you written permission from my end, but you need to deal with the army guys.' I was happy that at least things were moving in a positive direction. A staffer brought a letter in which my cameraman Sachin's and driver's details were typed along with our vehicle number. It took around 20 to 30 minutes to fetch that letter from the DSP and move ahead.

Delighted after getting the letter, we touched the highway again after around 20 minutes and drove towards the LoC. But our happiness was short-lived. We were stopped at an army checkpost after Uri town. Drivers had to get down and walk up to the chowki to furnish details about the car and its occupants. While our driver was completing these formalities, an army sentry posted at the gate walked up to us. He was a South Indian and sported a moustache similar to the dreaded sandalwood smuggler Veerappan.

'Why have you come here?' he asked roughly.

I was in two minds about whether to reveal my identity as a journalist, as I feared we would not get access if I said we were mediapersons. But then I thought that since the police had permitted us, there would not be any trouble.

'We are from the media—ABP News. This is the permission letter,' I said, firmly handing him the letter from the DSP.

He glanced at the letter and said, 'No…No…No. This letter won't do. Have you got permission from the army? We have got no intimation that you people are coming here,' he said.

I argued with him that since the police had permitted us, he couldn't stop us. But he refused to budge and took us to his superior inside the chowki. He asked us to deposit our identity cards and then called somebody to inform them about us. The officers asked us to wait inside the chowki until further instructions arrived. After ten minutes of waiting tensely, the officer's phone rang. He once again gave our details to the person on the other end. Half an hour later, his phone rang again. After a brief conversation, the officer turned towards us and said, 'You're permitted to go, but there is a procedure you have to follow.'

A military Gypsy led us to an office just a few metres ahead on the road. We were received by a lieutenant colonel who was very courteous and said that had we informed the army earlier, we would have escaped the trouble. Over tea, he briefed us about the area and instructed us on the dos and don'ts. The officer said that we would have to leave our vehicle at his office and an army vehicle would take us to villages at the LoC.

The condition of the army personnel's presence during the shoot dispirited me. I feared that the villagers would not be able to speak freely because of this and I would not get unfiltered voices. The army had been arranging shoots for TV channels from Srinagar in border areas, and I suspected that my shoot would be no different.

However, I thought that it would be imprudent to cancel the shoot, given we had gone through so much trouble to get access to the border villages. I decided to try my luck.

Fifteen minutes later, we left his office in a green Gypsy, accompanied by three armed jawans. Two trucks with more jawans followed us. We assumed that this arrangement was for our safety, since ceasefire violations were frequent, and to monitor what we were capturing.

After travelling a few kilometres, our cavalcade was joined by a cheerful major whose vehicle piloted us to a village very close to the LoC. He requested us not to take shots of him or his team members as that could reveal their identities to the enemy. As soon as the young officer stepped out of his jeep, an old villager rushed out to welcome him. He enthusiastically thanked the officer for some past help. Soon, a few more villagers gathered and greeted the officer with smiles. I noticed that the villagers were very fond of him.

As the officer led us towards the central area of the village, four–five kids between the ages of five and ten years surrounded him. 'Military Uncle, chocolate?' said a young girl, spreading her palm before him. The officer took out few chocolates from his pocket and gave them to the children.

'Do you often distribute chocolates to these children?' I asked.

'Yes, I fill up my pockets with chocolates whenever I come towards these villages. It feels good to see them happy. These children remind me of my four-year-old son,' he smiled.

'Where is your family?' I asked.

'In Delhi,' he replied.

'How many kids do you have?' the major asked me.

'I am the father of a seven-year-old son.'

'Good! Enjoying fatherhood?'

'Yup, but due to my profession, I am not able to spend much time with him.'

At this, the officer started laughing. I sensed sarcasm in his laughter. Soon I realized the reason. I was able to give more time to my family than the soldiers who were posted at the frontiers thousands of miles away in a hostile environment.

Life in the Shadow of Death

After climbing up a thin, rocky path, we reached the central area of the village. The LoC was visible from that height. A few men with beards and wearing skullcaps were sitting on a bench outside a grocery shop and chatting. These people were living the most uncertain life in India and the fear of death had become a part of their daily life. India shares a land border of 3,323 kilometres with Pakistan, including the LoC. The border passes through the states of Gujarat, Rajasthan and Punjab, but the longest stretch of 1,049 kilometres is in J&K—199 kilometres from Kathua to Akhnoor is the International Border, whereas 740 kilometres starting from Akhnoor is the unsettled LoC along the PoK. The remaining 110 kilometres accounts for the Actual Ground Position Line at Siachen.[1] The topography of the India–Pakistan border is diverse, with a mix of mountains, plains, deserts, rivers and forests. The hostility between India and Pakistan, and militancy have impacted the people residing in proximity to the International Border and the LoC, especially those in the border areas of J&K.[2] The LoC is one of the most militarized and capricious borders in the world.

Every village near the LoC in Uri has countless stories of death, destruction and fear. Unexploded shells often lie in open fields, and villagers are scared of going close to them. Parts of exploded shells are collected by village children and used as toys. Many villagers have lost their limbs and are living with just one hand or leg.[3] Sometimes when the shelling stops, relatives have to spend hours collecting the scattered pieces of the bodies of their loved ones.[4] The conversation among the villagers are often centred around the loss of relatives, cattle and homes, and the constant fear of war.

'After 5 August, we fear more shelling in this area. Around a month back, too, there was heavy shelling. A shell just fell at the door of my house. We had to stay away from home for many days.

We don't have any bunker here to protect ourselves,' said a villager.

A large area of Uri sector comprises hills, forest and rivers. The river Jhelum flows from Uri towards PoK. Often, militant organizations take advantage of this topography to infiltrate. Even after the 2016 fidayeen attack on the brigade headquarters and the following surgical strike, Uri has continued to be a preferred infiltration point for militant organizations.

On 19 August 2018, about a year before the abrogation of Article 370, an alleged militant attempting to infiltrate the border was killed near the Kasturi Naar forest range.[5] The latest case of infiltration had been reported just a couple of days before I visited Uri. The Indian Army claimed that it had foiled a major infiltration bid on 13 August. There was heavy firing from the Pakistani side. As per the security forces, this tactic is often adopted by Pakistani forces to give cover to the infiltrators. It was suspected that the infiltration bid was to disturb the first Indian Independence Day celebrations after the abrogation.[6]

Battle to Win Hearts and Minds

I was astonished to see the villagers' perception of the army. These people at the border were fond of the soldiers and spoke highly of the force. Yes, these people were Kashmiris and Muslims, and they praised the Indian Army. I felt that these people were expressing themselves from the heart. They didn't appear to be tutored or speaking due to fear of the army, which had worried me initially.

Shabbir Ahmad, a resident of the village, held his four-year-old son while speaking on my camera. His son was wearing a dress that resembled the army fatigues. 'I want my son Ibrar to become a high-ranking military officer,' he said. 'Since the 1990s till today, we have seen so much of shelling...we have seen so many casualties. We are standing with the army, and the army is standing with us shoulder to shoulder,' he said.

Shabbir supported the abrogation of Article 370. 'It will be good for us because earlier we didn't have access to the benefits of government schemes. Nothing reached people like us who reside on the hills.'

'Do you think there will be any change now?' I asked another villager named Arshad Hussain.

'Inshallah! We are surely going to see change. Earlier, we used to get only 10 per cent of all the funds and budgets, but now we feel that we will get all the benefits,' he replied.

Although Arshad welcomed the decision to remove Article 370, he was unhappy with the communication blockade. 'We are facing problems due to network. We live in a hilly terrain. Our relatives live in distant places. Even if somebody dies, we don't get to know. We are happy, but mobile phone network must be restored,' he said.

Arshad's neighbour told me, 'We believe that now progress and development will take place. Whatever didn't happen till today will happen now. Nobody comes here. Even you media people have come to this village for the first time. Whatever work must begin, it should be from Uri.'

'The army always stands with us. Whenever there is shelling, the army responds to it. We are with the force. Recently, we have seen two–three casualties. If the army had not been with us, it would have been difficult to survive,' said another aged man from the village.

Their affection for the army and welcoming of the abrogation of Article 370 originates in the fact that these villagers have benefitted the least from the government. In many border areas, the role that ought to be played by the civil government has been taken over by the army, which has become responsible for the safety and well-being of these villagers.

A Border Area Development Programme (BADP) was formulated as part of the Seventh Five Year Plan of the Planning Commission to help the people residing at the frontiers.[7] The BADP is a 100 per cent centrally funded plan to meet the special development requirements of inhabitants of remote and inaccessible areas near the IB. Schemes related to construction and maintenance of roads, water supply, education, sports, infrastructure and education of physically handicapped and backward sections and so on are supposed to be formulated under the BADP.[8]

When we think of the military, we think of guns, bullets, tanks and tough men in fatigues. But in the border areas of Kashmir, the benign face of the army is seen. Every military operation is conducted to win, whether it is combat with the opponent or to provide relief during some natural calamity. In 1998, the Indian Army launched a unique operation named 'Operation Sadbhavana' with an intention 'to win hearts and minds of people' in J&K, especially those who inhabit frontier areas, a scheme similar to corporate social responsibility initiatives. The mission is designed so that civilians don't perceive the people in uniform as hostile and instead consider them as their saviours.

The key areas of focus under Operation Sadbhavana are primary education, healthcare, adult literacy, vocational training, enhancement of agricultural output, empowerment of women, employment generation, the establishment of communication networks and the adoption of villages for development.

In 2005, the army announced that it was adopting Churunda village, which had been affected by a severe earthquake. Within a year, the army constructed 230 houses in the village, made a major connecting road, set up a veterinary centre and constructed tiled pathways. A school building, a dispensary, an amphitheatre, a vocational training programme for women, street lighting and water supply arrangements were also set up. The army undertook similar projects in the nearby Batgran and Thajal villages under the aegis of Operation Sadbhavana.[9]

Defence analysts believe that through Operation Sadbhavana a quid pro quo relationship is also maintained by the army with the people residing at the border. The border areas are vulnerable to OGWs and infiltrators. Goodwill with villagers helps the army keep a check on them. Suspicious activities at the IB or LoC have often been reported by the villagers, enabling the security forces to foil infiltration attempts.

The Pune Model

My interactions with the villagers reminded me of Sanjay Nahar, whom I met in Pune just a month before visiting Kashmir. He runs an organization named Sarhad that works in the border areas of J&K. He has been visiting Kashmir since the early nineties and has also worked during the insurgency in Punjab. Nahar spoke to me about the work his organization was doing in the Valley. He has come up with the 'Pune Model' to connect people residing at the borders with the mainstream and mitigate the impact of anti-Indian propaganda by Pakistan-based elements and separatists.

'Chhatrapati Shivaji Maharaj said that if you want to win a fort, then first you must win the villages surrounding the fort. We have adopted this philosophy,' said Nahar. He says that his organization attempts to reduce the 'trust deficiency' in the Valley and has been undertaking several programmes to that effect. A few years ago, he invited Gandhian Anna Hazare to Kashmir and organized a 'Sant-Sufi Sandesh Yatra' with the idea of propagating the teachings of peace by famous saints. Nahar said that he had noticed that even those youngsters who hated the Indian State were fans of Indian film stars and cricketers. Hence, he arranged a 'Know India' tour and brought Kashmiri boys to Mumbai. Nahar arranged meetings with Amitabh Bachchan, Shahrukh Khan and Hrithik Roshan and a few cricketers. He also arranged for a candid discussion with Bal Thackeray and Raj Thackeray.

Sarhad runs a school for orphans from Kashmir. The students are not only children of people killed in the crossfire but also those of militants who were eliminated in encounters with the security forces. Children of killed security personnel are also adopted by the organization. The students of Sarhad's school are helped with scholarships for further studies. 'So far, we have produced ten doctors and engineers,' Nahar told me.

There is a hamlet named Dardpora in the Kupwara district near the LoC. It is known as 'a village of half-widows' because there are around 200 women in the village whose husbands have been missing.

It is unclear whether they are dead or alive. These women are living a miserable life and have no support for the upbringing and education of their children. They survive on the meagre monetary support they get from relatives. Nahar claims that he has adopted several orphans from their village and has arranged for their education in his school. 'Orphans have the potential of becoming militants, so we focused on them. We strategized that these children can help us change the scenario in later years,' said Nahar.

Nahar's work in Kashmir has not been easy. He had to face various accusations, ranging from being an agent of the Intelligence Bureau to being sold out to Muslim propagandists and allegedly wanting to convert Muslim children in the guise of educating them. He has been targeted by radical elements belonging to both Hindu and Muslim communities. In fact, in 2018, he escaped an attack by a parcel bomb that exploded before it could reach his hands.

Trade and Grenade

After winding up the shoot, we headed back to the army office where we had left our car. En route, one of the jawans accompanying us in the Gypsy pointed towards structures on our left and asked, 'Aren't you going to include this in your report? Look how the place is looking today.'

The structures the jawan pointed towards were part of the Salamabad Trade Facilitation Centre. The centre was established as a confidence-building measure between India and Pakistan in 2008. The place was completely deserted and had a very depressing look. The whole complex looked like a ghost town. Till four months before I visited Uri, it had been a place full of life and brimming with people. Every morning, from Tuesday to Friday, trucks from PoK used to enter the complex with various commodities. Muzaffarabad is just 20 kilometres away from the centre. Traders from both sides of Kashmir had been allowed to deal in around two dozen items, which included spices, vegetables, dry and fresh fruits, carpets, embroidery items, shawls, clothes, wooden furniture. Salamabad's trade centre is one of the two cross-border trade centres. Another one is at Poonch in the Jammu region. It has been estimated that, since 2008, cross-border business has touched over Rs. 5,000 crore. The trade was conducted through a barter system on zero-duty basis. Over 800 traders have registered themselves for the trade through this channel. Due to the shutting down of the trade centre, the livelihoods of over 4,000 families have been affected. Some families had been directly involved in day-to-day operations, while others were engaged in providing services such as restaurants, mechanics and provisional shops.[10]

The trade had never stopped at this centre even after the massacre in Mumbai on 26 November 2008 or the terrorist attack on Uri's brigade headquarters in 2016, just a few kilometres away. In 2017, four militants were killed very close to the trade facilitation centre, but trade still continued. However, 2019 was different. The tension between India and Pakistan following the Pulwama attack in February seriously impacted cross-border trade. The status of Most Favoured Nation (MFN) was withdrawn from Pakistan. On 19 April 2019, the Ministry of Home Affairs suspended trade at the centre based on reports that the cross-LoC trade route was being misused by Pakistani elements for smuggling weapons, narcotics and fake currency.[11] The Home ministry received input that few persons involved in trade were clandestinely associated with banned terrorist organizations.

Whether the decision to stop cross-LoC trade is right or wrong is a subject of debate. However, it is also a fact that in the past few years, several cases of contraband have been reported. In 2013, the security forces recovered cocaine worth Rs. 13 crore from the trade centre. In January 2014, there was another major recovery of 114 packets of brown sugar. Total drugs recovered weighed around 100 kilograms and were valued over Rs. 100 crore in the international market. The series of seizures continued in 2015. In July 2017, security forces reported a major seizure of 25 kilograms of heroin from trucks coming from PoK.[12]

Weapons have also been seized at the centre, which, as per Indian security forces, were intended for militants. In March 2017, the Jammu & Kashmir Police recovered a cache of arms and ammunition from a truck, and the driver was arrested.[13] Apart from drugs and weapons, fake currency is seen as another menace.

The Indian government was also irked by reports that some businessmen were dealing in goods produced in a third country. It was also suspected that traders outside J&K used this trade channel to avoid taxes.

As I returned to the lieutenant colonel's office, I saw that Ghulam was waiting in a panicky state. 'Sir, it is too late now,' he said in a shaking voice.

'Yes, but I had to complete the shoot. You saw how long the army procedure took,' I said.

After thanking the officer, we headed back to Srinagar. I had shot the story in a travelogue format and while writing the script, I realized that I hadn't done a closing PTC. Our car was passing along the Jhelum River. I thought that the beautiful riverbank would be an excellent backdrop to do a closing PTC. When I asked Ghulam to stop the car, he pointed out that it was getting dark already. I shot the closing PTC but wasn't satisfied with the quality, so I shot two more takes. It took around 15–20 minutes in all. To stop there was an imprudent decision, which we realized soon.

9

STONE AGE

When we left Uri to return to Srinagar, it was already getting dark. By the time we crossed Baramulla, dusk had fallen. Ghulam seemed extremely disturbed and was murmuring prayers while driving. He said that there were some areas en route where stone-pelting was rampant. I asked him to stay back at the hotel that night after reaching Srinagar. As I was discussing the next day's plan with Sachin...SMASH...suddenly a stone struck the windshield. By the time we could comprehend what had happened, another stone hit the back left door. A stone-pelter was attacking us. We were horrified. Ghulam was shivering with fear, but he drove faster. He had turned out to be right. The windshield had a round hole that looked like a bullet shot. And more terrifying was the apprehension that there might be more attacks on the way.

A Sleepless Night

A few kilometres ahead, a few vehicles had queued up at the entrance of a river bridge. There were stone-pelters on the other side of the bridge, and they were attacking every passing vehicle. They had also placed burning tyres on the road to block the traffic. For half an hour, we waited, hoping that cops would come to clear the road, but nobody came. A few minutes later, a Maruti 800 car came up from behind us. A woman crying in pain was lying on the back seat and an older woman was stroking her forehead to comfort her. A worried man sat beside the driver's seat. When Ghulam spoke to him, he said that his wife was in labour. They were heading for a hospital in Srinagar. Everybody in the car felt helpless. The cries of the woman were getting louder every minute, and it felt like she would die if she didn't reach the hospital within minutes. The older lady and the man also started crying. All of sudden, a few youngsters from the other side of the bridge on motorcycles charged towards the vehicles. They had sticks in their hands. They started hitting the windshield of the vehicles and the people sitting in them while shouting expletives. Everyone, including the family in the Maruti 800, took a U-turn and rushed back towards Baramulla. Ghulam asked me to hide below the dashboard. He warned that in case the stone-pelters reached their car and saw non-Kashmiris and that too media people, then not only would we be lynched but the car would also be burnt to ashes.

We drove back for 5 kilometres and parked along the road after ensuring that the stone-pelters were not chasing us. No vehicles were coming from either side. Ghulam didn't know any other way to reach Srinagar, and it was not prudent to ask any villager for directions. Staying on the roadside for the night was also dangerous. It was 10 p.m. by now and the last we had eaten was the tea and biscuits at around 4.30 p.m. We were feeling hungry and scared at the same time. Thankfully, my wife had packed a few theplas in the bag when I left Mumbai, which satiated our hunger for a while.

Around 11 p.m., we noticed that a few vehicles had started coming from the Srinagar side. The road seemed to have cleared and traffic restored. As we were contemplating whether we should move, a convoy of the CRPF passed in front of us. I asked Ghulam to follow it.

He said it was a dangerous idea, as the CRPF men sitting in the trucks could fire at us. After the Pulwama incident, they view all private cars close to their convoy with suspicion. CRPF convoys were also targeted by stone-pelters, and we, too, could be hurt if we went close to them. So I advised Ghulam to maintain a distance of around 300 to 400 metres from them so that they didn't get wary. This way we could also stop if they were attacked by stone-pelters and take a U-turn.

Following the convoy, we again reached the bridge. As we crossed the bridge, we saw that the road was covered with glass pieces and the smell of burnt tyres was in the air. A few damaged vehicles were lying beside the road. Fortunately, we crossed that area safely and no stone-pelter was seen.

The CRPF convoy that we were following took a different route just before we were about to enter Srinagar. As we moved towards the road leading to our hotel, Ghulam noticed that three or four teenagers were throwing stones at every passing vehicle. He immediately took a right turn and used a different route to the hotel.

We reached the hotel around midnight with a damaged car and scared souls. I asked Ghulam to stay back at the hotel at night and took him along for dinner at the restaurant. After dinner, I wrote the script of my story to send it in the morning. I wasn't able to sleep that night. The cries of that pregnant woman and the faces of her helpless relatives haunted me. We didn't know what happened to her. I was also feeling guilty for not heeding Ghulam's advice of leaving Uri early. A big lesson learnt—in a conflict zone, never ignore the advice of a local.

Stone: An Instrument of Protest

I have seen stone-pelting by Shiv Sainiks in Mumbai during their numerous agitations. During the post-Babri Masjid demolition riots, I glimpsed rioters of warring communities attacking each other with stones and glass bottles. Recently, I covered a violent episode in Navi Mumbai where agitators of a particular caste pelted the police with stones demanding reservation in jobs and education. But this time, I wasn't just a witness covering the violence, I was a victim too.

Some historians record 13 July 1931 as the first incident of stone-pelting against the State in Kashmir. Around June 1931, a person named Abdul Qadir Gazi had addressed a meeting at a mosque in old Srinagar. The meeting had been preceded by severe communal clashes in various parts of the city. In the meeting, Qadir had said that the maharaja's rule was anti-Islam and 'Islam was in danger.' Pointing towards the maharaja's palace, he had said, 'It is a symbol of injustice, cruelty and slavery, and should be demolished.' Qadir had been arrested on charges of treason. The district administration had decided to conduct the trial of his case within the prison to prevent a deterioration of the law and order situation in the city. On 13 July, when the trial had commenced, a crowd gathered outside the jail premises. A large number of armed policemen had been deployed in anticipation of such a gathering. The people had offered themselves for arrest and demanded the release of Qadir. When some people had started offering namaz outside the jail, the cops had detained them. This action had enraged the crowd, and a violent clash had broken out. The sloganeering had intensified, and stone-pelting had begun. The police had retaliated by firing at the protestors. Twenty-two people had been killed and many others injured. Sheikh Abdullah had compared the incident with the Jallianwala Bagh episode.[1] The events of that day have been replicated hundreds of times in twenty-first-century Kashmir, although incidents of stone-pelting are less spontaneous now.

Stone-pelting in Kashmir against Indian security forces has occurred since the first phase of militancy in the late eighties. However, it metamorphosed into a systematic activity first in 2008 and later in 2016. It became a regular feature of street protests in the Valley along with anti-Indian slogans. The abrogation of Article 370 again brought stone-wielding protestors on the streets, now targeting not just the armed forces but also fellow Kashmiris. In 2019, approximately 2,000 cases of stone-pelting were reported. This number is second-highest after 2016, the year Burhan Wani was killed, when 2,653 cases were reported. The number of cases reported in 2017 was 1,412 and 1,458 in 2018.[2]

Motivations for Stone-pelters

Mostly, incidents of stone-pelting used to happen regularly every Friday post the afternoon prayers. It also occurred when some militant was killed or trapped in an encounter and with any major development that wasn't palatable to a separatist group.

My experience that night led me to ponder over the motivations for these stone-pelters. At an age when youth from others parts of India focus on their career or pursue their dreams, what compels these Kashmiri youngsters to pick up stones? What is it that overshadows the fear of authority in their consciousness? Why is it that they don't have any fear of getting beaten up, injured, arrested or, at times, even killed? Is it just hate that drives them or is there something else? I got multiple answers. Stone-pelters are driven by many factors, ranging from emotional to psychological and economic.

A large number of stone-pelters act on anti-India emotions, their desire for separation or feelings of being oppressed. The narratives of pro-Pakistani groups and separatists such as Syed Ali Shah Geelani influence these young minds, making them feel insecure and, consequently, generating hatred for the Indian state.

State and non-State actors from Pakistan have been overtly involved in brainwashing these youngsters. Since 1990, Pakistan has been observing National Kashmir Solidarity Day on 5 February every year. On this day, anti-India rallies are sponsored by the Pakistan government, where speeches are made and slogans shouted denouncing the 'Indian occupation of Kashmir'. In 2017, a video named 'Sangbaaz' (Stone-pelter) was tweeted by the spokesman of Pakistani defence forces, Major General Asif Ghafoor. Made using images of protests and violence in the Valley, the video glorified the stone-pelters and expressed solidarity with the youth who lost their eyes in retaliatory firing by the armed forces. The video ended with a text plate on screen, which read: 'An ISPR Production'. ISPR stands for the Inter-Services Public Relations agency of the Pakistan armed forces.[3] The song has been deemed as an anthem of the stone-pelters. However, the separatist organization Hurriyat Conference (Geelani's group) refuses to accept that Pakistan has a role in stone-pelting. Hurriyat Conference believes that stone-pelting has been used as a tool of resistance for long and that the people had also picked up stones against Dogra rule. 'Stone-pelting,' says Ajaz Akbar, the spokesman of Hurriyat, 'is a tool in the hands of deprived people.'[4]

Some youths have resorted to stone-pelting after witnessing coercive actions by the armed forces affecting their friends or relatives. Such stone-pelters are driven by personal vendetta.[5]

Another factor for stone-pelting is that it is considered heroic. In one of his articles, veteran journalist Shujaat Bukhari quoted a senior college teacher who said, 'Whosoever pelts the police with stones is seen as a warrior, and those who get killed in retaliatory action are martyrs.'[6] Most of the stone-pelters are aged between 15 and 30, and whenever anyone among them is injured or killed in retaliation by the forces, there develops an urge in the peer group for vengeance. It is not just the poor, unemployed youth who hurl stones but also educated youngsters from well-to-do families.[7] Many pictures published in newspapers show stone-pelters attacking the armed forces in their school uniforms.

In a sting operation broadcast in March 2017, India Today showed a few alleged stone-pelters confessing that they hurled stones because somebody paid them between Rs. 5,000 and 7,000 to do so. They were also given clothes and shoes. One of the alleged stone-pelters said that he used to get Rs. 700 for making Molotov cocktails. The alleged stone-pelters caught on camera disclosed that instructions regarding stone-pelting were circulated in WhatsApp groups.[8]

In 2017, two alleged agents of the Pakistani spy agency ISI were arrested. During their interrogation, they revealed that they got money from a Pakistani diplomat posted in India and distributed it to the stone-pelters.[9] As per a report, the ISI released Rs. 1,000 crore to separatist groups and its OGWs to fuel unrest in the Valley following Burhan Wani's encounter.[10]

Former CM Omar Abdullah rejects the idea that youngsters pelt stones for money. In his view, the feeling of Kashmiri people of being isolated from the rest of India is the reason behind stone-pelting.[11]

Observations of a Mumbai Cop

Regarding the motivations of the stone-pelters, I find the observations of my friend Sanjay Nikam from the crime branch of Mumbai Police relevant.

Nikam stayed for four months in Kashmir to trace and recapture a man accused of a murder in Mumbai. Nikam sometimes disguised himself as a hydraulic engineer or as a representative of a mobile company out to find locations for installation of mobile towers. Burhan Wani had been killed just a few months ago, and street protests were rampant. When heading to Srinagar airport with the accused after capturing him, Nikam was attacked by stone-pelters. He then found out that the outrage of these youths had been caused by a rumour that someone was cutting the braids of girls at the behest of the cops.

'This is one of the modus operandi of those people who instigate youths to pelt stones. They spread rumours that can't be immediately verified and soon youths start reacting to them by hurling stones,' said Nikam. 'But,' he said, 'rumour is just one of the factors of stone-pelting. Jobless youths who do nothing and those who are drug addicts also become part of stone-pelting groups.' As per Nikam, many of the stone-pelters just do the job like contractors for the sake of money and nothing else.[12]

What Nikam says can't be ruled out, considering the statistics indicating the monstrous problem of drug addiction in J&K. As per data from the Srinagar Police control room, most of the drug addicts are in the age group of 18–35 years. In 2019, 633 cases were registered, which went up to 1,978 by mid-2020. A de-addiction centre was started in 2008 and has treated over 10,000 addicts so far.[13] The situation has become so grave that Srinagar Police has opened a separate helpline to address cases of drug abuse.[14]

Advocate Mohammed Altaf Khan doesn't subscribe to the view that drug addiction is one of the motivations for stone-pelters. He has been doing his bit to prevent the youth from taking up violence. As a part of his efforts, he had interviewed 128 stone-pelters. I met Khan at his residence over tea.

'There will be very few who do it for money. There is so much anger in them. Many boys told me that they are doing it (stone-pelting) for resistance. A heroin addict needs 5,000 rupees a day to support his addiction. He can't be compensated for 500 rupees.

And once he takes his dose, he will not be able to fight. I have seen young stone-pelters with strong ideological and religious beliefs,' he told me.

A Menace for Fellow Kashmiris

When my car was attacked near Sangrama, there was nothing visible from the exterior to tell that I was a journalist. Mine was, unfortunately, one of the random vehicles that the stone-pelters chose to attack. It could have been any other vehicle with a Kashmiri driver and Kashmiri passengers, like that family with the pregnant woman. Many of the motorists who rushed to save themselves from the bike-borne youngsters were Kashmiris.

There have been very few instances where tourists have been targeted by militants, but stone-pelters are a different case altogether. One notorious incident is the death of a tourist named R. Thirumani in May 2018 as a result of stone-pelting. An analyst working for a BPO, Thirumani had come to Kashmir with his parents to get a break from the hot Chennai weather. He was on an eight-day tour in the state. As his car was passing through the Narbal area while going towards Gulmarg, stone-pelters attacked it. Thirumani succumbed to his injuries, while others travelling with him were severely injured. This incident reminded me of my meeting with Mehbooba Mufti at Mumbai's JW Marriot hotel in March 2017, when she was the CM. At the time, Mufti appealed to Bollywood to shoot in Srinagar and said that the situation in Kashmir was better. 'Kashmir is safe for tourists,' she said. It was an earnest effort by Mufti to revive the tourism industry in Kashmir, which was devastated by the events that followed Burhan Wani's death.

What happened with Thirumani could be dismissed as a one-off incident, but it spread an adverse message and scared away tourists from Kashmir. The visuals of the stone-pelting mob widely shown on national TV channels were also damaging the tourism industry in Kashmir. So who are the stone-pelters harming?

Saviours of Trapped Militants in Encounters

The incidents of stone-pelting had seen a surge after 2008, and the situation continued for the next three-four years. However, the incidents reduced around 2014. Two years later, in 2016, when Burhan Wani was killed, stone-pelting saw a resurgence. There were over 2,653 incidents of stone-pelting in 2016 alone.[15] In fact, when Wani was alive, his social media videos urged the youth to attack the army, police and paramilitary forces. In one of the last audio messages before his death, Wani urged youngsters to pelt stones on security forces during encounters.[16]

Wani's message could be seen implemented in the days following his death. Till February 2017, around 25 militants escaped after the stone-pelters protested and engaged security forces at the encounter sites. Abu Dujana, one of the most-wanted militants from the terrorist organization Lashkar-e-Taiba, was trapped twice, but he managed to escape, thanks to the intervention of a violent mob.[17]

In October 2018, a 22-year-old sepoy, Rajendra Singh, of the Quick Response Team (QRT) of the Indian Army was killed by stone-pelters. He was providing security to a convoy of Border Roads Organization (BRO) when, at Anantnag, a group of stone-pelters attacked. One of the stones hit Singh's head, and he succumbed to the injury.

In November 2018, a video was circulated revealing how a mob of stone-pelters helped LeT's most-wanted terrorist Naveed Jutt's aide escape during an encounter. The encounter took place at Kuthpora village of Budgam, in which two militants, including Naveed, were killed. However, Naveed's accomplice took advantage of the protests by stone-pelters and escaped.[18]

In November 2020, when there was an encounter between security forces and militants at Kawoosa town of Budgam, a group of stone-pelters started hurling stones at security personnel. This allowed the trapped militants to get out of the cordon and escape.[19]

Such incidents led to allegations that stone-pelters have become a part of the support system of militancy.

Backlash by Armed Forces

The armed forces see parallels between the militants and the stone-pelters. Both share the same hostility towards India. They get their ideological fodder from social media, especially from accounts administered by Pakistani elements. The intent of both these groups has been to harm, kill or maim security personnel. With the increasing attacks on security personnel and unsuccessful operations, the armed forces have begun taking strong retaliatory steps against the stone-pelters.

In Pulwama, once an army major proposed to hold a painting competition for students at the Government Degree College. As soon as he reached the venue in a Casspir vehicle, infuriated students began hurling stones. This led to retaliation from the army, and many students were injured, inciting further student protests across the Valley. To contain the agitation, schools and colleges were shut for the next ten days. Kashmiri journalist Shujaat Bukhari explains that what enraged the students was the major's arrival in a Casspir vehicle. The Casspir is known for its impact in militancy-prone areas, as its landmine-resistant, ambush-proof build protects it from firearms and is used to transport soldiers. It has become a symbol of hate for the militants and stone-pelters alike.[20]

On 7 July 2018, three youngsters, including a 16-year-old girl, were killed when army personnel opened fire on a violent mob in Kulgam district which was protesting the arrest of Asiya Andrabi, the leader of the separatist group Dukhtaran-e-Millat, by the NIA. In a statement, the army claimed that it had to resort to firing when a patrolling unit was attacked by a mob of 500 people and petrol bombs were hurled at it, and that the mob had been warned before shots were fired.[21]

A day after, when an army soldier was killed in a stone-pelting incident, then Army Chief General Bipin Singh Rawat called stone-pelters OGWs of terrorist organizations and said that they must be dealt with sternly. Speaking to reporters, he asked, 'If stone-pelters can kill people with such acts, are they not becoming like a terrorist?'[22]

In an interview given to the Press Trust of India (PTI) few months after the abrogation of Article 370, he said, 'People are throwing stones at us, people are throwing petrol bombs at us. If my men ask me what do we do, should I say, "'Just wait and die! I will come with a nice coffin with a national flag and I will send your bodies home with honour." Is it what I am supposed to tell them as chief?' General Rawat dared stone-pelters to fire bullets instead of throwing stones so that he could retaliate in a fitting manner.[23]

Human Shield Incident

Any account of stone-pelting in Kashmir is incomplete without a mention of the incident on 9 April 2019. A by-election was necessitated in Srinagar parliamentary constituency due to the defection of sitting MP Tariq Hamid Karra from the PDP to the INC. The polling day was marred by violence. That day, an incident at Utligam polling station led to widespread outrage and debate over the army's tactics to deal with the stone-pelters. We have two versions of the story.

One version is of Major Leetul Gogoi of the 53 Rashtriya Rifles. As per Major Gogoi, he got a distress call from the polling station saying that the electoral staff and Indo-Tibetan Border Police (ITBP) jawans deployed at the polling station were surrounded by a mob of over a thousand people, including women and children, who were hurling stones and petrol bombs at them. As Gogoi reached the location along with his men, he, too, was attacked by the mob. At this, he verbally warned the crowd but was ignored. Gogoi noticed that a man standing close to him was the leader of the stone-pelters. He arrested the man and returned to the polling booth to rescue the ITBP jawans and polling staff. As he was leaving the place, his mine-resistant vehicle got stuck in the mud. This gave the stone-pelters another opportunity to attack them. At that moment, an idea struck Gogoi. He tied the suspected leader to the bonnet of his vehicle. Gogoi said that stone-pelting stopped after that.[24] 'I did this only to save the local people. Had I fired, there would have been more than 12 casualties. With this idea, I have saved many people's lives,' he claimed.[25]

The man who was tied on the bonnet was Farooq Dar, a 26-year–old-resident of Chill village who earned his living by embroidering shawls. Dar's version contradicted Gogoi's and claimed that Major Gogoi had lied to save himself. Dar maintained that he never hurled stones at anybody in his life. As per Dar, he cast his vote that day at the polling booth in his village[26] and was accosted by Gogoi while passing through Utligam. He was pulled down from his motorcycle and roughed up by the army men. He was then tied to the jeep. Dar claims that he was taken to the army camp after being driven around in 20 villages. He was let off when the sarpanch of his village reached the camp and convinced the officers that he was not a stone-pelter.[27]

The video of this incident soon went viral on social media platforms and was shown on national television news channels. A month later, Major Gogoi was awarded a commendation by then Army Chief General Rawat for his efforts in counter-insurgency operations. However, a year later, Gogoi had to face ignominy when an army court indicted him for fraternizing with a local woman and being absent from the place of duty. Dar, who suffered from depression after the incident, expressed his satisfaction at Gogoi being punished.[28]

Bullets for Militants, Pellets for Stone-Pelters

After the 2010 protests, the Valley was introduced to a new kind of crowd control device—a 'pellet gun'. It soon became the most dreaded, hated and controversial weapon in Kashmir. The pellet gun was considered non-lethal and was being used across the world by security forces to deal with unruly mobs. A pellet gun's cartridge contains a few hundred lead pellets. The cartridge releases several pellets in a range of a few hundred metres upon being fired. It is expected to inflict pain and deter the protestors but not kill them.[29] So far, pellet guns have been used as a crowd control measure only in J&K. However, its use has been resisted by several quarters.

While responding to a public interest litigation (PIL), the CRPF revealed that from 8 July till 11 August 2016, it had fired 1.3 million pellets.[30] According to a report, between July 2016 and February 2019, pellet guns have killed 18, blinded 139, injured 2,942 and caused eye injuries among 1,459 people.[31]

In January 2020, Chief of Defence Staff (CDS) and former Army Chief Bipin Rawat explained how the stone-pelters were getting injuries on their face. Rawat said that a soldier doesn't aim for the face of a protestor but his legs. But when that protestor bends to pick up stones, he gets hurt. 'Security forces can't be blamed for such injuries,' said CDS Rawat.[32]

Various human rights groups have asked the Indian armed forces to discontinue the use of pellet guns. In September 2017, then executive director of Amnesty International, Aakar Patel, asked for the immediate renouncement of pellet guns as a crowd control measure.[33] In March 2017, the Supreme Court asked the Centre to consider alternate means to deal with stone-pelters. A bench headed by then Chief Justice J.S. Khehar expressed concern over injuries suffered by minors due to pellet guns. In December 2016, Mehbooba Mufti, then CM, also requested the security forces to stop using pellet guns.[34]

The opposition from all corners compelled the armed forces to reconsider their use. Although they were never completely discontinued, other non-lethal methods of crowd control were considered. In October 2017, the CRPF received 21,000 rounds of plastic bullets developed by the Defence Research and Development Organization (DRDO) that are considered less lethal than lead pellets.[35] The forces also began using chilli shells that cause a burning sensation in the eyes and irritation in the nose, mouth and throat upon explosion. Another device used was Pelargonic Acid Vanillyl Amide (PAVA) ammunition that temporarily immobilizes the target.[36] Although these measures are not as dangerous as pellet guns, they, too, have been deemed as hazardous for health, especially for people with lung conditions.[37] In 2019, there was a report that the government was going to procure a 'sound cannon', which is programmed to emit sound waves and cause ear pain, also called long-range acoustic device (LRAD). It was used in

Pittsburgh to disperse protestors during the G-20 Summit. However, so far there has been no official report of its procurement.[38]

Although the use of pellet guns has not been officially discontinued, due to heavy criticism, it is now being used sparingly.[39]

From Stone to Gun

One of the common motives of a stone-pelter and a militant is that both intend to cause injuries to the security personnel and articulate themselves using violence. The difference is that a stone-pelter attacks with stones, which are considered less lethal than the guns and grenades used by a militant. Militants are more organized than groups of stone-pelting youngsters and receive formal training from Indian or Pakistan-based militant organizations. However, stone-pelting is seen as a first step towards militancy.

The case of 25-year-old Sajad Gilkar is worth mentioning here. Sajad was allegedly a chronic stone-pelter and had been booked in numerous cases, though his parents claim that he was named even in cases in which he was not present. Due to so many cases, he had to attend court frequently. Sajad found these court hearings excruciating. One morning, he left home without his mobile phone. When he didn't return, a missing person complaint was filed at the local police station.

Thirteen days later, Sajad called his father and informed him that he had joined the militant organization Hizbul Mujahideen. In an emotional voice, Sajad told his father that the village where he was hiding was encircled by security forces and a confrontation with them had begun. Sensing that he would not be able to get out alive, Sajad wanted to speak to his mother for one last time. But his father was not at home, and by the time he reached home to his mother, Sajad was killed. Many youths like Sajad turn to militancy, frustrated with frequent rounds of police stations, courts and prisons. Youths with previous cases of stone-pelting often find it hard to lead a normal life, as they are picked up and interrogated every time there are fresh protests.[40]

In July 2017, Reuters published a report that carried quotes from stone-pelters. One of them said that if he had access to a gun, he would prefer joining militancy instead of throwing stones.[41] Five out of six local militants have a history of stone-pelting.[42] In August 2019, 15 Corps commander Lieutenant General Dhillon said that 83 per cent of all youths who become militants start with throwing stones for Rs. 500. Elaborating with statistics, he cautioned parents of stone-pelters to keep a check on their wards, as most of the youths are killed within a year of joining militancy. He informed them that 7 per cent of them are eliminated in the first week, 9 per cent in the first month, 36 per cent in the first six months and 64 per cent in the first year.[43]

The J&K administration has adopted a variety of measures to curb stone-pelting. Apart from jailing numerous stone-pelters, it has been announced that those who have been involved in stone-pelting will not get security clearance for passports and government jobs. The weekly stone-pelting on Friday is no longer seen and, by 2021, there was an 88 per cent decline in incidents. One of the reasons for such low numbers was the enforcement of the lockdown due to the Covid-19 pandemic.[44]

10

PAKISTANI PROPAGANDA: VIRTUAL WAR, REAL IMPACT

Social media and affordable data have made revolutionary changes in the way the world works. Social media has augmented content creation, sharing and monetization, and helped micro entrepreneurs and small businesses to market their products and services. It has opened new avenues of livelihood. Facebook and Twitter have compelled governments to listen to their citizens and companies to their customers. WhatsApp has become an inseparable part of daily life for most of us.[1] Social media has helped generate a huge fan following for chefs, actors, musicians, doctors, politicians and—militants!

Yes, there is a different dimension to this virtual world. Along with a host of benefits and ill effects, social media has also emerged as a new tool of militancy. Particularly, in the context of Kashmir, it is being widely used by the deep state of Pakistan to further their anti-India propaganda and fuel unrest in the Kashmir Valley. From the perspective of a wide section of the Kashmiri population, social media has been a medium to vent their dissent. During the past decade, the impact of social media has been multidimensional in Kashmir, especially since 2016.

Internet Era of Militancy

Social media is being used in Kashmir to radicalize youngsters and recruit them to militant organizations. The new militants are very different from the ones of the nineties. They are young, informed, educated, technology savvy and not faceless. They post selfies and pictures, flaunting their guns or playing cricket on social media. The internet has greatly helped glorify militants and violence.[2] Videos uploaded by militants have led to the humanization of insurgents to the common population and allowed them to put forward their viewpoints. They are seen; they are known. They penetrate people's mobile phones and computers.[3] Social media has been observed as an effective instrument for garnering public support and sympathy for militants.

The biggest and one of the first faces of social media-oriented militancy in Kashmir has been that of Burhan Wani. His case is different from the conventional understanding of violence in Kashmir. Wani used his social media skills to change the face of militancy by crowdsourcing support from the likes of Arab Spring agitators and Islamic State of Iraq and the Levant (ISIS). In 2012, he created the Twitter handle @Gazi_Burhan2 to upload photographs of alleged atrocities by security forces and anti-India content. He made emotional appeals to youngsters to join the jihad by using verses from the Quran and called for the establishment of 'Nizam-e-Mustafa' (God's Government) in Kashmir. He was one of the first militants to post his picture with his face uncovered along with other accomplices from locations near Srinagar. Through his videos and Twitter messages, he highlighted his fight against the Indian establishment. In 2015, he uploaded a video on Facebook appealing to the youngsters to join his organization to establish 'khilafat' in Kashmir. In that video, Wani was seen with two other militants wearing military fatigues, holding Kalashnikovs and displaying the Quran. The video rapidly went viral. Wani said that Kashmiri Pandits could come and reside in the houses and land they owned, but 'Israel type' colonies would not be tolerated. In the same video, Wani urged people to attack Indian security forces. His tirade on social media had a real impact on the ground. There was a rise in the number of attacks on the army, paramilitary forces and police since then. A police officer and his family members, including women, were beaten up by a mob provoked by Wani's speech.[4]

Social media platforms have been widely used to induce youngsters to join militant organizations. After Burhan's death, thousands of pictures and videos were uploaded on these platforms to expose alleged atrocities and human rights violations by the armed forces. Stone-pelters often shot videos of their clashes with security personnel and uploaded them in real-time, accompanied with commentary about the retaliation of armed forces.[5] The propaganda material consisted of dying declarations of militants trapped in an encounter, their last telephonic conversation with family and friends, and so on. The content from militant organizations included training videos of recruits in the jungle, selfies depicting bonhomie among them, videos of militants playing cricket and so on. Such social media content was becoming part of the popular culture.[6] Militant organizations often announced recruitment on social media and also posted pictures of recruits, sometimes with their educational qualifications, date of joining and their aliases.

Social media has been used as an instrument to generate fear and discourage activities opposed by militant organizations. Before the Republic Day parade, a school principal was threatened at gunpoint so that his school didn't participate in the parade. The video of the principal pleading for mercy was circulated to scare others. Often, videos were uploaded to mock the security forces and convey that militants were one step ahead of them. In 2018, a LeT commander named Naveed Jutt escaped from Srinagar prison but was soon seen in a video walking fearlessly in the streets of Anantnag.[7]

The complicity of elements from Pakistan in fuelling unrest and encouraging violence in the Valley has been overt. Social media is not just a communication tool but a weapon of war for them. A year after Burhan Wani's death, around 320 WhatsApp groups and 30,000 Facebook accounts were found originating from Pakistan.[8] As per a report, Pakistan's intelligence agency, ISI, ran around 18,000 social media accounts on Twitter, Facebook and WhatsApp for anti-India propaganda.[9] In December 2015, LeT chief Hafeez Sayeed launched a cyber cell, allegedly inspired by ISIS, with a motive to propagate the group's ideology, propaganda and fuel unrest in the Valley. Many

WhatsApp groups emerged, whose members were mostly from the Kashmir Valley but whose admins had Pakistani mobile numbers.[10]

Internet Curfew

This bitter experience prompted the authorities to shut down internet services before the abrogation of Article 370 and bifurcation of the state. It was the longest ban since the introduction of the internet in the Kashmir Valley. Indian Foreign Minister S. Jaishankar defended the shutdown. In an interview, he asked, 'How do I cut off communication between terrorists and their masters on one hand but keep the internet open for other people?'[11] Before 2019, internet services were blocked for around four months after the death of Burhan Wani in 2016. In fact, since 2012, there have been over 35 instances of total or partial shutdown of the internet in the state, the highest in India. The view of the administration was that social media platforms and instant messaging services were being misused and were detrimental to the peace and tranquility of the state.[12] So to counter online propaganda and hate-mongering, the administration resorted to shutting down internet services, along with identifying and blocking hostile social media accounts. Post Burhan Wani's encounter, in April 2017, 22 social media sites were banned.[13]

This policy of internet curfews is a matter of debate and its effectiveness has been questioned. It has been reported that many people were using VPNs to overcome the ban.[14] Many people from Srinagar took the train to Banihal town around 100 kilometres away at the periphery of the Jammu region to access the internet.[15] The train was unofficially named 'the Internet Express'.

Collateral Damage

A section of the population saw the internet ban as an attempt by the State to crush their voice, but those dependent on activities using the internet had to suffer tremendous hardships.

With no internet connectivity, the lives of seven million people reverted to the pre-internet era, affecting business, education, medical services and the media. To renew a driving licence, apply for a passport, fill admission forms, check emails or register for medical school exams, people travelled to Banihal. This became possible only after train services resumed in the second week of November. Although broadband internet was available in Banihal, people had to struggle to get their tasks done. There were long queues outside a limited number of internet cafes, and people had to wait for hours for their turn.

Speaking of the situation in the Valley, journalist Afshan Anjum said, 'If 4G phones and round-the-clock Wi-Fi connected laptops are part of your life, you might not be able to comprehend how different is the daily life of the population living without the internet. Like other parts of India, there are no shopping malls or cinema halls in Srinagar. Like Delhi and Mumbai, there are no football academies every few steps nor are there ample cooking, music and foreign language classes. In such a scenario, the life of children and youngsters from the middle class or upper class gets confined within the academics of schools and colleges. Many coaching centres give more importance to online classes, through which students keep in touch with their teachers in Delhi and Mumbai. With a temperature as low as -5 degree Celsius, these students cover a major chunk of their syllabus at home through the internet. However, this year, the children were deprived of a medium to study as well. Are these children eligible to get less than what children in other parts of the country are getting?'[16]

The IT industry, worth Rs. 500 crore, was impacted and many people lost their jobs. During the initial few months, 74,500 people in tourism and 70,000 craftsmen lost their livelihood due to the ban. The dreams of many who were planning start-ups and small portals were shattered.[17]

'It would be difficult to forget those days for people who were sick. It wasn't possible to avail of certain schemes and services in Srinagar's government hospitals since doctors didn't have digital access. For those who wanted to consult doctors from other cities or order medicines, email was their bridge between life and death,' said Afshan.[18]

Journalists reporting from the Valley had to depend on a limited number of computers in a government-run centre to file their reports. In early December, WhatsApp accounts that were inactive for over 120 days started getting deactivated.

In November, conditional internet access was allowed to businesses, but it was only by March next year that people were able to use social media again. 'On 5 March 2020,' said Afshan, 'all of sudden there was a deluge of messages on my mobile. It was after a long time that I was hearing a notification sound on my phone. I picked up the phone and was relieved. Internet was back in Kashmir. But then I thought it might be a temporary relaxation by the government. I hastily started making video calls to my friends and relatives. Since the past month, we had started getting internet in parts.'

Whether an internet ban is an effective method to prevent violence, rumour-mongering, recruitment of militants and counter-propaganda by Pakistani groups or whether it has been counter-productive is still a matter of debate. The security forces believe that it has definitely prevented the spreading of misinformation, rumour-mongering and organized protests.

Section III

NEW KASHMIR

11

NEW COLOURS OF POLITICS

The August 2019 decisions resulting in the abrogation of Article 370 and bifurcation of the state have altered the political discourse in J&K forever. In the years following the landmark decision, new alliances have been taking shape, new political formations emerging and different issues coming to the fore. Some are now struggling to maintain their relevance in the changed scenario, while others have had to swallow the bitter pill. Kashmiri politics earlier revolved primarily around three political parties—the PDP, the NC and the Congress. After 2019, the game has changed with the entry of new players. The upheaval in Kashmiri politics was ongoing while this book was being written.

Freed Birds?

In the days leading up to the abrogation of Article 370 and bifurcation of the state, the political class of Kashmir was first kept under preventive detention and later slapped with the PSA, which allows the government to keep people under detention for a prolonged period. Leaders and political workers were either kept under house arrest or at places like the Sher-e-Kashmir Convention Centre and MLA Hostel, which were designated as sub-jails. Many were sent into prisons outside J&K.

When their release slowly began, the first prominent face to be freed was the NC leader and former CM Farooq Abdullah, who made a public appearance with his wife on 13 March 2020, after seven months of detention in his house. Eleven days later, on 24 March, his son, Omar Abdullah, drove out from Hari Niwas, where he was held captive for eight months, to have lunch with his parents. Abdullah looked very different with his grey beard. Both father and son avoided speaking on the decisions of August 2019 after their release. Omar Abdullah's discharge was preceded by a petition by his sister Sara Pilot in Supreme Court alleging that his detention was unconstitutional.

Shah Faesal, a bureaucrat turned politician, was prevented from boarding a flight from New Delhi to Istanbul on 14 August 2019. Faesal was brought to Srinagar and detained till 4 June 2020. He had floated a political outfit named Jammu and Kashmir People's Movement. He was accused of advocating 'soft separatism' through his tweets, articles and social media posts.

Sajad Lone of the People's Conference was released on 31 July 2020, just five days short of completing a year under arrest. Lone said that he was not physically tortured but the experience was 'psychologically draining'.

In the case of Saifuddin Soz, a Congress stalwart and MP, the administration maintained that he had never been detained, but he had to approach the court for being allowed to move around. On 20 September 2020, Soz claimed that he was verbally informed that he was free.

The last among the big names to be released was the PDP chief and former CM Mehbooba Mufti. Her detention ended on 13 October 2020. Among all the former CMs, her 14-month detention was the longest. She was first detained at her official residence then moved to a government building near MLA Hostel and then to her residence on Gupkar Road.

The politicians were out, but the politics was yet to begin. Many had kept mum on the August 2019 decisions after being freed, although a few statements made news, like Omar Abdullah saying that he would not contest elections while J&K remained a Union Territory and that the UT assembly would be disempowered. Mehbooba Mufti, too, echoed Abdullah's stance and announced that she would not contest elections till Article 370 and the special status of J&K were restored. However, before their abstinence could be mistaken as them quitting politics, they came up with a strategy to keep themselves and their parties relevant in the Valley's politics.

Gupkar Alliance and the Cracks Within

The political history of Kashmir throws many examples of enemies becoming friends and vice versa. The PDP–BJP alliance in 2014 was the most recent one. A similar arrangement happened again in 2020. The new umbrella, under which most non-BJP parties came together irrespective of their mutual differences and acrimonious past, is known as People's Alliance for Gupkar Declaration (PAGD). The collective treatment meted out to them by the Centre unified them. But how cohesive is their bond and how durable is their alliance?

The first major stir after August 2019 in the political sphere of Kashmir was seen exactly a year later, on 22 August 2020, when the parties issued a statement under the banner of the PAGD calling the abrogation of Article 370 unconstitutional and a measure to disempower the people of the erstwhile state. It was a follow-up meeting of the resolution passed on 4 August 2019, when representatives of various political parties met at Farooq Abdullah's residence on Gupkar Road. It was resolved in the 2020 meeting that all the parties would collectively fight for the restoration of the special status of J&K. Leaders from six political parties participated in the conference, including the NC, the PDP, the Congress, the People's Conference, the CPI and the Awami National Conference.

In a later meeting, held at Farooq Abdullah's residence in Jammu, it was decided that the amalgam would transform itself into an electoral alliance. The first election to be contested under this banner was for the District Development Council (DDC) to be conducted in December 2020. The parties resolved to come together to stop 'the divisive politics' of the BJP. In an interview to a TV channel, Abdullah said that the actions of China at the LAC in Ladakh were due to the abrogation of Article 370 and, with their support, he was hopeful that Article 370 would be restored.[1]

The Congress appeared to be cornered by the BJP, which questioned the party's nationalist credentials. Shortly after Amit Shah's tweets, Randeep Surjewala, spokesman of the party, issued a statement disassociating the Congress from the PAGD and said that the Congress was not part of the Gupkar alliance. He said that there was no electoral alliance with them and the Congress was fighting on its own. However, Ghulam Ahmed Mir, state party president, announced that there were seat-sharing arrangements with the constituents of the PAGD at the district level.[2]

The PAGD received another setback when Sajad Lone's party, the People's Conference, severed its relationship with the alliance.[3] Shah Faesal, who was seen as an emerging name in Kashmiri politics, not only quit his party but also withdrew from politics. It was seen as another setback to the PAGD, as Faesal had brought intellectual weight to the alliance.

DDC Elections Set the Ball Rolling

The DDC elections served as a drill for the much-awaited assembly elections. It helped reactivate the political system that had been largely dormant since 2018. The elections were also being touted as the commencement of the democratic process in the Valley. Mainstream political parties like the NC and the PDP didn't find it expedient to boycott the elections, fearing that new players like the BJP and the Apni Party would occupy the political space. It allowed political parties to connect with the people and helped many leaders to keep their political career going, albeit in an unusual manner.

Faced with political uncertainty and the desire to keep themselves politically relevant, parliamentary and assembly representatives contested elections. Former minister Taj Mohiuddin, a Congress leader and an MLA from the Uri seat, told a newspaper, 'Who knows when the assembly elections will be held? This is the right moment to contest elections and move forward for the people.'[4]

The DDC polls were not only the first major democratic exercise after August 2019 but also entirely conducted during the ongoing pandemic. It was a matter of high curiosity among political commentators, psephologists and Kashmir watchers to determine the public participation in the polls. As has been the trend, the Jammu region saw a high voting percentage, between 65 to 75 per cent, whereas in the Kashmir Valley it was 30 to 40 per cent. The voting percentage in the militancy-infested areas of south Kashmir, like Shopian and Pulwama, were as low as 14 per cent and 8.5 per cent, respectively.[5] In some polling centres of north Kashmir, a good turnout was seen despite bad weather and sub-zero temperatures. The administration, concerned about militants disrupting the elections, provided security cover for the candidates. Except for a few minor incidents of violence, the elections were conducted peacefully.

The DDC elections weren't devoid of historic religion- and region-based polarization in the erstwhile state, which was reflected in the voter turnout as well as the election results.[6] However, some commentators caution against deducing the turnout in the Valley as acceptance of the 5 August decisions and assuming that everything is alright in the Valley. Despite internal issues, the PAGD was able to perform well in its first electoral contest. Out of the total of 280 seats, the constituent parties of the PAGD won 102 seats. Although the alliance was victorious with the highest number of seats, the BJP emerged as the single largest party with 75 seats.[7] The BJP had participated in the elections aggressively, with some national leaders joining the campaign. The party made full use of its 'Gupkar Gang' jibe to target its opponents. However, the success of the BJP is linked to the high turnout of voters in the Jammu region.

The successful DDC candidates had to elect the chairman of their respective district councils. In this contest, the PAGD was able to secure only five out of ten councils in the Valley, while two seats went to Apni Party and others to independents. The alliance was able to get three seats in the Jammu region (Kishtwar, Ramban and Rajouri), whereas the BJP won six seats.[8] The Congress was not able to win the chairperson's seat in any of the 20 districts. It was alleged by members of the PAGD that there was horse-trading, coercion and malpractices during the election of council chairpersons.[9] Whatever its performance may be during DDC polls, the PAGD is being seen as a potent force with regards to the upcoming assembly elections.

A New Political Outfit

'There is an attempt to create a system where not only the government is yours but also the opposition is yours,' remarked a Kashmiri journalist, when asked about the new political parties coming up after August 2019 in the Valley. In his view, such parties are tacitly supported by the BJP to strengthen its influence in the Valley's political system.

'I see this as a strategy to finish the existence of parties like the PDP and the NC to create alternatives,' he said.[10]

Apni Party, a newly floated political outfit by multimillionaire businessman Altaf Bukhari, has sparked a buzz in the political sphere of the Valley after August 2019. From apple juice plants to agro-chemicals, Bukhari has diversified business interests. He was earlier associated with the PDP and was part of Mufti's cabinet, holding portfolios of Education and Finance. His membership was terminated from the party when the PDP got a whiff that he was about to quit. Bukhari's distancing of the PDP was noticed when he remained absent in important party meetings and rallies. A year after his expulsion from the PDP, Bukhari announced his political party named Jammu and Kashmir Apni Party, on 8 March 2020.

At the time of the announcement of the party, Bukhari indicated that the prime issue to be taken up by his party would be the restoration of the statehood of J&K.[11] Protection of jobs, implementation of domicile laws and return of Kashmiri Pandits were other issues that he stressed upon while launching the party.

Bukhari has not been shy about his alleged proximity with the Centre. A news portal reported him saying, 'We have to do business with Delhi, whosoever rules Delhi. We don't look at Delhi from the point of who is ruling in Delhi today. We look at it from the government of India. We have no hesitation in dealing with the government of India. There is an atmosphere of mistrust and we want to end the mistrust between New Delhi and J&K.'[12]

Apni Party tasted its first success when, in November 2020, Junaid Azim Mattu, the mayor of Srinagar, joined the outfit. Its political potential was first tested in the DDC elections, held from 28 November to 22 December 2020. It was a quadrangular contest fought between the Gupkar alliance, the BJP, the Congress and Apni Party. Out of a total of 280 seats, Apni Party managed to win only 12 seats. Although, numerically, the party's performance was not impressive, it was successful in making its presence felt on the ground. Also, Apni Party secured more seats than Sajad Lone's People's Conference, which is an older party and won only eight seats.[13] Apni Party also managed to win the DDC chairman's posts in Srinagar and Shopian. These little victories gave the message that Apni Party had the potential to become a considerable player in the assembly elections in future.

Six days after announcing the new party, Altaf Bukhari led a 24-member delegation to meet PM Modi on 14 March 2020. While interacting with the media after the meeting, Bukhari praised Modi abundantly by saying that he was a man of commitment and his heart beats for J&K.[14] The next day, the delegation met Home Minister Amit Shah. After over a two-hour long meeting, Bukhari said that Shah had assured him that there would be no demographic changes in J&K.[15]

The reception of Bukhari by Modi–Shah and the subsequent statements by him offered enough fodder to judge Apni Party's leanings and raison d'être. Omar Abdullah has been calling Apni Party 'BJP's B team'.[16] Political commentators observe that Apni Party has been taking up issues that aren't a nuisance for the Centre, such as opening up mineral resource exploitation by the administration to outside bidders. Issues like the restoration of J&K's special status and Article 370 are not touched by the party.[17]

Commenting on Apni Party, veteran journalist Bashir Manzar told me that the party's birth was 'premature'.[18] 'Apni Party has been born at a time when Kashmiris have a suspicion in their mind that

Delhi is playing some game to initiate the political process here,' said Manzar. Remarking about the allegations of the Apni Party being pro-Delhi, he said, 'When the PDP was established, then also people suspected that there was Delhi's hand behind it. In Apni Party, there are all old faces of politics in Kashmir; however, except for people like Altaf Bukhari, age is not on their side. Their innings are over.'

'I don't say that Apni Party will be unsuccessful. It will have its role in politics, but I don't think it will be like the PDP, which became a game-changer in 2002,' said Manzar.

Haseeb Drabu, who quit politics but continues to write on the UT's power equations, looks at the formation of Apni Party from a historical perspective. 'Nobody can be a puppet of any political party but of the deep state of India. We have examples of Ghulam Bakshi, Mir Qasim and Sadiq who have been seen as Delhi's men. Today there is BJP in power, so such people might be with the BJP. If Congress would have been in power, they would have been with them,' he said.[19]

Drabu says that he expects a few more parties to be formed. 'In Jammu, there are just two major parties, the BJP and the Congress, but seats in the Valley will get distributed among many different parties. The next government will be formed from Jammu and there will be some partners from Kashmir. Population-wise, Muslims are in the majority here but have become a minority politically,' he said.

Roshni Scam and Politics

Just before the DDC elections commenced, an alleged scam rocked the politics of the land. The BJP called it 'one of the biggest scams in the history of Jammu and Kashmir.'[20] The alleged scam had the names of almost all the mainstream parties, their leaders, senior bureaucrats and businessmen, and gave the BJP good material to target its opponents.

The genesis of the alleged Roshni Scam was in an act passed by the Farooq Abdullah-led National Conference government in 2001. It was known as Jammu and Kashmir State Land (vesting of ownership and occupants) Act, 2001. It gave land ownership to occupants of government land after a fee payment. Initially, the cut-off year was set as 1990. In 2005, the then CM Mufti Mohammad Sayeed extended the cut-off year to 2004, followed by Ghulam Nabi Azad extending it to 2007. A premium of 25 per cent of the market rate was fixed by the government, and free ownership rights were given to the farmers for agricultural land. As the stated objective of the act was to generate resources for power projects, it was called Roshni Act, 'roshni' meaning 'light' in Urdu.

In 2014, the comptroller and auditor general (CAG) termed the dealings under the act as a scam of Rs. 25,000 crore, pointing out several irregularities that had benefitted influential people. The State Vigilance Organization also filed an FIR against some people who had been accused of not satisfying the criteria but had managed to get ownership of the land. In October 2018, the then governor Satya Pal Malik repealed the act and cancelled all dealings undertaken based on it. This was followed by the Anti-Corruption Bureau ordering an investigation. A petition was filed in the High Court of Jammu & Kashmir and Ladakh with a plea to transfer the probe to the Central Bureau of Investigation (CBI). In October 2020, the court declared that the act was 'illegal, unconstitutional and unsustainable', and cancelled all allotments as invalid.[21] The court ordered the CBI to investigate the matter and asked the J&K government to release the names of people who had been the beneficiaries of the act.[22]

As per the court's order, hundreds of names were made public, including those of politicians, bureaucrats and businessmen. The J&K administration claimed that Omar and Farooq Abdullah had encroached on seven kanals of land to construct their residence in Sunjwan in Jammu. Their party, the National Conference, denied the charge. Allegedly, a few leaders of the PDP were also beneficiaries of the scam and the party's office in Jammu was built on three kanals of encroached land. Mehbooba Mufti was riled up at the charge and produced receipts that said that the party office was on government land, for which rent was being paid.[23]

Mehbooba Mufti hit back at the BJP by saying that if it was serious about the issue, it should go after the big fish and not behind the poor. Omar Abdullah slammed the accusations, calling them malicious, and said that the timing and motive of the charges were driven by (the DDC) elections.[24] Nevertheless, the BJP didn't miss the opportunity to capitalize on the issue. In most meetings during the election campaign, it was mentioned that the alleged beneficiaries of the Roshni Scam would be brought to book.[25]

Central Agencies as Instruments of Politics?

An established belief in the Indian political discourse is that whichever party holds power in the Centre uses agencies like the CBI, the Enforcement Directorate (ED) or the Income Tax (IT) department to settle scores with its political rivals and suppress them by initiating investigations. In recent years, the TMC government in West Bengal and the Maha Vikas Aghadi government in Maharashtra have accused the BJP-led government at the Centre of misusing the central agencies to meet its political ends. J&K has not escaped this trend. Most of the prominent faces from the mainstream parties of the UT are caught in the net of central agencies. Although the CBI is investigating the Roshni Scam as per the court's order, the ED is also probing political stalwarts for other cases.

Veteran politician and NC leader Farooq Abdullah is at loggerheads with the ED over a 10-year-old case where the ED has accused him of siphoning off funds from the Jammu and Kashmir Cricket Association (JKCA) when he was president from 2006 to 2012.[26] Abdullah has refuted the charges against him, saying that he was being framed in the case to smear his political image. His party said that the very first probe by the police had been ordered by the Abdullah government itself. There have been discussions in the political corridors over the timings of his being called for questioning by the ED.

Another big politician to make the rounds of the ED office has been the PDP leader and former CM Mehbooba Mufti. On 25 March

2021, she was summoned to the ED office in Srinagar for an enquiry about a case of money laundering. Mufti attempted to quash the summons by approaching the High Court of Delhi but to no avail.

Allegedly, the money from the CM's discretionary fund was diverted and a few lakh rupees were transferred into Mehbooba's mother Gulshan Nazir's account.

The PDP slammed the action against Mufti and her mother, calling it an act of political vendetta. The party alleged that the central agencies were being misused against the Opposition.[27]

Clamour for Statehood: New Issues in Kashmiri Politics

To reach out to people, political parties need issues. Once all the major political leaders were released, there was a curiosity in the political corridors about the shape of the new politics. What are the issues that different parties are going to take up in the run-up to the first Vidhan Sabha elections after J&K was stripped of its statehood and special status? A rough observation of the developments in 2020 gives us some idea.

The Gupkar alliance is seen as a landmark event, as historically rival parties formed a joint front to keep the BJP from gaining a foothold in the Valley's political discourse. But some note that the BJP is making a tacit entry into the system through organizations like Apni Party. Political pundits say that one should not be surprised if there is a pre-poll or post-poll alliance between the Apni Party and the BJP in future elections. If the BJP and the PDP could come together in the past, there is more likelihood of the BJP and the Apni Party coming to some sort of political arrangement. Politics remains an unpredictable game in India.

Apart from the restoration of Article 370 and the special status of J&K, reinstating J&K as a state seems to be the prime agenda for all political parties. Leaders of the PDP appear to be pursuing the demand even more aggressively than the NC and others. There has been no change in the PDP's old demand that India and Pakistan must sit together for peace in Kashmir. A journalist requesting anonymity said that although parties like the PDP and the NC know that the reversal of August 2019 decisions is impossible, they will keep on demanding it to maintain an emotional connect with the people.

Apni Party has been the most vocal in demanding the restoration of statehood. Party founder Altaf Bukhari said that statehood would be a panacea of development.[28] The Congress has also been demanding it and have organized street protests over the issue. This demand is convenient for the BJP, and the Centre has promised that it will happen. But in March 2021, the president of the J&K BJP unit, Ravinder Raina, surprised everybody by saying that if statehood was restored, 'the same old people' would come back to power and form governments and 'scrap all good laws'.[29] In his view, J&K being a UT is the best way to overhaul the governance. In February 2021, Home Minister Amit Shah assured the Lok Sabha that statehood would be granted to J&K at an 'appropriate time'.[30] From the speeches and statements of the BJP leaders, one can deduce that although their party is not averse to granting statehood, it will not be accorded anytime soon. The party would prefer the political discourse of the Valley to be centred on this issue rather than anything else.

Muslim Rashtriya Manch

When I visited Kashmir again in the last week of March 2021, one of my objectives was to meet members of the Muslim Rashtriya Manch (MRM) and understand how they were able to establish themselves in the Valley, what their motivations were to join the organization and how they operate at a location where being openly identified with the RSS can lead to jeopardy.

There have been attempts by the RSS to get the Muslims of the Valley on-board to further its agenda. The MRM is a product of one such attempt. Since its inception in 2002, the MRM has been able to spread its presence to some of the districts and tehsils of the Valley. It has also attempted to build inroads into rural Kashmir by inducting sarpanchs into the organization. The groundwork to form this organization was done by Indresh Kumar, who has worked in J&K for almost two decades.

'We thought that the RSS is dangerous and anti-Islam...but when I heard Indresh Kumar for the first time in a conference, my views changed. He understood and respected our religion. He was concerned about Muslims,' said Mir Nazeer, convenor of the MRM in J&K.[31]

In one of the narrow streets of the Shivpora area of Srinagar, a small office of the MRM, guarded by local cops, is being run. In a space-crunched, dimly lit room, Nazeer sat in front of a table with the Indian tricolour displayed on a wall. When I went to meet him, Nazeer was in a meeting with some of the members of his organization, which included the MRM's spokesperson Dr Shamshul Haque.

Narrating how the MRM became active in Kashmir, Nazeer said, 'I, along with few others, had formed a group called Nationalist Movement with an agenda to work for our country. In 2003, Rekha Chowdhary, a BJP leader from Jammu, introduced me to Indresh Kumar at a conference. He said that issues of Kashmir can be resolved with discussions on the table and suggested merging the group with the MRM. Till 2012, we didn't have an office. Our meetings were conducted either at somebody's residence or in some ground.'

When I asked him how many members the MRM had in Kashmir, Nazeer took out a register and, after turning few pages, said, 'Somewhere around 15,000 to 18,000. We have a unit in every district of the Kashmir Valley.'

'And who are the people joining your organization?' I asked.

'They are people who have a nationalist mindset,' said Nazeer while pointing towards a poster on one of the walls in the room, which read: 'Release PoK, Gilgit, Baltistan! Khali karo! Khali karo! Khali karo!'

I sensed that there was another reason for people to join his organization. My observation was seconded by a few others with whom I spoke later on. The reason was militancy. Many of the members of the MRM had lost their near and dear ones after being targeted by militants; Nazeer himself exemplified this. Three of his brothers had been shot dead by militants. Apart from being victims of militancy and holding personal grudges, other motivations included funding and the proximity to power, which helped get things done. Most of the members of such organizations come from border areas and hilly locations, whose inhabitants have a distinct identity and thought from other Kashmiris, I was told. 'I have escaped a few attacks on myself and have been threatened several times. The separatists are warning people to beware of us by saying that the RSS is operating under the guise of the MRM. A religious leader said that we work for an organization that is an enemy of Muslims. The politicians also have misled people about the MRM. However, we strive to connect people and not to divide them.'

Dr Shamshul Haque said, 'The MRM is a platform for Muslims across India. In Kashmir, people openly say that we are RSS men. We are practical. We do neat and clean work for the people. People come to us with their grievances and we forward them to the authorities.'

He told me that the MRM conducts youth development programmes like drug de-addiction and counselling. 'Our endeavour,' he said, 'is to connect people with mainstream India. I am sure that in the coming days, people will themselves unfurl the Indian flag here.'

I spoke to Indresh Kumar in Mumbai before coming to Srinagar. 'The MRM is not an organization of the RSS. It is an outfit of the Muslims and for the Muslims,' he said.

Kumar told me that aim of the RSS in Kashmir is to change the mindset of the Muslim population towards contentious and inflammatory issues. Through its programmes, the Sangh attempts to convince Kashmiri Muslims that they are being used as puppets by elements in Pakistan. People are told how Articles 370 and 35A have been perilous for the welfare of the Valley. They are told that their betterment lies in moving along with mainstream India and there is no point in shedding blood upon the instigation of a hostile neighbour.

The MRM urges the youth to shun guns and stones by arranging meetings with community leaders and sitting with the stone-pelters to convince them to give up violence. The outfit has also decided to set up legal cells to help youngsters who have been booked on charges of stone-pelting and get them into the mainstream.[32] Discussions on the history of Kashmir are also arranged, where the role of Muslims freedom fighters in India's struggle for independence and the bravery of Muslim soldiers who fought against India's enemies are also highlighted.[33]

Trifurcation? Not Now

One of the major demands by the RSS about J&K was its trifurcation. The Sangh wanted the erstwhile state to be divided into three regions based on religious grounds—Jammu with a Hindu majority, Kashmir with a Muslim majority and Ladakh with a Buddhist majority. In September 2000, *The Times of India* published a statement by then RSS spokesperson M.G. Vaidya, where he said that the RSS was in favour of the trifurcation of J&K, as that would help contain violence in the Valley. In his view, the trifurcation would accelerate development in Jammu and Ladakh. Vaidya said that only the Valley needed special status. Later on, the RSS adopted a formal resolution supporting the demand.[34]

Ram Madhav, who was the joint spokesperson of the RSS in 2002, reiterated the Sangh's demand in Pune, citing the example of Punjab. He said that if the former 'Vishal Punjab' had been divided into three states, with Sikh-dominant Punjab, and Hindu-dominant Haryana and Himachal Pradesh, then there was nothing wrong in trifurcating J&K.[35]

In 2002, the Vishwa Hindu Parishad (VHP) leader Giriraj Kishore asserted that the trifurcation would help displaced Kashmiri Hindus.[36] Kishore's views echoed the rationale of the Sangh, which believed that the Hindu majority of Jammu was being discriminated against by the Muslim politicians from the Valley, and so Jammu needed to be separated from Kashmir.

However, trifurcation was one issue where the BJP and the RSS seemed to be at loggerheads. The BJP stalwart and then union Home

Minister L.K. Advani rejected the idea of trifurcation outright. Advani had said that the focus of the government was the integration of the Kashmiri people with the rest of India, and the government was clear that there would be no division of J&K.[37] Then CM Farooq Abdullah had warned that any such move would trigger communal strife. He said that the Muslim-majority districts of Jammu, like Poonch, Rajouri and Doda, would not like to be part of Jammu, if the trifurcation happened.

Although the trifurcation of J&K has been pursued by the Sangh for the past decades, it has gone soft over the demand post-August 2019. I got an impression of the Sangh's softened stand during my conversation with Indresh Kumar. 'Discussion on the trifurcation is not required now. We will deal with it later on. As for now, we are satisfied with the reorganization of J&K,' he said.

12

KASHMIRI PANDITS: HOPE OR ILLUSION OF HOPE?

'It is not rocket science to settle me back in my homeland! But they are not doing this because I am a commodity and they need to sell me again and again in different election markets.'

'When we will go to Kashmir, we will not go to return. We want to go there permanently.'

'Ghar Wapsi is a political lollipop.'

These voices full of rage and disillusionment are of different Kashmiri Pandits. I met some of them in person or spoke to them on the phone. They hold diverse views over the resettlement of members of their community in the Valley. Although the abrogation of Article 370, bifurcation of J&K and withdrawal of statehood has had no direct implications for Kashmiri Pandits, the Modi government's focus on Kashmir has led to the perception that the displaced Kashmiri Pandits will be resettled in the Valley. After all, there is a strong government in the Centre that adheres to Hindutva ideology and, in today's India, Kashmiri Pandits are one of the biggest examples of religious victimization. While the August 2019 decisions have given some of them hope, others are sceptical.

The Pandits of Kashmir are Hindu Brahmins, but their rituals, customs, festivals and food habits differ from Brahmins in other parts of India. For example, Kashmiri Pandits consume meat and offer it to God as well. For them, the biggest festival is Mahashivratri, unlike Deepawali or Holi. The religious and cultural traits of Kashmiri Pandits have been largely influenced by the Muslim rule in the Valley. Many changes occurred in the community due to their subjugation and to avoid persecution. A brief look at history reveals that Kashmiri Pandits have been persecuted time and again in the past few centuries, first by the Muslim Sultanate in the thirteenth and fourteenth centuries, then again in the fifteenth century, and later on during the Afghan rule. Kashmiri Pandits who once dominated the demography became a minority in the Valley due to repeated persecution, forced conversion and migration over the centuries. However, the biggest blow that the community received was at the dusk of the twentieth century, in the late eighties, with the advent of militancy in the Valley.

Numerous accounts describe in detail the atrocities that Kashmiri Pandits had to endure during that period—how they were threatened, kidnapped, tortured and killed. Their houses were burnt down and property seized. Kashmiri Pandit women were molested and raped. They didn't get any protection from the police, nor were their Muslim neighbours able to keep their word to shield them. On the contrary, in some cases, neighbours aided the militants in the carnage.

Many Kashmiri Pandits regard 19 Januray 1990 as 'Holocaust Day'. On the night of 18 January, announcements were made from mosques asking Pandits to convert, leave the Valley or get killed. In urban areas of Kashmir, like Srinagar, militants identified Pandit families and eliminated them. In rural areas, there were mass killings, like the Wandhama Massacre, where, on 25 January 1998, militants gunned down 26 people, including women and children.

There were clearly differences between Kashmiri Muslims and Kashmiri Hindus. Muslims perceived Pandits as a privileged class under the maharaja's rule. They dominated the government jobs and owned most of the land. However, this perception was not true, as all Kashmiri Pandits were not affluent, which Sheikh Abdullah acknowledged in a statement in 1940.[1]

Despite harbouring sentiments of bitterness and feelings of inequality, prolonged coexistence led to shared community living. Both Pandits and Muslims had a common culture, language and the pride of being Kashmiris.[2] There were few communal riots in the past between the two communities, but Pandits never imagined that a time would come when they would have to abandon their homeland.

Pakistan-backed militancy influenced by the Wahabi version of Islam in the Valley contradicted the Sufi traditions of Kashmir. Wahabism propagated intolerance and hatred towards non-Muslims, and it was one of the reasons why the Pandits were targeted. A narrative was built suggesting that the Pandits were 'agents of India'. There was also a perception that they worked for Hindu organizations like the RSS.

One of the reasons for hatred towards the Pandits was the reappointment of Jagmohan as the governor of J&K in January 1990.[3] During his reign, armed forces were allegedly given a free hand to deal with separatists and militants. Several incidents occurred that were deemed tyrannical, such as the Gawkadal Massacre, in which numerous protestors were shot dead by security forces. It was propagated that Jagmohan had been sent to Kashmir to 'massacre Muslims'.

Kashmiri Pandits fled Kashmir as they felt that they were not safe in the Valley. However, another narrative tells us that it was Governor Jagmohan who didn't attempt to stop the exodus and instead facilitated it. A four-member committee, named Initiative on Kashmir, visited the Valley from 12 to 16 March 1990. Its report said that the administration in general and Jagmohan, in particular, were responsible for the flight of Hindus. Transportation for fleeing Hindus was arranged by them.[4]

In his autobiography, *My Frozen Turbulence in Kashmir*, Jagmohan has refuted the allegation of facilitating the exodus of Kashmiri Pandits. He wrote that the findings of the committee were not credible and were based on hearsay. Jagmohan stressed that no evidence was produced to suggest that government vehicles were provided to fleeing Kashmiri Pandits. In his view, the trigger of the exodus was the killing of 71 Hindus between December 1989 and 15 May 1990.

Today, Kashmiri Pandits can be divided into three categories. One category is of people who are living in refugee colonies, like Jagti in Jammu. Another is of people who have migrated to other states and settled there. The third category is of people who didn't leave the Valley during the exodus and continue to lead miserable lives.

Is a Rebuilding of Trust Possible?

'Is there a dialogue happening with Kashmiri Muslims for the return of Pandits?' asks Ashish Kaul, a Kashmiri Pandit settled in Mumbai, whom I interviewed. As an author, Kaul has written extensively on the plight of Pandits residing in refugee camps.

He says that work at the grassroots level and people-to-people contact is necessary to generate trust. 'Kashmiri Pandits,' says Kaul, 'left because they were let down by the Muslim majority. They lost trust. Is the Muslim majority willing to come forward and say that they are open to rebuilding that trust?'

To explain how Pandits lost trust in their Muslim neighbours, Kaul narrates a painful incident that happened with his relatives.

'My mausi (maternal aunt) worked at HMT and mausa (maternal uncle) worked at the Broadway Hotel in Kashmir. They stayed in the Chinkral Mohalla of Srinagar. During the exodus, we requested them to leave the Valley with us, but they refused. They told us that their Muslim neighbours had assured them that nobody would be allowed to harm them. Soon, our fears turned true. One morning, militants stormed their home and killed them. Another couple who resided on a floor above them was also killed. For two days, their bodies were lying in the house. The neighbours who had promised to defend them didn't even come to shift their dead bodies to the hospital.'

Kaul believes that the alienation of Kashmiri Pandits began since Sheikh Abdullah's regime. *Bhattloot*, according to Kaul, is the word used to describe the robbing of Kashmiri Pandits.

'At an emotional level,' says Kaul, 'we want to go back...but we don't want to live in isolated colonies. We want the Kashmir of the 1980s, where we could move around freely and where Hindus and Muslims lived in harmony.'

Kaul stressed that the return of Kashmiri Pandits must be comprehensive. People must get the means for sustenance along with residences. They must get jobs as per their educational qualifications.

Although Kashmir-based militant organizations are not opposing the return of Kashmiri Pandits (slain militant Burhan Wani, in one of his last videos, asked Pandits to come back), Kaul remains sceptical about security. He explains his fears in as many words, 'Today's Kashmiri society has tasted blood. Terrorism has become a micro-economics in Kashmir. Many people have become dependent on terrorism and are enjoying the fruits of terrorism.'

I spoke to Ashoke Pandit, a film-maker based in Mumbai. Pandit was born and brought up in Mumbai and is credited with the documentary *And the World Remained Silent*, on the plight of the Kashmiri Pandits. He has been associated with various organizations working for the resettlement of the Pandits.

'We need to rebuild trust with the Muslim community and that, for now, seems difficult. The wounds will take time to heal. The bonding between the two communities will begin only by the time of the next generation,' Pandit observed.

Pandit, who takes pride in introducing himself as a hardcore right-winger, has welcomed the abrogation of Article 370 and the withdrawal of statehood. He believes that such decisions will lead to better law and order conditions, and will create an environment conducive to peace. Pandit stresses that any discussion or formulation of strategy over the fate of Kashmiri Pandits would be incomplete without taking the aggrieved community into confidence. 'This is a matter of the heart. Only bureaucrats can't make the strategy of our return. You have to deal with people who are hurt. When we will go to Kashmir, we will not go to return.'

I spoke to Dr Agnishekhar, a prominent writer and convenor of the organization Panun Kashmir. Although he was happy with the abrogation of Article 370, he was full of bitterness against the central government. 'Kashmir changed after 5 August 2019, but Kashmiri Pandits are still living in 4 August. There is no change in our status,' said an agitated Agnishekhar.

Voices from Jagti

If there is any place that could be called the biggest symbol of the exodus of Kashmiri Pandits, it is Jagti Township. Located 21 kilometres away from Jammu city, it is like an island of people with stories of grief, suffering and struggle. These people escaped being shot, burnt alive or thrown into the river with their throats slit. Many are surviving with the hope that they will be able to spend their old age on their ancestral land, whereas others have died waiting for their hopes to materialize.

Jagti Township was set up in 2010 for migrant Kashmiri Pandits as part of a resettlement and rehabilitation programme introduced by the Manmohan Singh government. It has 4,224 residential units housing around 18,000 people. Although the shelter in Jagti is better than living in tents, it is far inferior to the lifestyle they enjoyed in their native land. Families live in crunched tenements of 350 square feet consisting of a bedroom and a living room. Just having a concrete building isn't enough. They have had to struggle for necessities. For the initial few years, there was no regular electricity supply and residents had to resort to agitation to get it. They still lack clean drinking water. For survival, every refugee gets Rs. 3,250, and the amount is capped at Rs. 13,000 per family. Residents have been clamouring for the past few years to increase the relief amount.

I approached the residents of Jagti with several questions in my mind. Do they want to go back to Kashmir? What are their fears? What do they expect from the government? How do they view the abrogation of Article 370 and other decisions? There was no unanimous answer to these questions, making it difficult to infer what Kashmiri Pandits want.

'I have been elected as sarpanch of my village, but I have not stepped there since my election,' said 37-year-old Ravindra Pandita. Pandita has been residing in refugee camps since he was four years old. In the last few years, he began to visit his native village of Tumlahal in Pulwama. In 2019, Pandita contested the panchayat elections as a BJP candidate and was elected unopposed. However, he has not been able to visit his village due to security concerns since then. He just goes to the block office in Pulwama with police security for official work. There have been several cases of assassinations of sarpanchs after the elections.

'Who doesn't want to return to their home? Who wants to live in a place where temperatures go up to 50 degree Celsius? We want to live in our motherland. It is shameful that we are refugees in our own country,' said Pandita vehemently, when I asked him if he wants to return to the Valley. However, he said that the environment was not conducive for Pandits to return.

'There are many issues that need to be addressed. Things are happening just on paper. It is just eyewash. We are not feeling secure to go back to our villages. While the land of many Pandits was usurped, some sold their land in distress. The administration is stuck in the old mindset. I can show 200 cases where even the court orders have not been implemented by the administration.'

Who will Punish the Perpetrators of the Genocide?

Another major grievance that most Kashmiri Pandits I spoke to had was that the people responsible for the exodus have not been punished.

'Ajmal Kasab was hanged for the 26/11 attacks, Yakub Memon was hanged for the Mumbai serial blasts and Afzal Guru was hanged for the attack on the Parliament, but, tell me, who has been punished for killing Kashmiri Pandits, burning their houses, raping their women and forcing them to flee?' asked Pandita.

In Ashish Kaul's view, the government has been nonchalant about punishing perpetrators of crimes against Kashmiri Pandits.

'You (the central government) activated the whole machinery for Sushant Singh Rajput's death case. The CBI was asked to investigate the matter because you wanted to convey that you were taking the case seriously, but the same enthusiasm has not been displayed in the case of atrocities against Kashmiri Pandits. Till the time perpetrators are punished, everything will be considered just political rhetoric...'

Ashoke Pandit concurs with Kaul's views. 'Not a single case has been filed against the genocide of Kashmiri Pandits. The perpetrators have been booked in other cases but not for the murders, rapes and loot of Kashmiri Pandits. They need to be punished. When we approached the court through a PIL, we were told that the matter was too old.'

Pandit says that the current dispensation at the Centre is capable of punishing the perpetrators and is hopeful that some action will be taken in that direction.

Demand for a Homeland

Since the exodus, there has been an increasing demand for a homeland for Kashmiri Pandits. Panun Kashmir, an organization founded by Dr Agnishekhar and others, has been pursuing this demand through various platforms. The organization believes that providing a homeland is the only viable solution for the rehabilitation of Kashmiri Pandits.

Dr Agnishekhar explained the rationale behind this demand. 'Is there any guarantee that I will not be attacked again or I will not be compelled to escape once more? We need a new Union Territory. Make a new Chandigarh in Kashmir. We can go and settle there for our future generations. A politico-administrative security setup is required,' said Agnishekhar.

Agnishekhar says that Kashmiri Pandits have suffered three kinds of genocide. One was the physical genocide, where they were killed, their women were raped and their property was usurped or damaged. Another was an economic genocide, where the source of livelihood of Kashmiri Pandits was attacked by snatching their farmlands, shops and jobs. The third was a cultural genocide, when there were attempts to eliminate the distinct identity of Kashmiri Pandits.

'The downtown area of Srinagar has been named as Sheher-e-Khas. The government had also changed the name of Hari Parbat. Anantnag is referred to as Islamabad. Such renaming of locations is an attack on our culture. This has been done since Sheikh Abdullah's regime in 1975, when the names of several villages were changed,' said Agnishekhar.

The proposed homeland that the Kashmiri Pandits are demanding encompasses an area north-east of the river Jhelum. It includes the districts of Anantnag, Pahalgam, Sonmarg and some parts of Srinagar. As per Panun Kashmir, the homeland must have 4 per cent of the total area of united J&K, which existed before 1947.

'The geopolitical aspirations,' said Agnishekhar, 'of Kashmiri Pandits must be fulfilled, and the blueprint of a homeland by Panun Kashmir is a way to do that.'

However, Ashoke Pandit said that the ghettoization of Kashmiri Pandits must not be done, and the homeland is the way for providing them justice.

Those who Stayed Back

'There used to be 32 families of Kashmiri Pandits in this locality; now just mine remains here,' said 54-year-old Sanjay Tikoo, who heads one of the 808 families that remained in Kashmir after the exodus.

After speaking to scores of Kashmiri Pandits who were staying in Jammu's Jagti camp and elsewhere, I wanted to understand what made people like Tikoo stay back. Were they not harmed? Were they not scared? How did they survive those days in the early nineties? How have they been living in the past three decades in the Valley? To seek answers, I headed to Tikoo's residence in the Barbarshah area. Tikoo stays in his ancestral house, which is a ground-plus-one structure that can be approached through a maze of narrow lanes.

Before answering my questions, Tikoo insisted on knowing which other Kashmiri Pandits I had met and what they had told me. After listening to my impression of displaced Kashmiri Pandits in detail, he harked back to 1990 and said that whatever I was told about the exodus of Kashmiri Pandits was not completely true. 'The narrative about Kashmiri Pandits has been exaggerated from both sides,' he said.

'It is not correct to say that exodus began on 19 January 1990. In reality, the exodus began on 15 March and continued till 30 May. However, it was shocking to see that on 19 January, within an hour, thousands of people were on the road. That was not the time of mobile phones and internet, but it was pre-planned, and the intelligence agencies were unable to detect it,' he said. Tikoo said that it is misleading to say that Pandits were attacked and looted on the way when they were fleeing. 'If that would have happened, not a single Pandit would have survived.'

According to Tikoo, the Kashmir Liberation Front and Islamic Students League had done a study in the mid-eighties to estimate how many Kashmiri Pandits were employed in central and state government jobs and the amount of land possessed by them.

Tikoo recollects, 'Sweepers, vegetable vendors and milkmen had been sources of the militants during the exodus. They reported to local commanders about how many families had left. During those times, a list of Kashmiri Pandits and National Conference workers used to be given in local mosques. Killings were done according to that list. Once, a Muslim friend, after offering the evening namaz, alerted me. He had seen my cousin brother's name, who was staying with us, on the list. We sent him to Jammu the next morning. Due to this timely alert by that Muslim friend, my cousin's life was saved.'

Tikoo says it is absurd to portray all Kashmiri Muslims of the early nineties as extremists. There were numerous instances where Muslim neighbours had supported and protected Pandits. 'I remember that out of 100 people, 60 supported us,' he said.

There had been two incidents when Tikoo's family thought of leaving Kashmir, but eventually they stayed back. A threatening letter in Urdu from a group named Al-Umar Commandos was stuck at the entrance of the lane leading to their house. It alleged that informers had visited Tikoo's home and that he must leave with his family within seven days. Tikoo went to the local mosque for help, but they refused to intervene. Then, Tikoo published an advertisement in *Srinagar Times* in response to the threatening letter, which read, 'We will leave, but then whatever will be the fate of Barbarshah, we will not be responsible.' Tikoo said that his family had packed all their belongings but then thought of leaving everything to God and stayed back.

In May 1990, the killings of five Kashmiri members from a family in the Ali Kadal area got the Tikoo family worried. Again, they packed up to leave. 'I walked up to Naaz cinema and paid

500 rupees in advance to a truck driver to pick us up the next morning. When I returned home, my emotional mother pleaded to stay back for a few more days. We never thought of leaving after that,' recollected Tikoo.

'1990 to 1992,' said Tikoo, 'was a time when we felt that nobody was with us. But apart from Kashmiri Pandits, non-state actors killed Muslims and Sikhs also.'

He recollects that in rural areas, if any Kashmiri Pandit wanted to travel outside the Valley, they had to take permission from the local mosque. A green card with a date was given to them, mentioning the date by which they had to return. If the person didn't return by that date, he had to pay with his life. 'Militants suspected that those going out could be giving inputs to security forces. A number of killings of Kashmiri Pandits after 31 May 1990 were of those who returned later than the given dates,' said Tikoo.

Apart from the looming threat of death at the hands of militants, the Kashmiri Pandits who chose to stay back were at the receiving end of harassment by the security forces also.

'In our storerooms, we used to stock a good quantity of food grains to be used during the harsh weather months. They suspected that we were feeding the militants and destroyed our stocks. Such treatment was meted out to the majority (Muslim) community also,' he remembered. 'The officers,' he said, 'who come from outside of Kashmir don't know ABC of this place.'

Since 2003, Tikoo has been running an organization named Kashmiri Pandit Sangharsh Samiti and is currently its president. He has been one of the most vocal faces of Kashmiri Pandits residing in the Valley and has been instrumental in connecting the 808 families that are spread out in different parts of the Valley.

Tikoo said that today there is no community-to-community relationship between Kashmiri Pandits and Kashmiri Muslims, but individual-to-individual relationships between members of the two communities. 'Today also our family distributes water-soaked walnuts as a tradition to Muslim friends on Mahashivratri,' he said. In his view, the situation of Kashmiri Pandits today is much different from what it was in the 1990s. The daily life of Pandits is running smoothly for most of the 808 families residing in villages. Weddings and other ceremonies happen freely.

He doesn't see any problem in Kashmiri Pandits returning to their homes and leading a normal life. 'Only when some turmoil happens, like the Amarnath land row, Macchil encounter or Burhan Wani's killing, then our activities get restricted,' he said.

Tikoo got riled up when I asked him what his expectations were from the central government after the 5 August decisions. 'A BIG ZERO,' he said loudly, in an angry voice. 'After the abrogation of Article 370, we haven't got any benefit. My sociopolitical, economic or religious freedoms have not changed. In fact, after 5 August, there is nobody to listen to us. There is a political vacuum. Earlier, there was a government who used to listen to us and redress our grievances to some extent.'

Referring to PM Modi, he said, 'I just want him to follow what late Atal Bihari Vajpeyee ji advised him. Follow "Raj Dharma". I am telling Modi ji that there are alarm bells for the coming days. He must fulfil all the promises he made. Due to the sudden lockdown, the life of lower-class people has been miserable. Their lives need to be restored.'

Ghettoization of Kashmiri Pandits

Sanjay Tikoo informed me that over 4,000 Kashmiri Pandits have returned to the Valley under the Prime Minister's Relief and Rehabilitation Scheme initiated during Manmohan Singh's tenure. He said that now there is no problem with resettling Kashmiri Pandits in the Valley, but the model of a gated community adopted by the government is absurd. Kashmiri Pandits who have returned are mostly employees of the government. They live in one- or three-storeyed buildings that have been built as 'transit accommodation' and are heavily guarded by the CRPF and the local police. Most of these people originally resided in other parts of the Valley. The gated colonies restrict the assimilation of people of different communities and the rebuilding of mutual trust.

I spoke to Mahendra Kumar (name changed), who has been residing at Vesu camp, one of the half-dozen colonies in the Valley built as transit accommodation for Kashmiri migrants. Only two colonies have concrete houses, while the rest of the colonies are made of prefabricated material. Mahendra and his family live in one such colony.

Mahendra told me that life in such colonies has been pathetic, with a lack of space and privacy. The conditions get worse during the cold months. 'This time, in winter, there was abnormal snowfall. The snow had covered the area around our houses up to 6 feet. Our houses were damaged. It was a natural calamity. We sent SOS calls to the authorities to rescue us. However, it was only local political workers who reached us first. Near our houses, there were several under-construction, multi-storeyed buildings, which we were told would be allotted to us on completion. So, the families who got stuck in the snow were temporarily kept in those buildings. So many lives were saved, but after that something unexpected happened. FIRs were filed against us for trespassing. Since we were government employees, letters were written directing a pay cut.'

Despite these problems, the government has plans to come up with more such colonies. In 2020, an order by the J&K government's Revenue department reserved 5 acres of land for transit homes of Kashmiri Pandits. The proposed colony is to be built in a village in Shopian. In 2015, a blueprint of the rehabilitation project was disclosed, showing heavily secured, self-contained colonies for Kashmiri migrants, with amenities like shopping malls, schools, hospitals, playgrounds and so on.

Mahendra concluded the conversation by saying, 'In such an arrangement, you can't socialize and mingle with other communities. We need to develop chemistry between the Hindu and Muslim communities. We have returned, but we have not been rehabilitated.'

13

THE NEW GOVERNANCE

Jammu and Kashmir has lost its statehood, its special status and a big section of it has been converted into a UT. How have these decisions affected the lives of people in the Valley? How is the administration shaping up in 'new Kashmir'? What are the fresh issues occupying the minds of Kashmiris? Through my visit to the Valley and interaction with the people there, I endeavoured to seek answers to these questions.

From Governor to Lieutenant Governor

'The governor has no work to do. A person who is the governor of Jammu and Kashmir usually drinks wine and plays golf,' said Satya Pal Malik, the former governor of J&K, in March 2020.[1] This description of the governor's work shocked some and amused others. Some felt offended and derided Malik for his comments. Shiv Sena in its mouthpiece *Saamana* called his statement an insult to the governor's office. However, the office of the governor in Jammu and Kashmir became non-existent after Malik was transferred to Goa.

Since J&K was made a UT from a full state, the constitutional post of the governor was replaced by the lieutenant governor, like it is in Delhi and Puducherry. A lieutenant governor is appointed by the President of India for a tenure of five years and enjoys executive, legislative, financial and discretionary powers more or less similar to that of a governor.

Satya Pal Malik was succeeded by Girish Chandra Murmu as lieutenant governor, who was replaced nine months later by Manoj Sinha. Various constitutional experts have warned against appointing a person who has been active in politics as governor or lieutenant governor, but this has not been followed in Kashmir. Manoj Sinha was an active politician just months before his appointment. He was a three-time MP and a minister till the end of PM Modi's first tenure in 2019. After assuming office in Srinagar, one of the major challenges before Sinha has been the recovery of the economy, which has been in peril since 5 August 2019, due to the twin lockdowns.

New System of Grassroots Governance

The first visible change in the governance at the grassroots level post 5 August 2019 decisions came up in the form of District Development Councils (DDC). This new unit of governance substituted the erstwhile District Planning and Development Boards.

For every district, there is also a District Planning Committee (DPC), which is required to guide the formulation of development programmes and prioritize various schemes, take up issues related to development and finalize periodic plans and budgets.

The Centre justifies the introduction of the DDC system as an effort to revive the Panchayati Raj system. The DDCs are touted as effective representative bodies for development at the grassroots level.

The new system was initially criticized by most local political parties as 'tokenism' of the democratic process, for giving more power to the bureaucracy and curtailing the role of MLAs. The system was also accused of creating confusion over the administrative structure. However, all parties participated vigorously in the DDC elections in November 2020.

No Jammu and Kashmir Cadre

An IPS officer who has been serving in Srinagar, surrounded by hills, can now discharge his duties from the beaches of Goa. He can also be transferred to beautiful Puducherry for policing a town full of heritage buildings reminiscent of the French rule in India. One of the most significant changes in the civil services of J J&K

after August 2019 has been the merging of the J&K cadre with another cadre.

Since J&K has lost its statehood and has become a UT, its cadre had to be discontinued and merged with the Arunachal Pradesh, Goa, Mizoram and Union Territories (AGMUT), in January 2021. The change implies that henceforth an officer from the erstwhile J&K cadre can be posted in any of the nine UTs or the states of Arunachal Pradesh, Goa and Mizoram and vice versa. The merger applies to the officers of the Indian Administrative Service (IAS), Indian Police Service (IPS) and Indian Forest Service.

Discontinuing the J&K cadre has a political message too. The central government sees the decision as a part of the process of turning J&K into a UT and integrating it with mainstream India. The decision has also led to a discussion that the restoration of the statehood of J&K is unlikely to happen. Another factor necessitating this change has been the reluctance of the erstwhile J&K cadre officers to work in the Ladakh region due to harsh working conditions. The government now has a large pool of officers to be deployed in various regions.

Shah Faesal, a former IAS officer who participated in Kashmiri politics for a few months, shared his observations with me about doing away with the J&K cadre. Faesal said, 'These are transitional decisions and taking a long-term view is going to be rather difficult. But then IAS/IPS are all India services and I don't think cadre matters much here. There is already a lot of mobility between the Centre and states and it has worked well so far. It may be difficult for senior officers to move out of the J&K cadre at a stage of life when stability matters more than anything else. But besides that, I am not sure what major complications the cadre merger can cause. Maybe if the statehood is returned someday, the cadre may also be returned.'

Delimitation: A Can of Worms?

The bifurcation of J&K has necessitated the reorganization of electoral constituencies. A Delimitation Commission was constituted for this purpose on 6 March 2020.

Referring to the 2011 Census, the commission has to determine the number of electoral seats and boundaries in such a manner that the population in all the constituencies is equal as far as possible. The commission also has to fix the number of seats to be reserved for women, Scheduled Castes, Scheduled Tribes and several other groups. It is expected to provide representations to Gujjars, Bakarwals, West Pakistani refugees and Gorkhas.

The commission has a very complex task as it deals with an issue that has far-reaching political implications. The status quo of the total number of seats shared between the Jammu and Kashmir regions is likely to get disrupted. So far, it is the Kashmir region that has had an upper hand in deciding the government of the erstwhile state. All the chief ministers, except Ghulam Nabi Azad, have been Kashmiri-speaking Muslims. Presently, the Kashmir division has a 56 per cent population share and Jammu has 44 per cent. However, Jammu holds 62 per cent of the total area and 38 per cent is with the Kashmir region. There is a clamour that the delimitation must be done based on area rather than population. It has also been alleged that the 2011 Census being used has anomalies.[2]

Some groups have begun expressing their expectations from the delimitation process. On 26 March 2021, a delegation of Kashmiri Pandits and Sikh activists met the chairman, Justice Ranjana Desai, and other members of the commission and acquainted them with their demands. The delegation stressed that to secure the political rights of minorities like Kashmiri Pandits and Sikhs in the UT, measures like reservation or nomination of seats for them must be adopted. In addition to the above, the delegation also demanded one seat each in the Lok Sabha and Rajya Sabha.

The Delimitation Commission is working slowly, and its tenure has been extended by a year from 5 March 2021. The assembly elections are likely to be held only when the commission completes its process. In the first week of July 2021, when the delimitation panel visited the Valley to get views of political parties and UT officials, there was a mixed response from constituents of the

Gupkar alliance. Representatives of the NC and CPM met the panel, but the PDP refrained by saying that the commission lacked constitutional and legal mandate. Representatives of the Congress, the BJP and few other parties met the panel.

When I asked veteran journalist Bashir Manzar for his view on the delimitation process, he said, 'Delimitation in Kashmir is happening before time. However, historically, such exercises have been taking place time and again, during which some communities of voters are shifted here and there.'

In December 2021, the commission proposed the addition of six seats for the Jammu division and one seat for the Kashmir division. It also proposed reservation of 16 seats for candidates belonging to the Scheduled Castes and the Scheduled Tribes. The acceptance of the proposal would increase the seats of the Jammu region from 37 to 43, while Kashmir, with one addition, would have 47 seats. The constituent parties of the Gupkar alliance have opposed the proposals. Altaf Bukhari's Apni Party also protested against the proposal.

Domicile and Land Laws

In June 2020, a printed document that read, 'This is to certify that Shri. Navin. K. Choudhary, son of Deokant Choudhary, resident of, at present Gandhinagar, Jammu, is a domicile of UT of J&K,' went viral on social media.[3] IAS officer Choudhary was the first among the bureaucrats to get a domicile certificate under the new law. He hails from Darbhanga in Bihar and has served in the erstwhile state of J&K for over 26 years. Granting domicile to Kumar is an instance of how things are shaping up in Kashmir.

One of the major developments in J&K after August 2019 has been the implementation of a new domicile law. The law has been an issue of contention and has implications for the demographics of the UT. On 31 March 2020, the central government issued a notification for domicile rules, stating that any person living in the UT for 15 years or those who have studied in Kashmir for 7 years and appeared for 10th and 12th class exams are eligible to acquire domicile status. As per the new guidelines, children of those who have worked or studied in the UT for the stipulated period are also eligible. Those who have worked for the government for a minimum of 10 years are also eligible to benefit from the new system.

The new domicile law replaces the earlier system of issuing permanent resident certificates (PRC), under which only permanent residents were entitled to own property, apply for jobs and seek admissions in educational institutions of J&K. The PRC system was defined under the now-scrapped Article 35A of the Indian Constitution.[4]

The process has been made easy and swift. Within a year of the new domicile rules coming into force, over 32 lakh people have got their certificates. Around 31 lakh of them have been holders of the PRCs, which have now been replaced by the domicile certificates.

Except for the BJP, all other parties have been critical of the new domicile rules and have viewed it with suspicion. Farooq Abdullah of the NC said that the new system is not acceptable as it is illegal and unconstitutional. His son, Omar Abdullah, questioned the hurried manner in which the domicile law was being implemented.[5] The PDP also targeted the law through a series of tweets. The official Twitter handle of the party said, 'The domicile law as it appears is not only trying to shake the boundaries of an already existing state but is also trying to give massive problems for residents of J&K. It is further alienating the people and depriving them of constitutional rights.'[6] Apni Party also condemned the law, saying that it was a casual attempt by New Delhi to deceive the people of J&K.[7]

Voices of protests against the 'domicile reforms' came from non-political quarters also. Kashmir's Grand Mufti Nasir-ul-Islam slammed them by saying that they were against the interests of the people of Kashmir. Mirwaiz Umar Farooq condemned it and suspected that it was an attempt to alter the demographic character of the UT. A statement from the separatist organization JKLF called the reforms undemocratic and contrary to international laws and obligations.[8]

An order issued by the Ministry of Home Affairs on 26 October 2020 substantially altered the legal system for land ownership.

Amendments were effected to 14 laws of the erstwhile state of J&K, and 12 laws were repealed. The most significant amendment has been made to the Jammu and Kashmir Development Act, 1970, where the phrase, 'Permanent Resident of the State', has been deleted. This implies that any individual can buy land in the UT.

Former bureaucrat Shah Faesal has a positive view towards changes in the laws. He told me, 'These are natural consequences of the abrogation of Article 370. The intent has been to fast-track development in J&K. If by making land allotment easier the government succeeds in promoting industrial activity and bringing in large investments, then this might be remembered as major policy reform.'

New Era, New Rules

In April 2021, the J&K administration formed a Special Task Force (STF) for taking action against public servants suspected of involvement in activities against the 'security of the State'. The order empowers the administration to terminate an employee without conducting any enquiry against the person on grounds of security of the state. The chief of the STF is an additional director general of police (Addl. DG) rank officer. A few other police officers are also members of the STF along with members of the Law, Justice and Parliamentary Affairs departments.

The brief of the new STF includes compiling records of employees suspected of activities requiring action under the aforementioned Article. The STF is also permitted to seek assistance from other agencies and departments, if required.

The formation of the STF was not taken well by some political parties. Communist leader M.Y. Tarigami opposed it by saying that it was arbitrary, draconian and against the interests of employees. He said that the order could be used as a 'tool for the government and bureaucrats to suppress their subordinates'.[9]

Darbar Move Discontinued?

J&K had been the only state in India with two capitals—Jammu city and Srinagar. From May to October, the government offices function from Srinagar, and, as winter sets in, the operations move to Jammu city for the next six months. The exercise of shifting government employees, files and other systems of administration from one capital to another has been known as the 'Darbar Move'. This tradition is said to have commenced during Maharaja Gulab Singh's regime in 1872 to adjust to the harsh weather of the region and make the government available to people from both Jammu and Kashmir.[10]

For Darbar Move days, holidays are declared in government offices and hundreds of trucks and buses are arranged to transfer files and other documents between the two capitals. Every year, around Rs. 200 crore is spent for the Darbar Move, which covers transportation, accommodation and various allowances of the government employees.

Over the years, the practice has been criticized as a waste of money, time and resources, and there has been a clamour to do away with it.[11] The present dispensation also doesn't seem to be eager to continue with the tradition. An indication of the administration's view became apparent in April 2021, when a circular was issued by the UT administration that only sensitive files would be moved from Jammu to Srinagar. Considering the pandemic, physical movement of the files was discouraged and governmental work was to be done through the e-office. Unlike the hundreds of trucks arranged every year, it was announced that only ten trucks would be made available. For the first time in its history, Darbar Move was deferred in 2021.[12]

14

GUNS DON'T JUST KILL

'Kashmir has seen its worst. What more could happen now?' a CRPF commandant counter questioned me in August 2019, when I asked him if he had anticipated the situation in the Valley would deteriorate after the decisions taken by the central government.

It was feared that there would be violent reactions to such decisions, so there was a clampdown and a communication blockade in the Valley. Due to the extensive presence of security personnel all around, the incidents of organized stone-pelting were minimal. Militant groups didn't react immediately, suggesting that militancy in Kashmir was fading away. But they reacted!

I am a foodie and I have identified locations of delicious vegetarian food in almost every city of India that I have visited. For Srinagar, my favourite was Krishna Vaishno Dhaba near Dal Gate, famous for its rajma pulao and baingan ka bharta. This modest eating house at a walking distance from Dal Lake has been popular among local vegetarians, members of the armed forces, tourists and pilgrims alike. Often people have to wait to get a table during lunch and dinner hours. The last time I visited this eatery was in February 2019. When I went back in August that year, the eatery was shut throughout my stay in Srinagar. Two years later, in March 2021, once again I reached the eatery and found the area around it desolate. Its shutter was down, even though that day there was neither any curfew nor a call for hartal by any separatist group. The reason for its closure broke my heart.

On the evening of 17 February 2019, when Krishna Dhaba was brimming with customers, Akash Mehra, the 21-year-old son of the eatery's owner, was handling the cash counter. All of sudden, two masked men armed with pistols walked in and fired point-blank at Akash. He was rushed to Sri Maharaja Hari Singh Hospital with bullet injuries to his abdomen. He succumbed to the injuries after 11 days of struggle. His murder added another number to the civilian victims of militancy in Kashmir.

The murder of Akash Mehra shocked locals and visitors like me alike. No harm had been done to Krishna Dhaba or its owners even during the three decades of insurgency, then what had happened now for them to be targeted? The owners of the eatery never antagonized local politicians, separatists or militant organizations. They were always sensitive to the local situation and kept the eatery shut whenever there was any protest or a call for a bandh. Another question is: How did the militants manage to execute such an incident, as Krishna Dhaba is located in one of the highly secured areas of Srinagar? The killing of Akash Mehra implies that if militants can kill unarmed civilians in this area, then they can kill them in any other area easily.

On the same day, several envoys of European Union countries and members of the Organization of Islamic Countries were in Kashmir and were accommodated in a hotel just two kilometres away from Krishna Dhaba. The time of attack suggests that the militants wanted to convey a message to the foreigners that any projection of normalcy in Kashmir by the Indian government was false and that resistance against the Indian State was continuing. The recent decisions had not weakened the forces of militancy in the Valley. Another message was directed towards non-Kashmiri residents and Hindus—they were not safe in the Valley. It was believed that the militants had adopted this modus operandi to create a fear psychosis among Hindus and non-Kashmiri residents.

A day after Mehra was fired upon, the police arrested three youngsters. They were said to be members of a militant organization Muslim Janbaaz Force, which is seen as an offshoot of the LeT. The pistol allegedly used to shoot Mehra and the shooters' motorcycle were also recovered.[1]

Earlier, in January, militants had shot dead an elderly jeweller named Satpal Nischal.[2] He had been settled in Srinagar for the past five decades. Just a few days before his murder, he had reportedly gotten his domicile certificate, which was seen as one reason of his coming on the radar of the militants. A militant organization named Resistance Front took the responsibility for the killing. Hours after the killing, a message allegedly from the group went viral. It said, 'Any Indian, irrespective of faith, caste and colour, who comes to Kashmir intending to settle here, will be treated as an agent of RSS and not as a civilian.' However, Satpal's son denied that the killing of his father was linked to the domicile certificate.[3]

Incidents of the killing of non-Kashmiris by militants began just days after the abrogation of Article 370. An analysis of these killings indicates that despite the heavy presence of armed forces and the prolonged communication blockade, the insurgents have been able to indoctrinate the youth, provide them with guns and use them to deliver violent messages. However, the police claim that the situation is under control. The rise in the number of killings of non-Kashmiris indicates that the new domicile policy will be arduous to execute in the Valley. Peace is yet to arrive.

Old and New Militancy

Today, militancy in Kashmir is very different from what it was in the 1990s and 2000s. In the early days of militancy, Kashmiri youths crossed the LoC to get arms training in camps set up in PoK and some locations in Pakistan. They had to spend days in the jungle and in rough, hilly terrains to participate in extensive training programmes lasting for many weeks, and sometimes even months. They had to follow elaborate training modules—like Daur-e-Sufa (religious training), Daur-e-Aam (weapons handling training), Daur-e-Khaas (specialized combat training) and Daur-e-Ribat (intelligence gathering).[4] The recruits learnt to operate different kinds of weapons, including rocket-propelled grenades. Their co-trainees were often Afghan mujahedeen and recruits of the Pakistani Army. Once combat-ready, they were infiltrated back to the Indian side.

However, heightened vigilance at the LoC and fencing has now made it arduous to cross over to the other side. Now, recruits do not cross the border for training and are not as rigorously trained as their predecessors in the 1990s. They get rudimentary training in the jungle or orchards from mostly policemen and members of security forces who have joined militancy.

The kind of training militants got in different eras reflects in their performance during encounters with the Indian security forces. The militants of the 1990s proved to be battle-hardened and it often took time to neutralize them, whereas today's poorly trained militants don't last long in combat with the security forces. This explains the increased number of local militants being killed during encounters of late. An example of this is the encounter of Burhan Wani, which is said to have been concluded within 15 minutes. Today's militants focus more on propaganda with pictures and intimidating audio messages.[5]

Ajay Bachloo, my colleague in Jammu, spoke to Lieutenant General Y.C. Joshi of the Northern Command. He cited the successful conclusion of the DDC elections and said, 'People's faith in democracy has strengthened.' Joshi said that there is a three-pronged challenge for the army in J&K. The first challenge is from Pakistan, which is continuously attempting to smuggle arms inside the UT. The second challenge is from China, which is playing mischief at the LAC. And the third challenge is to maintain the internal situation in J&K.[6]

Although the number of stone-pelting and other law and order incidents have reduced, militancy is still a big concern.

In 2017, 'Operation All Out' was launched as a joint campaign by the Indian Army, the J&K Police, the BSF, the CRPF and the IB to flush out militants. Many such operations led by the armed forces—'Operation Rakshak', 'Operation Calm Down' and 'Operation Sarp Vinash'—had been launched in the past to combat militant organizations.

ISIS in Kashmir: Reality or Hoax?

It was around mid-2013 that the world learnt about the militant jihadist group ISIS through videos showing its brutal methods and its dream of a global Sunni Caliphate. Images of the beheading of journalists, mass executions of Iraqi soldiers and policemen, and other such acts of unimaginable cruelty shocked the world. After Osama bin Laden was killed by the US Navy Seals in 2011, the ISIS chief Abu Bakr al-Baghdadi became the new face of global terror. In fact, ISIS appeared to be more lethal than Osama's Al-Qaeda, as, through online radicalization, it encouraged youth across the globe to reach Iraq and join the war.

Kashmir has been a battleground for foreign terrorists since the 1990s, but the news of the entry of ISIS around 2014 alarmed the security system.

In 2014, after the devastating floods, ISIS flags were displayed in the Valley for the first time. In the interrogation of the flag bearers by the law enforcement agencies, it was revealed that they didn't have much knowledge about the ISIS. Their intention was just to provoke the authorities. The bodies of some militants killed in encounters were draped in the ISIS flag. There have been numerous incidents of flag displays after 2014, but their connection with the ISIS was not substantiated. But the ISIS's interest in the Valley couldn't be ruled out completely.

After 2017, the ISIS has been taking credit for several skirmishes of militants with law enforcement agencies and killings of security personnel. In May 2019, it made a low-key announcement through Amaq News Agency about the beginning of its India branch named Wilayah-al-Hind. In June 2019, some youths holding the ISIS flag pelted stones at security forces in Nowhatta. Such incidents were repeated after Eid prayers in 2020 in the same area. In April 2020, an attack on the CRPF patrolling party in Anantnag that resulted in the death of a jawan was claimed by the ISIS.[7]

Security agencies have been refuting any considerable presence of the ISIS in the Valley. None of the militant organizations have announced their affiliation to it. Moreover, in 2016, separatist leader Syed Ali Shah Geelani of the Hurriyat Conference rejected the ISIS, saying that it is a terrorist organization that kills innocent people and doesn't represent Islam.[8] The rhetoric of a global Caliphate has neither appealed to the separatists nor pro-Pakistani militants. So far, the presence of the ISIS is primarily limited to the online sphere.[9]

Al-Qaeda, however, did make serious efforts to make inroads in the Valley. Zakir Musa, who succeeded Burhan Wani, established a group named Ansar Ghazwat-ul-Hind (AGH), pledging its affiliation to Al-Qaeda. Although the number of militants associated with AGH was very low, it had made its presence felt through a few violent incidents.[10] However, before AGH could advance, there was a heavy crackdown on it by the security forces. Most of the members were killed in encounters, including Zakir Musa himself. But before the security forces could assume that AGH had been wiped out from the Valley, a few more incidents happened. The latest news of encounters between the security forces and AGH members came on 10 April 2021. In two separate encounters, in the southern Kashmiri areas of Tral and Shopian, the security forces killed seven militants of AGH. The police told the media that one of the slain militants was tasked with attacking the Amarnath Yatra.[11]

Drone Terrorism

Early in the morning, on 27 June 2021, two explosives-laden drones crashed at the Indian Air Force station at Jammu airport. One exploded on the roof of the building, whereas another blasted in an open area. Two personnel were injured and a part of the building was damaged in the attack. It was the first such incident in India. The security forces suspected that the drones had been operated by LeT from the Pakistani side. Days after the blasts at the Jammu airport, numerous drone sightings were reported from border areas and near security installations. A month later, on 23 July, a drone carrying explosives was shot down by the J&K Police near Guruchak village of the Akhnoor Sunderbani sector.

Since early 2018, there have been reports of drone sightings and dropping of weapons, explosives, currency and narcotics around the IB and LoC. Drones have also been used for reconnaissance at the border areas. However, they have now advanced to dropping bombs as well. This has posed a new challenge for the Indian security forces. Although anti-drone technology has been developed, drones continue to be difficult to detect and intercept. For terrorist organizations, drones have come up as an inexpensive means of inflicting damage without infiltrating humans.

Although there was no loss of life and property reported in the Jammu airport drone attack, it underscores the fact that brains on the other side of the border are constantly trying to find new ways to execute their designs. First, the heightened vigilance by Indian forces at the border pushed them to recruit members locally in the Valley through online propaganda and now the same is being done through drones. Indian security forces have responded to this new threat by installing anti-drone jammers at a few locations.

The Mantra of a Veteran

'Don't push everything at one time. A healing touch is required. If you are serious about resolving the problem in Kashmir, then you can't push just a single political agenda.'

These are the words of Lieutenant General D.S. Hooda, who retired after serving as general officer commanding-in-chief of the Northern Command. It was during his tenure that the Indian Army conducted a 'surgical strike' in September 2016 in PoK in response to the storming of an army base at Uri by terrorists. Hooda was responding to my question over what he thought was a way for the restoration of peace in Kashmir.

Hooda sounded moderate in his views. Serving for long years in the region has made him a cognoscente of the security situation in J&K, and he is seen as one of the most credible voices on the issue.

'For now,' said Hooda, 'let us not give weightage to contentious issues. Keep them aside. There is a slow and steady way to do things.

Keep local sentiments in mind and focus on development. People will automatically accept you when their life is improving.'

Elaborating on what exactly needs to be done, Hooda said, 'I sense that we need to take a long-term view of the situation. While we continue to counter terrorism and see that no infiltration takes place, we need to do three to four things.'

Hooda's suggestions are:

1. Reach out to the people: There are widespread feelings of alienation and anguish, which need to be dealt with. Political activity must be restored. Elections must be held. People must feel that they are not just governed by Delhi.
2. Engage with the youth: A large part of the population is below 30 years of age. They are vocal about issues, and the government needs to engage with them.
3. Tackle radicalization: There is worry among the people that their identity is under threat. They fear that outsiders will buy land and settle down. The Hurriyat takes advantage of this. Controversial decisions that could trigger widespread protests must not be implemented. Cultural sensitivities must be kept in mind.
4. Development: Article 370 has been diluted, but then people must see fruits of development on the ground. This needs to be sped up.

'Bury the Past and Move Forward'

One of the major developments with regard to security measures in J&K post the abrogation of Article 370 happened on 25 February 2021. Both India and Pakistan announced that they have agreed to strictly adhere to previous agreements on a ceasefire along the LoC and other border areas. The decision was taken at a meeting held between the directors general of military operations (DGMO) of the two countries. The security scenario in Kashmir has been in flux for the last two decades. A ceasefire understanding was worked out between India and Pakistan in November 2003, which later facilitated a meeting between Vajpayee and Musharraf in Islamabad on the sidelines of the South Asian Association for Regional Cooperation (SAARC) summit.

The ceasefire agreement was largely followed from 2003 to 2008, but after the Mumbai attack on 26 November 2008, the situation gradually began deteriorating. Ceasefire violations became frequent, and they increased dramatically after 2012. As per the data of the Union Home ministry of India, 10,752 cases of ceasefire violations have taken place along the India-Pakistan border between 2018 and 2020, in which 72 security personnel and 70 civilians were killed.[12] Both countries have been accusing each other of ceasefire violations, and Pakistan has its own figures. In such a scenario, many perceive the ceasefire announcement of February 25 as a significant step towards extricating the Valley from violence.

Lieutenant General Hooda told me, 'It is a good step. The local population was most affected by ceasefire violations. Many civilians were getting killed. All aspects of life were getting affected—from the schooling of kids to tending of fields.'

Hooda noted that whenever relations between the countries have improved, terrorist violence has gone down. Hooda's experience tells him that talks and confidence-building measures have a direct impact on violence.

'Launching a bus service between the two countries, starting trade and so on have led to the cooling down of the situation. If you look at data starting from 2002 till 2012, there is a consistent decline in violence levels. Terrorist violence was down even during the Amarnath land row. After that, the violence level started rising,' said Hooda.

Although both the countries have announced that they will not violate the ceasefire, just a few months ago, cases of drone sightings were reported on the Indian side of the border. Numerous cross-border tunnels were also unearthed, some as long as 150 metres, which were to be used for the infiltration of militants.[13] Increased instances of ceasefire violations and strategies such as using drones and tunnels suggest that the Pakistani side had been actively pursuing violence in the Valley. In such a scenario, Pakistan's resolve to adhere to the ceasefire agreement has aroused scepticism.

'Considering past experiences, do you think that such an agreement will last for long?' I asked Hooda.

'That depends on Pakistan. If Pakistan stops infiltration, then I think it will. If both countries see this as a step of coming together, then things will get better,' he said.

The agreement was followed by a few more events that raised hopes that a peace process would soon commence between the two warring neighbours. A significant development in this regard was a speech by the Pakistani Army Chief Qamar Bajwa at the Islamabad Security Dialogue on 18 March 2021. In his address, he stressed non-interference of any kind in the internal affairs of Pakistan's neighbours and other regional countries. Although he mentioned Kashmir, saying it was at the heart of the problem between the two countries, Bajwa sought a peaceful resolution of the dispute. His words 'Bury the past and move forward...' shocked everyone, and many foreign policy commentators saw this as a major policy shift.[14]

A few days later, on 29 March 2021, PM Imran Khan wrote a similar letter to his counterpart in India. In response to Modi's greetings on Pakistan National Day, Khan wrote back, 'The people of Pakistan also desire a peaceful, cooperative relationship with all neighbours, including India. We are convinced that durable peace and stability in South Asia is contingent upon resolving all outstanding issues between India and Pakistan, in particular, the J&K dispute. The creation of an enabling environment is imperative for a constructive and result-oriented dialogue.'[15]

Many believe that Pakistan's softened stand vis-à-vis India has been a consequence of its financial condition.[16] The military and civil leadership in Pakistan is alarmed at the deteriorating economic scenario, and, among the numerous damage control measures, one is mending the relationship with India.

However, soon after this, Imran Khan's government, under the influence of the hawks, took a U-turn on the imports of sugar and yarn from India. PM Imran Khan rejected the proposal of the Economic Coordination Committee for such imports. Pakistan's foreign minister, Shah Mehmood Qureshi, said that the relationship with New Delhi can't be normalized till the special status of Kashmir is restored. This again ignited doubts over the future of bilateral relations.

A Soothing Story

'I see personnel of armed forces in Kashmir as victims of conflict. They have come here without an understanding of what is happening. They are naïve and they suffer every day,' said Advocate Mohammad Altaf Khan while sitting on a traditional baithak at his home in the Sanat Nagar area of Srinagar. I had heard about him and his wife Fouzia through Sudhakar Solomonraj, who was head of the Political Science department at Wilson College when I studied there.

Altaf and Fauzia are striving to keep the youth of Kashmir away from violence in their own way. The couple doesn't run any NGO but conducts workshops on ethical leadership for schools, colleges and other platforms, working with young people in J&K as well as the armed forces.

'We stress that whatever your thoughts and ideologies, they must be based on non-violence. If you adopt violent means, then your voice will not be heard, you will lose moral authority and you may be killed. We rely on Mahatma Gandhi, who stressed that if you have to change the world, you have to change yourself first,' said Khan.

'I tell youngsters that the only thing that can take us away from the conflict is our values. If we stick to our values, we will win. We provide a platform where people share their feelings and tell them what they can do about their problems,' he told me.

The couple presents various conflict resolution techniques to its audience, and one of them is role-play. 'For example, we suggest people to imagine themselves in the shoes of Kashmiri Pandits and understand their perspective and likewise,' said Khan.

During his conversation with me, Khan expressed his unhappiness towards the politicians of Kashmir. 'People don't protest when Omar Abdullah, Farooq Abdullah and Mehbooba Mufti are jailed, for they represent India in Kashmir and not Kashmir in India,' he said.

Citing the example of politician Waheed Parra, Khan said, 'He was seen as close to the Indian Home ministry but was jailed. People took sadistic pleasure in that.'

The Khan couple seems to be a ray of light at the end of the tunnel. Kashmir needs more people like them who could propagate the futility of violence.

15

PARADISE AND ITS PATRONS

In the last week of March 2021, I travelled to Kashmir again for the sake of this book. From Mumbai, I took the Rajdhani Express to New Delhi and then a flight to Srinagar. There was a jubilant ambience in the cabin. Most of the passengers were tourists with families. Excited kids, youngsters, senior citizens and newlyweds occupied seats around me. Most of them appeared to be from middle-class families and were going for a holiday for the first time after the Covid-19 lockdown had been lifted. There was a minuscule number of Kashmiris also on the flight. When the flight touched down around 1 p.m., the temperature was 14 degree Celsius and it was drizzling. All the passengers landing at Srinagar airport had to mandatorily get tested for Covid-19 infection. The process was smooth and was completed within 10 minutes.

At the airport, I met Naved Dar (name changed), who works as ground staff for an airline. I had got acquainted with Naved Dar during my previous visits to Srinagar.

'I have done an MBA, but look at what I am doing for the last 10 years! Issuing boarding passes to passengers and pasting stickers on their bags. I feel like quitting this job, but then what will I do? There are no jobs these days,' said an infuriated Naved. Before joining the airlines, he had worked as a freelance journalist. Every time I met him, Naved appeared to be a cheerful man content with his life. This time he was different. Although Naved was in his mid-thirties, he seemed older. While talking to me at the airport's coffee shop, he recounted the ordeal he went through during the pandemic. The airline which employed him was non-operational for many months and, consequently, his salary was cut. To add to

Naved's woes, his son, Zeeshan, born prematurely in August 2020, developed serious health complications. To save Zeeshan's life, it was essential to hospitalize him in Delhi. Meanwhile, Naved's wife needed urgent medical intervention for asthma. All this took a severe toll on Naved financially, and his savings evaporated. He had to borrow money from friends and sell off his family gold.

'I tweeted and tagged many celebrities who were in the news for their charity. Nobody responded to my plea,' said Naved.

While we were talking, a youngster passed by. Naved told me that before the pandemic the youngster worked at a shop inside the airport that had to shut down, as the owner couldn't pay the heavy rent, so he now worked at another shop with a lower salary.

Naved said that the double lockdown had caused tremendous distress to the people of Kashmir, and many Kashmiris found it difficult to survive. The 'double lockdown' that Naved spoke about was something that I was going to hear repeatedly during my visit to Kashmir. The pandemic had caused distress and job losses all across India, but for Kashmir, it was indeed a double whammy.

As I got out of the airport premises, I saw that Ghulam was already there to pick me up. My colleague Asif had booked a room for me in Hotel Al Zahoor in the upscale Rajbaug area. I was surprised to find that on my way from the airport, there was not a single security check, unlike my last visit in 2019. The intimidating presence of weapon-wielding security personnel was also sparse. The hustle-bustle on the streets was like any other Indian city. The ubiquitous tension was gone.

Zahoor, owner of Hotel Al Zahoor, also runs a general store nearby. It was this backup occupation that helped him survive the double lockdown that had impacted the livelihood of people in Kashmir.

'After security measures imposed post the abrogation of Article 370 were lifted and business was getting restored, the pandemic made an entry. The hotel was completely shut for around seven months. Even when the lockdown was lifted, I couldn't operate. Most of my staff had gone. With much persuasion, I have been able to keep some people to work,' said Zahoor.

It was evident that the hotel was understaffed. The man at reception doubled as the restaurant manager. In a hotel of around 20 rooms, there were just two men to attend to the guests, maintain the rooms and carry luggage.

The Amarnath Yatra and pilgrimage to Vaishno Devi in the Jammu shrine contribute majorly to the tourism in Kashmir. However, since August 2019, there had been no yatra and the number of visitors coming to Kashmir after visiting Vaishno Devi had also diminished. But the end of 2020 brought good news.

'There has been a heavy rush of tourists since November (2020) and I have to manage with just these men. In the hospitality industry, you can't hire just anybody. You need people who are attentive towards guests, not the guys who put wires in their ears and are busy in their own world.'

I noticed that many rooms, which were probably shut for months, were being repaired and refurnished. The influx of tourists had compelled Zahoor to make full use of his capital to ensure all the rooms were ready to use.

I remember that since January 2021, many tour operators in Mumbai had begun publishing full front-page advertisements in leading newspapers showcasing their packages for Kashmir. One advertisement read: 'Deluxe Package for 6 nights and 7 days at Rs. 39,750 and Premium Package for Rs. 74,750 per person. The package includes return airfare, accommodation, breakfast, dinner, all transfers, all sightseeing and Covid insurance.' Such advertisements were an indicator that Kashmir had started receiving tourists.

After staying for two days at Zahoor's hotel, I shifted to Hotel Royal Comfort facing Dal Lake. Like Al Zahoor, this hotel was also booked to the capacity. At breakfast, I met a railway officer from Ratlam who had come with his family for a vacation. He told me that before deciding to visit Kashmir, his friends and colleagues who had visited the Valley before him assured him that the place was safe now.

'Yesterday, I went to Gulmarg to show snow to my children. Today, we are going for a shikara ride at Dal,' he said enthusiastically.

When Dal became Dull

'A day will come when the houseboats of Dal will just be seen in pictures and school books!' sighed Mohammed Yaqoob Dunoo while talking to me in the office of the Kashmir House Boat Association. Dunoo is the spokesman of the association that represents owners of 910 houseboats operating in Dal Lake, Jhelum River and Chinar Baug.

The reason I met Dunoo was to understand the impact of the post August 2019 situation on Kashmir's tourism in general and on the houseboat industry in particular. Dal Lake and the houseboats floating on it for around 150 years have become an iconic symbol of Srinagar, drawing tourists from across the globe. Dal's providence to Srinagar is multifaceted. The lake is also a hub for fishing, and its floating gardens produce a variety of vegetables. However, the core economic extraction from Dal is through its houseboats and shikaras.

'From 1990 to 2019, there was uncertainty in Kashmir. Gun culture was there, but still, tourism, which is our lifeline, didn't get impacted the way it has been for the last two years. We survived (the protests after) Maqbool Bhat's hanging, the execution of Afzal Guru and the encounter of Burhan Wani. The flame of tourism in Kashmir was kept alight by houseboat owners like us, but today we are struggling,' said an agitated Dunoo.

Dunoo's rage stemmed from his inability to repair and reconstruct his houseboats. There has been a restriction since 1983 on the reconstruction of existing houseboats and construction of new ones due to environmental concerns, and the matter is subjudice. The administration believes that its policy will help prevent pollution and, thus, preserve the lake. The guidelines issued in April 2020 made it mandatory to obtain a no-objection certificate from numerous agencies to repair houseboats. The houseboat owners are furious about the lack of support from the government.

'Since 15 December 2020, houseboats have drowned due to lack of repairs. We had neither money nor permission to repair them,' he said. Dunoo informed me that many houseboats have not been repaired since 2010 and a few of them are going to sink soon.

Stressing that houseboats are a quintessential feature of Kashmir tourism, he said, 'The PM says that we have to make new Kashmir, but will that new Kashmir be without houseboats? In most advertisements to promote Kashmir tourism, pictures of houseboats are used, but in reality, our industry is dying.'

'On 2 August 2019,' said Dunoo, 'the administration issued an advisory, and after that, not a single tourist was to be seen in the Valley. Everybody dependent on the tourism industry was impacted for the next six months. It was a time I had never witnessed in my life before. Internet blockage had devastated online businesses. After that came the pandemic, which ruined us.'

'In the name of relief, we have been provided just 3,000 rupees per houseboat for the past three months. They are treating houseboat owners at par with shikarawalas (small boats). The average cost of a houseboat is around 3 crore rupees,' he said.

Dunoo is sceptical about the visible influx of tourists. In his view, this surge is going to be short-lived.

'People felt suffocated due to the lockdown, so now they have started to travel and visit places like Kashmir. However, we will see this rush of tourists in Kashmir only till the time regular international flights are not operational. Today, the people who generally prefer Singapore, Malaysia, Thailand or Europe are touring Kashmir. Once regular air travel resumes, the number of tourists will diminish. In any case, air travel to Kashmir from other parts of India has been costlier when compared with flight tickets to Southeast Asian countries or the Middle East.'

Remembering the old times, Dunoo said, 'This industry began in 1888. During the maharaja's rule, there was a Motmi Durbar that took care of tourism in the Valley. Earlier, foreigners used to stay in houseboats for three to four months, unlike tourists of today who just stay for two–three days. After the 1990s, the number of foreign tourists has reduced drastically. Foreign governments issued advisories warning their citizens not to go to Kashmir, although some came at their own risk. Our industry became totally dependent on domestic tourists then.' Dunoo was referring to the aftermath of an incident that happened in 1995 in which five Western tourists were kidnapped by a militant organization named Al-Faran. A Norwegian named Christian Ostro was beheaded. The incident had caused huge international furore.

Dunoo concluded his conversation with me with these words, 'Kashmir was an active volcano. Now it has become a dead volcano. We don't know what will be the impact on us when this volcano erupts.'

After meeting Dunoo, I walked towards Dal Lake. While walking along the promenade, one can see numerous houseboats anchored beside one another. Most of the houseboats have fancy names in English, like *Mermaid, Butterfly, Monalisa, Royal Glory* and so on. Houseboats were given such names to cater to the tastes of tourists from Europe, Australia and America. In some cases, due to prolonged and repeated stays, many foreign patrons formed friendly relations with the owners and requested them to rename the houseboats after their wife, girlfriend or daughter. Hence, one can see houseboats with names like *Shiela, Jasie, Katherine, Isla.*[1]

May 2021 brought news of some relief for the houseboat owners when Lieutenant Governor Manoj Sinha announced a new policy for houseboat repairs. Committees would be set up to meet every three months and review applications for repairs from the houseboat owners, which could be submitted online.

Shikaras: Boats in a Storm

At Ghat number 7, I met 40-year-old Javed Ahmed who owns a houseboat named *Young Manhattan*. Ahmed's family—his mother, wife and two children—is dependent on him for their survival. He was worried that another lockdown would be imposed for some reason or the other.

'Since the past two years we have been suffering. Whenever tourism begins, something bad happens. After the abrogation of Article 370, when tourism was shut, I worked as a labourer and earned

500–600 rupees per day. When restrictions were eased, everybody became hopeful. But then this pandemic destroyed everything.'

At the ghat, I saw numerous shikara-owners waiting for customers. Some were playing cards, while others were busy gossiping or engrossed in their mobile phones to kill time. The operation of shikaras is intertwined with houseboats, as the guests of the houseboats need their services to cross the lake. They also deliver essential supplies and utilities to houseboats and take tourists for rides. These dwarfed, multi-coloured boats with the capacity to seat around four passengers are integral for transportation within Dal. There are 25 ghats at Dal, and every ghat has a fixed number of shikaras attached to it. Ghat number 7, where I stood, had 54 shikaras.

Twenty-three-year-old Adil Bashir was intently listening to my earlier conversation with the houseboat owner. He wanted me to know about the plight of the shikara-owners as well.

'I am of marriageable age, but due to the prevailing uncertainty, I can't think of getting into wedlock. Many like me want to get married but are not doing so due to our low income,' he said.

Rowing shikaras has been Adil's family occupation for generations. He had to drop out after class 8 to help his father earn for the family. Apart from his old parents, Adil has two younger sisters dependent on him.

'During the lockdown, we sat idle at home with no work. Sometimes, I got a job as a labourer when somebody wanted to construct or repair their house. That was not a regular source of income. Many shikara-owners have got the pandemic relief amount, but that is not sufficient. Few haven't got even that till now,' said Adil.

'Tour operators,' said Adil, 'take away a big chunk of our earnings. They book packages for tourists and take away a major part of the profit. Most of the tourists you are seeing here have come on a package basis. We don't earn much from them. We want tourists to approach us directly.'

Adil was also enraged at the national media for presenting a fearful image of Kashmir, which scares away tourists. In his view, any incident happening in the Valley is blown out of proportion.

'We respect tourists and offer them our hospitality. A tourist is as safe here as he is in any other tourist location of India,' he said.

Are Tourists Safe in the Valley?

'Kashmir is one of the locations where tourists want to go again and again,' said Sunita Vanarpe, owner of Kaustubh Tours based in Mumbai. In the last week of March 2021, she had organized the second tour of the year in the Valley with 15 tourists. Her first tour was in the first week of March. 'It was a ladies' special tour with 10 women,' she said enthusiastically.

Sunita's travel firm has been organizing tours to Kashmir since 2008. She recollects that during the early days of her company's operations, 25–30 people per day travelled to Kashmir through her firm. For a few days in 2016, clients cancelled bookings due to adverse law and order situations following the killing of Burhan Wani. Her business picked up again in 2017.

'Just before the announcement of the abrogation of Article 370 in August 2019, we were in Kashmir. We were asked to leave. Another group of 50 tourists was all set to fly in, but then we had to cancel the tour. We started again in January 2020, but then had to stop due to the lockdown in March.'

'Have there been any security concerns?' I asked.

'So far, we have never faced any uncomfortable situation. The trouble happens mostly in border areas and not where tourists go for sightseeing. If there are any concerns, our local coordinators, who are Kashmiris, take care of it. They treat us like their family members,' she said.

'In Maharashtra,' she said, 'right now people are scared due to widespread cases of Covid-19 infections. Once the situation comes under control, we expect more tourists,' she informed.

It is not that tourists have never been attacked in Kashmir. There have been several cases of attacks on the Amarnath Yatra pilgrims. After Burhan Wani's encounter in 2016, many tourists present in the Valley were distressed. The last attack was on R. Thirumani in

May 2018. Since then, no other attack on any tourist has happened till the time of writing this book. Militant organizations realized that targeting tourists would antagonize the local population against them.

Bollywood is Back

'I was offered a short role of a doctor in a South Indian movie. They gave me dialogues written in Malayalam, which I didn't understand. I requested them to give me lines in Hindi or English and then get them dubbed,' said my driver Ghulam, who also provides transportation to film units that come to the Valley for their shoots. Before August 2019, Ghulam was busy less with tourists than with film crews.

The picturesque Kashmir Valley has been a hotspot for film-makers since the advent of cinema in India. A tourist guide in Gulmarg would never forget to show tourists the Shiva temple where the famous song '*Jai Jai Shiv Shankar, kata lage na kankar*' from movie *Aap Ki Kasam* (1974) was shot or the bungalow where the movie *Bobby*'s (1973) song '*Hum tum ek kamre me band ho...*' was filmed. Insurgency in the 1990s halted everything. There were very few exceptions, like the movie *Mission Kashmir*, which was shot in the late 1990s amidst detailed security arrangements.

Ghulam recollects that film-makers returned in 2005, when militant activities were at their lowest. Films like *Saat Khoon Maaf* (2011), *Jab Tak Hai Jaan* (2012), *Ye Jawani Hai Deewani* (2013), *Haider* (2014), *Bajrangi Bhaijaan* (2015) and so on were shot here. Film shoots got disrupted again in 2016 when Burhan Wani was killed. Ghulam narrated to me an incident where he narrowly escaped getting beaten up and his vehicle getting damaged. A college had been booked for a shoot near Srinagar. There was a shot where an actor had to wave the Indian tricolour. As soon as the news spread in the surrounding areas, hundreds of stone-pelters gathered and began vandalizing the film set. Equipment for the shoot was damaged and the crew had to rush to safety. A few days later, the scene was shot at a different location. The production in-charge this time paid local stone-pelters in advance and, in fact, employed some of them to carry out minor tasks.

Film-makers returned to the Valley again in 2017. 'For two years, the situation in the Valley remained conducive for film shoots, but then came August 2019 and everything came to a standstill. First, it was due to security measures and then due to the pandemic,' said Ghulam.

After the lockdown was lifted, film-makers once again began returning steadily. Film-maker Madhur Bhandarkar was spotted in Gulmarg in April. When I spoke to him, he didn't reveal whether he had some project based on Kashmir but said that Kashmir was once again becoming a hotspot for Bollywood shoots.

'In the seventies and eighties, there was a time when five to six shoots happened simultaneously in Kashmir. That discontinued after 1989 due to an upsurge of militancy. However, now Bollywood has returned to Kashmir. In the last few years, many big films with big stars have been shot in Kashmir. We have everything in Kashmir. Why do we need to go to Switzerland? If we shoot here, local people will get work,' said Bhandarkar.

Many film-makers from South India had begun shooting in Kashmir. Since international travel was not easy due to the Covid-19 situation, many film-makers were shooting in Kashmir to replicate Switzerland or other exotic destinations.

Ghulam told me, 'Recently, I went for the shoot of a South Indian horror movie named DSP at Pahalgam. The actress was from Punjab and the actor was from the South.' However, just like other members of the tourism industry, Ghulam was not sure for how long the commands of 'lights, camera and action' would be heard in the Valley. 'The security situation and weather of Kashmir are like the fashion of Mumbai. You never know when they change,' he said with a worried smile.

Film-makers wishing to shoot in Kashmir received good news on 5 August 2021, the second anniversary of the abrogation of Article 370. In a function that evening, Lieutenant Governor Manoj Sinha, in the presence of actor Aamir Khan, film-maker Rajkumar Hirani and producer Mahaveer Jain announced the film policy of J&K. The policy aimed to provide a secure and convenient environment for film-makers to shoot in Kashmir. Those wishing to shoot in Kashmir could apply on the special website launched for the purpose.[2]

A Hub for Winter Sports

Maria Samuel, who was my colleague at Star News in Mumbai till 2005, is now running a winter sports facility in Kashmir. She is the director and founder of Gulmarg Ski Academy, which was set up in 2018. Gulmarg has been one of the busiest tourist destinations in Kashmir. The cable car ride amidst the snow-clad landscape, which continues till late March, draws scores of tourists here. 'Gulmarg has powder snow, which makes the place conducive to winter sports,' said Maria.

'Did you have any inhibitions while setting up the academy here?' I asked her.

'In 2017, I came to Kashmir as a tourist with my daughter. We didn't have any issues. People were very hospitable and cooperative. However, running a business here is a different thing. In 2018, when I started here, the first question was about safety, but so far that has not been any issue. People now feel that Kashmir is safe and approachable. A lot of development is coming up here,' she said.

'How has the situation been post August 2019?' I asked.

'Yes, there were apprehensions after the abrogation of Article 370, but so far the situation has been conducive to the sports industry,' said Maria.

'Post Diwali 2020,' she said, 'Kashmir has been selling out like hot cakes. Gulmarg is an important destination on the international skiing map, and skiing enthusiasts across the world have come here in the past.'

Maria appeared to be content with the support she got from the local administration and people. 'Our ski guides are local Kashmiris. They have been learning from foreigners and are picking up well,' she remarked. In her view, there are areas like Pahalgam and others in south Kashmir where the snow is better than Gulmarg and so have the potential to be developed as skiing destinations.

Maria is one of the beneficiaries of the central government's policy to make Kashmir a hub of winter sports. While virtually inaugurating Khelo India Winter Games in February 2021, PM Narendra Modi stated the government's intent by saying, 'This is a step towards making India's presence felt in the international winter games arena and also make Jammu and Kashmir a hub of winter sports.'[3]

After the abrogation of Article 370, there have been two editions of the Khelo India Winter Games in Kashmir in February 2020 and 2021. Khelo India Winter Games is a platform for multidisciplinary winter sports, including skiing, snow rugby, snow baseball, snow mountaineering, ice hockey and speed skating.

The success and peaceful organization of two editions of the winter games prompted Modi to say that J&K is ready to reach new heights of peace and development. 'The Games,' he said, 'will strengthen the resolve for "*Ek Bharat, Shresth Bharat*".'[4]

16

THE APPLE: NOT JUST A FRUIT

'Sir, the last apple you ate in Mumbai might have come from Kashmir,' said Ghulam while driving me through an ill-maintained and pothole-filled road towards Budgam from Srinagar. The road passed through numerous apple orchards and walnut trees. Ghulam informed me that he had bought some land for an apple plantation.

'The situation in Kashmir is very volatile, and I thought there must be an alternate source of livelihood. So, just for financial security, I have decided to invest some money in the apple business,' he said.

India ranks seventh in the production of this fruit across the world. Around 80 per cent of the apples produced in India come from J&K, where apple cultivation dominates the rural economy and fetches a revenue of around Rs. 1,500 crore. Around 3.5 million people in the Valley are dependent on the apple trade. In Kashmir Valley, apple cultivation is prevalent in districts like Srinagar, Ganderbal, Budgam, Baramulla, Kupwara, Anantnag and Shopian. Around five districts of Jammu also produce apples, albeit in a smaller quantity.[1]

After the abrogation of Article 370, a sense of fear and uncertainty prevailed among apple farmers and traders. Within two months after the historic decisions, militants killed three truck drivers in Shopian. On 24 October 2019, militants waylaid three trucks that were registered in Haryana, Punjab and Rajasthan. Two of the three trucks were burnt down.[2] The deadliest attack happened on 29 October, when a delegation of lawmakers of the European Union was visiting the Valley to assess the security situation. The militants stormed tenements of orchard workers from West Bengal and killed five of them. Such attacks happened at a time when the apple trade was recovering after the lifting of security restrictions. Over 10,000 trucks filled with apples left the Valley that week and hundreds of apple-laden trucks were leaving every day.[3] Scared due to the attacks, many labourers and apple traders from Rajasthan, Haryana and Punjab left, while some of them even left the stock for which they had paid some advance amount.

The apple trade was eventually restored and went on smoothly till lockdown was imposed due to the Covid-19 pandemic.

In a village of Budgam, I met Mohammad Ashraf, an apple cultivator who owns an orchard of around 500 trees.

'After the removal of (Article) 370 not only was our identity taken away, but the blockades imposed during that time also impacted our business heavily. That decision was a shock to us, but to survive, you need to work, you need to eat. So, we came out of our homes and worked. However, much of my apple produce perished in 2019, as I wasn't able to sell it,' said Ashraf.

Ashraf had 10 Bihari workers on his farm who left in August 2019. Sitting in one of his orchards, he told me about the several problems apple producers were facing. In most of the cases, he compared the situation of Kashmiri apple cultivators with those of Himachal Pradesh, which is another apple-producing state. Ashraf told me that people like him were feeling discriminated against.

'They (Himachal apples) fetch a rate of 200–300 rupees per kilogram. We get a maximum of 50–60 rupees. From March, we begin the cultivation by spraying fertilizers, and after June, the fruits start coming in. However, fungicides, pesticides, etc., are costly here. There is a price difference of around 1,000 to 1,500 rupees when compared with Himachal. They, too, are often of substandard quality and so our produce gets spoiled. An orchard that fetched us 6 lakh rupees earlier, now gives us produce worth 1 lakh only due to faulty insecticides,' complained Ashraf.

Ashraf also had complaints about people's behaviour with Kashmiri sellers in other states.

'Some people behave with us in a step-motherly manner. They know that this work is our backbone, so by breaking it, they want to break us. We face trouble when we go to cities like Delhi to sell apples. After finishing our business, when we roam around to see the city, the police trouble us and look at us with suspicion. On the contrary, we treat outsiders in Kashmir very respectfully. If sometimes, due to heavy snowfall, some tourists or Amarnath Yatris get stuck on the way, we give them shelter in our homes.'

In Budgam, I met another apple cultivator named Riyaz Ahmed who owns an orchard of 300 trees.

'The removal of 370,' said Riyaz, 'is like the sky falling on us. I am asking you, if people were really happy with the decision, then why was there a need to impose a curfew?'

Riyaz said that his days of despair began in August 2019.

'We have not been able to recover since then. We have been producing apples but not getting fair rates. Now, there is no bargaining over rates with the trader. We ask them to pick up the produce at whatever rate they pay us. Many have still not received their payments. Earlier, we earned enough to run our home and save some money also, but now things have changed,' he said.

Riyaz owns a few walnut trees also and informed that the plight of walnut producers is no better than the apple cultivators'.

'Walnuts are being imported in large quantities, so we are getting lesser rate. Due to losses, some people have cut down their walnut trees, which is illegal,' he said.

Most of the farmers I spoke to wanted more governmental support for their businesses. The apple and walnut producers especially urged for more support from the Horticulture department. They were also wary of increasing imports as the pandemic slows down and international transportation is restored.

Artisans are Alive

When I last visited Kashmir in August 2019, the downtown area of Srinagar was out of bounds for me. It was perilous to move around in this locality as a TV journalist. Around two years later, I reached downtown again, and this time I was not a TV journalist with a microphone and camera but a writer carrying nothing more than a notebook and ball pen. The area resembles Bhindi Bazaar or Dongri of old Mumbai or Ballimaran Market of Delhi. Making my way through the crowded, noisy and narrow streets between old buildings, I reached the 150-year-old Khwaja Shawl House in the Haval area. The ground-plus-one structure is a shop-cum-residence of its owners.

There, I met Mudassar Ali Khwaja, who is in his late thirties and the fifth generation of his family to work as an artisan. Mudassar has his own handlooms. He manufactures and sells pashmina and woollen shawls. Before I could ask him any questions, Mudassar enthusiastically displayed his artwork to me. He spread a shawl and requested me to look at the minute *sozni* (needlework) with which it was embellished. Another one had *aksi* (double-side work) on it. Some had *jama* embroidery work on them. Mudassar told me that depending on the detailing of the work, it takes two months to four years to complete a shawl.

Answering my question on how his family survived during the past two years, Mudassar said, 'Today we are living on our savings. It has become difficult to run our home. I have 45 artisans working for me. I paid them and looked after them during the lockdown. Things have changed now. Earlier, we used to sell shawls as costly as 1 to 2 lakh rupees, but now we are hardly able to sell shawls costing a maximum of 10,000–20,000 rupees.'

He said that earlier showroom owners from outside Kashmir also ordered stocks from him, but that has diminished now. However, Mudassar was hopeful that his business would recover. 'Since the past few days, customers have started coming in. I expect business to improve in the coming few days.'

Like Khwaja Shawl House, I saw numerous other shawl stores. They had attractive artworks on display but were mostly empty. At some of the shops, a few customers were visible but they were locals. Ghulam told me that there was a time when a rush of foreigners and domestic tourists was seen in this area, but the security situation during the past few years wiped out everything. Considering the sensitive nature of the locality, Ghulam told me that cab drivers were discouraged from bringing tourists downtown.

Other artisans like carpet weavers, papier-mâché craftsmen, embroidery workers and artisans who make copperware, known as *trams*, have also suffered. The lockdown had posed several problems to them, such as the scarcity of raw materials and transportation of finished products. Many artisans travelled to other states to sell their products in handicraft exhibitions, like Delhi Haat, Bangalore Art Fair, Surajkund Crafts Mela and so on, but the pandemic brought all of it to an abrupt halt. There were 2.5 lakh people in the region who were dependent on the handicrafts industry for their livelihood, which fetched foreign exchange of around Rs. 1,700 crore[4] every year, but the twin lockdown has been detrimental for business. Almost half of the artisans are women. During the past two years, many artisans have quit their traditional work and have taken up meagre jobs to make ends meet.

The craft traditions of Kashmir can be traced back to the fifteenth century when a king named Zainulabideen ruled the region from 1420 to 1470.[5] Unlike some of his predecessors, Zainulabideen had a liberal approach towards art and culture. On his invitation, many craftsmen and artisans came from central Asian cities and taught the fine arts to Kashmiris, which had then been passed on from generation to generation. With the artisans switching to other jobs, Kashmir is gradually losing its 600-year-old heritage.

Economic Overview

Apart from meeting people linked to tourism, apple production and artisans, I met Shaikh Ashique Ahmed, chairman of the Kashmir Chamber of Commerce, to understand the wider economic picture of the Valley. Speaking to me at his office on Residency Road in Srinagar, Ahmed sounded worried about the scenario.

'In 2019, between 5 August and 5 December, we had submitted a loss report of Rs. 18,000 crore to the Union Commerce ministry and the J&K government. After security restrictions were eased, there was a breathing period during January and February 2020, and then came March with another lockdown. We rebounded from one lockdown to another. By August 2020, business losses reached approximately Rs. 40,000 crore. Around 5 lakh people have become jobless. The GDP has been impacted. We took top-down feedback from all sectors and nobody contested our report,' said Ahmed.

Ahmed informed me that handicraft exports have been hit badly. 'It's a chain. Since exports suffer, the traders and artisans are impacted. Also, the carpet industry needs to be revived, otherwise we will lose our heritage,' he said.

The description of Kashmir's economy by Ahmed has been confirmed by other sources as well. As per a report by the Union Ministry of Commerce, there has been a slump in exports by approximately USD 35 million in 2019–20. In 2019, exports were around USD 130 million in comparison to USD 97 million in 2020. A large chunk of Kashmir's economy is dependent on exports.[6]

A report by a think tank named Centre for Monitoring Indian Economy reveals that the unemployment rate in J&K is 14.2 per cent, which is graver than the national average. J&K is ranked fourth among the high unemployment states in India.[7]

'Last year (2020), on 18 March, our delegation met Union Home Minister Amit Shah and Finance Minister Nirmala Sitharaman and apprised them of our situation and suggested ways on how businesses could be revived. They acknowledged our views and assured us all the help in reviving Kashmir's economy. We also met Lieutenant Governor Manoj Sinha in August and acquainted him with the situation. He formed a five-member committee to work on the modalities of economic revival,' said Ahmed.

In September 2020, a month after meeting with the delegation, Sinha announced a package of Rs. 1,350 crore for the business sector. A 50 per cent rebate in electricity and water bills was also announced. This was apart from the Rs. 1,400 crore announced for J&K under *Atmanirbhar Bharat Abhiyan* (Self-reliant India campaign).[8] Although Ahmed had initially welcomed the package, he told me, 'We expected a marathon package. We wanted sick and non-performing units to be revived. Those demands have not been met. We want every business to run rather than close down.'

Ahmed suggested that there should be some model to help young entrepreneurs and rehabilitate old investors. 'Revival of business,' he said, 'would lead to the generation of employment. All local people applying to start businesses must get assistance on priority. We have appealed to Kashmiri youths to come up with start-ups.'

The blocking of the internet has been a major cause of damage to Kashmir's economy. 'The IT sector and e-commerce were badly hit,' says Ahmed. Mobile phone services with 4G internet were fully restored only in February 2021. But by then, the internet shutdowns had devastated the e-commerce industry, affecting bulk orders and foreign clients.

The Union Budget of 2020–21 has brought some hope for Kashmir's economy. A total budget of Rs. 108,621 crore was announced for the UT. Out of this amount, Rs. 39,817 crore was reserved for capital expenditure, whereas Rs. 68,804 crore was kept aside as revenue expenditure.[9] The amount earmarked for capital expenditure includes spendings on the connectivity of villages and completion of 4,500 kilometres of roads. The budget aims to extend financial support through various schemes to 15 lakh youths by engaging them in sports activities. A provision of Rs. 2,008 crore has been made for the agriculture and horticulture sectors, while Rs. 786 crore have been kept for the tourism sector.[10]

Responding to the Budget, Lieutenant Governor Manoj Sinha stated that 'the quantum jump in the allocation of all sectors speaks about the strong resolve of the PM towards the development of J&K'.[11]

In April 2021, the J&K administration approved the industrial policy for 2021–30, which aims to make the UT an aspiring investment destination in the next 10 years and stresses on the ease of doing business. It makes provisions for basic infrastructure, last-mile connectivity and setting up of industrial parks for industrial units.[12]

In August 2021, *The Indian Express* reported that the industrial policy was yielding results. Quoting sources in the J&K administration, the report said that the UT was getting investments worth Rs. 23,000 crore and four big Indian corporates from the steel, telecom, cyber optics and hosiery sectors were in various stages of land allotment. The new investment worth Rs. 11,000 crore would be in Kashmir Valley, while Rs. 12,000 crore would be invested in the Jammu region. The newspaper reported that around 3,000 hectares from the government's land bank of 6,000 hectares have been earmarked for industrial projects, and the government has also been contemplating land acquisition. A single-window system is being planned so that projects don't get stuck in paperwork. It is expected that industrial growth in the Valley will boom after the Katra–Banihal section of the railway line is functional.[13]

EPILOGUE: KASHMIR IN A TIME MACHINE

The word 'new' is not new for Kashmir. In 1944, Sheikh Abdullah talked about making a different Kashmir with his plan of 'Naya Kashmir' submitted to Maharaja Hari Singh. Once again, 'new' became a buzzword for Kashmir when the decisions of August 2019 were announced. A 'new Kashmir' is being visualized by the BJP and the RSS as well. In September 2019 PM Modi said, 'New winds are blowing in Kashmir. We will all build a new Kashmir together that will be for everyone.'[1]

In the previous chapters, I have attempted to enunciate how different stakeholders in Kashmir have been impacted post August 2019; however, questions remain about what the long-term impact of the developments will be and what undercurrents are being noticed today. What will Kashmir be like 10 years from now? Will Kashmir ever be free of militancy? What will the political discourse in Kashmir look like? Will there be significant demographic changes? Is there any scope of the special status of J&K being restored? To seek answers, I spoke to a wide range of people, from common Kashmiris to former politicians, ex-bureaucrats and journalists. Here, I am summarizing their views.

As mentioned in a previous chapter, Haseeb Drabu is no ordinary Kashmiri. Since he quit politics, Drabu has independent views devoid of any political influence. While speaking to me, he was critical of the mainstream parties of Kashmir. 'Obviously, there has been a major change since 2019; however, the long-term impact of August 2019 decisions is uncertain. But those who spent all their time supporting the accession, their credibility is finished. Political parties like the NC or the PDP, who were accessionists, have lost their vision. Now, only two thoughts will survive—integration or separation. There is a certain degree of crudeness in the politics of Kashmir today. It is very difficult to predict right now where it is heading.'

Drabu said that since the 1950s, the Jan Sangh and, subsequently, the BJP have been saying that Article 370 would be abrogated. 'The narrative they came up with was of development, but no significant developmental work is taking place,' Drabu remarked. 'Nationally a majoritarian discourse is building up, which is also impacting Kashmir, considering it is a Muslim-majority place. A developmental framework needs to be evolved that satisfies different stakeholders, which is not happening. They (the Centre) have to realign the political narrative in Kashmir. Indian federalism is getting spoiled. It is becoming a majoritarian republic.'

I spoke to another man who had a short stint in Kashmiri politics and now observes the goings-on as an outsider. Shah Faesal, a former IAS officer, spent a chunk of his life as a politician in the sub-jails of Kashmir post August 2019. In January 2019, Shah Faesal announced his resignation from the civil services on Facebook. Two months later, he formed a political party named Jammu and Kashmir People's Movement. After his release in June 2021, following ten months of detention, Faesal decided to quit politics.

'What made you disillusioned with politics?' I asked Faesal.

'The events of August 2019,' he said, 'were quite overwhelming for me. We had understood Kashmir in a certain way and suddenly there was a situation where all of us were proven wrong. My basic presumption for coming into politics was to focus on good governance and answer the question for myself whether electoral politics had any role in bringing peace to Kashmir. The abrogation of Article 370 and abolishing the state was a signal that electoral politics must restrict itself to quotidian issues of governance and leave political questions to the Union government. I didn't want to build a career by spinning new lies and telling Kashmiris that look here, vote for me and I will get the Kashmir "issue" resolved. The Kashmir issue had already been resolved in 1947; it was just that while rooting for India, we Unionists were not vocal enough about India's stated position on Kashmir. I decided that rather than leading Kashmiris down a garden path, I must place the facts before them and tell them that look, this is where we stand now and the experience of the last 70 years suggests that the clock can't be turned back. Kashmir has acceded to India, and anyone who tells people that borders can be changed by joining militant outfits or supporting political parties with soft-separatist agendas is basically selling snake oil to Kashmiris. It was my moment of reckoning and I quit with all humility.'

When I asked Faesal about his views on the future of Kashmir, he referred to the pre-2019 period. In his view, politics then was conducted in three broad forms. One was separatist politics, rooted in the historical struggles for people-hood, which go back to the Mughal annexation of Kashmir in 1586. The second was the Unionist politics that recognized the finality of accession in 1947 and looked at Kashmir as an integral part of the Indian Union. Soft-separatism was a unique variant of electoral politics that operated within the framework of the Indian Constitution but looked at Kashmir as a disputed region, whose future was to be determined as per the roadmaps of separatist politics.

'Interestingly,' said Faesal, 'the liberal Indian state gave space to all three forms of politics to co-exist. But the decisions of August 2019 changed the political structure in such a way that separatist politics and soft-separatism lost their right to exist. With J&K becoming a UT, the political rhetoric of parties who participated in elections had to undergo a monumental shift. It was now a choice of being with India or being against it. The grey zone was eliminated. How this will work in the long-term is an interesting question. Soft-separatism was a conscious strategy to engage a new generation of disaffected Kashmiris with electoral politics and let them experience the fruits of Indian democracy without compelling them to take a pro-India position on the lingering questions of history. This did work well for some time...The experience from across the world also suggests that ethno-religious conflicts have been addressed by greater federalization, autonomy and decentralization, with subnational identities being allowed to survive. So, in the coming years, as South

Asian politics takes new turns due to the rise of China, the US exit from Afghanistan and the emergence of the Quadrilateral Security Dialogue (QUAD), Kashmiri politics will also undergo significant changes. But at the moment we are undergoing a transition from the old to the new, and this is a very tricky moment for making long-term predictions. But one thing is for sure that in the post-370 world, politics in Kashmir is never going to be the same again.'

Faesal opines that the government has to take quick steps in implementing the vision that PM Modi had been talking about in the context of the abrogation of Article 370. 'People,' he wrote, 'are impatient, and if there is a discernible change in the ground situation, issues of day-to-day survival get resolved, political activity returns and the process of internal reconciliation between Delhi–Srinagar picks up, then we might see Kashmir entering a phase of peace and prosperity. If there is complacency and the abrogation of Article 370 is seen as an end in itself without sufficient effort to change the lives of the people at the grassroots level, then Kashmir is going to give us many surprises in the future.'[2]

One of the people I spoke to was Bashir Manzar, a veteran journalist. He has experiences from both sides of the fence. For a short period in the 1990s, Manzar was in charge of publicity for a militant organization. Today, he is part of mainstream Kashmiri media and runs a 16-page daily named *Kashmir Images*.

To my question on the future of Kashmir, Manzar said, 'Ten years from now, I see Kashmir in a worse state, if there is no correction from Delhi. They (the Centre) should show what big developmental work they have done in Kashmir. Corruption is still there. Earlier, it was done by Kashmiri politicians and is now being done by people who have come from other states. You want to run a stick-wielding government that shows a tulip garden and says that everything in Kashmir is good…but that is not true. For you to make people love the tricolour, you need to generate confidence in them.'

In Manzar's view, the political process in Kashmir has been paralyzed. He sees the Centre's style of functioning as scuttling the political process.

'How durable do you think the Gupkar alliance will be?' I asked.

'The way it has come up,' said Manzar, 'I don't think it will be as durable as the UPA or the NDA. The reason for that is there are two big political parties in Kashmir—the NC and the PDP. Historically, these two parties have mutually struggled to snatch each other's space, like Nitish Kumar and Lalu Yadav in Bihar. Once they came together, but their alliance was not successful. Lalu will grow only when Nitish will go down and vice versa. The same is true with the NC and the PDP. As far as DDC elections were concerned, it was okay, but I don't think this Gupkar alliance will survive for long. Every party will pursue their own agenda.'

Manzar was also dismayed over the lack of Kashmiri presence in the top bureaucracy. 'In the top bureaucracy, there is no Kashmiri, and we will see its impact in further days,' he said. On the question of the feared demographic changes in the Valley, Manzar said, 'See, Article 35A disallowed non-Jammu and Kashmiris to buy land in Kashmir, but it didn't restrain people of Jammu to do that. One must dig deep and see how many Hindus or Muslims from just Jammu have bought land in Kashmir. I don't think many. The reason is that Kashmir is good as a tourist location, holiday home or to make a summer hut, but settling here is not easy. The harsh weather doesn't allow it to happen. So I cannot digest that there would be a demographic change. Another factor is security. I don't think a Gujarati would be able to make his mansion at Tangmarg near Srinagar. If people from other regions are settled in protected Israeli-pattern colonies, that's a different case.'

In Manzar's view, the only fear is of new land laws. People feel that government land will be given to big industrialists. 'New land laws disempower people. Those who oppose the revocation of 35A, you call them separatists, but at the same time, Article 371 of the Indian Constitution has features of special provision for several states,' he said.

Anuradha Bhasin, editor of *Kashmir Times*, has earned a reputation for fearlessly articulating her anti-establishment views that have often got her and her newspaper in trouble. When I asked about her image of Kashmir 10 years from now, she couldn't stop laughing for few moments.

'We don't know what is happening today and you are asking about ten years from now,' she said while trying to control her laughter. Turning solemn, she continued, 'Everything seems irrelevant in today's politics. You have taken away political power and the entire leadership was kept behind the bars for around a year. Even if the assembly is formed, it will not be relevant. Politicians have been threatened.'

In Bhasin's view, future South-Asian politics will have repercussions in Kashmir. The situation in Afghanistan would also have an impact. 'People are not happy and their silence must not be misinterpreted. Youngsters are still willing to pick up guns,' she said.

Talking about new domicile laws, she said, 'The agenda of the RSS for the solution of the Kashmir problem has been to convert J&K into a Hindu-majority state. They attempted to disempower people and make demographic changes.'

Bhasin observes that the August 2019 decisions would have more impact on Jammu Hindus, but they are being seen as 'collateral damage'. 'Most of the personnel of the central forces have spent over 10 years in Jammu and Kashmir. Most of the migrant labour have stayed here for a long time, since the situation was conducive and there were advantages like free schooling and so on. So, this (domicile policy) will impact them as well.'

'After August 2019,' said Bhasin, 'many in Jammu were happy thinking that Kashmiris have been shown their place, not realizing that they are in the same boat. That is why later on some Hindus from Jammu demanded Himachal-like arrangements.'

Apart from talking to intellectuals, I also approached commoners for their views on Kashmir's future. One of them was Manzoor Sofi, who runs a small transport business that arranges logistics for movie shoots in Kashmir. He resides in Srinagar with his wife, a son and a daughter, who is studying in a secondary school. 'I will send my children out of Kashmir for their studies and jobs. Although the situation is much better than what I have seen in the 1990s, there is so much uncertainty. The kind of peace we are expecting is not happening. I am aware of the kind of behaviour meted out to Kashmiris outside the Valley, but I would have not thought of sending my children outside if the situation was peaceful and there was more clarity.'

The Icebreaker

After the abrogation of Article 370 in 2019, 24 June 2021 was a significant day for Kashmir. A group picture was clicked in which all the major political faces of J&K, including Farooq Abdullah, Omar Abdullah, Mehbooba Mufti and Ghulam Nabi Azad, were seen standing beside PM Modi and Home Minister Amit Shah. They all met in Delhi to discuss the future political course in the UT. Some expressed surprise that the group of leaders that had been referred to as the 'Gupkar Gang' by Amit Shah was invited for talks. It was the first meeting between the Centre and mainstream politicians of J&K after the August 2019 decisions. The meeting was important in several ways. It displayed the eagerness of the Centre to begin a dialogue with Kashmiri politicians and indicated that the political process in J&K had been initiated. Overall, 14 leaders from J&K, including four former CMs of the erstwhile state, were present at the meeting. NSA Ajit Doval and Lieutenant Governor Manoj Sinha also participated in the discussion.[3]

Minutes after the three-hour-long meeting ended, PM Modi tweeted that his government's priority was to strengthen grassroots democracy in J&K.[4] It was reported that in the meeting, Modi conveyed to the leaders that he was aiming to reduce '*Dilli Se Aur Dil ki Dooriyan*' (Distance with Delhi and the heart). After the meeting, Omar Abdullah reacted by saying that the distance couldn't be reduced by just one meeting. He said that there was no need for a delimitation exercise, as it created suspicion among people.[5]

In the first week of July, the People's Alliance for Gupkar Declaration issued a joint declaration and demanded the restoration of statehood of J&K before holding assembly elections. Through the statement, the PAGD expressed its disappointment over the outcome of the meeting in Delhi and said there were no confidence-building measures like the release of political prisoners.

The seminal decisions of 5 August 2019 have led to a beginning of several changes in the Valley. Kashmir's future depends on how various stakeholders of the Valley respond to the changed scenario and their willingness to disremember the acrimonious past. The top priority for the dispensation in New Delhi should be to build trust among the Kashmiris through its words and actions. The aspirations and concerns of Kashmiri youth must be addressed too. Efforts must be made to create a sense of belongingness with the mainstream. The regional political parties could play a major role in this. The people in the rest of India must also reflect on their attitude towards Kashmiri people. If we say 'Kashmir is ours', we also need to say, in the same spirit, that 'Kashmiris are ours'.

ACKNOWLEDGEMENTS

I was in two minds about writing this book. It was my friend and senior journalist Sunil Mehrotra of *Navbharat Times* who motivated me to go ahead with the project. Another person who encouraged me to write was D. Sivanandhan, former director general of police of Maharashtra and police commissioner of Mumbai, who is a voracious reader and has been an acquaintance since my days as a cub reporter. He has read all my previous work and has been giving me valuable feedback.

I was also greatly supported by my colleagues at ABP News. Ajay Bachloo in Jammu and Asif Qureshi in Srinagar provided good insights and helped me with resources to work on the book. I am also grateful to my former editors at ABP News, Milind Khandekar and Rajnish Ahuja, who sent me to Kashmir to cover almost all the momentous news events that happened in the Valley during the past decade. Most of the content for this book comes from those tours.

Sudhakar Solomonraj, my teacher and head of the Political Science department at Wilson College, Mumbai, connected me to a few people in Kashmir who provided valuable inputs for this book.

I am grateful to my friend Dhaval Kulkarni, author of some great books on politics, who spared his time to get me acquainted with some good resource centres and libraries.

I am thankful to Lieutenant General D.S. Hooda, Indresh Kumar, Haseeb Drabu, Shah Faesal, Anuradha Bhasin, Bashir Manzar, Dr Agnishekhar, Sanjay Tikoo and many others for sparing their time for me and enriching this book with their insights.

I am also indebted to my driver in Srinagar, whose name has been changed to Ghulam in this book, for not only manoeuvring through the volatile streets of Kashmir and keeping me safe but also providing me good insights about life in the Valley and sharing his personal story with me.

I am grateful to Yamini Chowdhury for giving me the opportunity to write on this subject, and to Aurodeep Mukherjee for his sharp edits to improve the book's readability. I thank Upama Biswas and the team at Rupa Publications for coming out with this book smoothly and swiftly. It was a pleasure working with them.

I am grateful to my wife, Rimpi, and son, Vedaanta, for their support and sacrificing their claims on my post-office hours so I could devote time to writing this book.

NOTES

Chapter 1: 2014: Record-breaking Elections

1. Pallavi. 'Report of the Group of Interlocutors for Jammu and Kashmir', The PRS Blog, 25 May 2012, https://bit.ly/3GFJ37g. Accessed on 18 January 2022.
2. 'Jammu and Kashmir voters brave boycott call, weather to record 70% turnout', *India Today*, 25 November 2014, https://bit.ly/3FzoduB. Accessed on 18 January 2022.
3. '71% voting recorded in 2nd phase of Jammu & Kashmir poll', *The Times of India*, 2 December 2014, https://bit.ly/3nB2dnc. Accessed on 18 January 2022.
4. Sardesai, Rajdeep. *2019: How Modi Won India*, HarperCollins, New Delhi, 2019.
5. 'Fact check: Did Modi lie about hoisting the national flag at Lal Chowk in 1992?', *OpIndia*, 14 February 2019, https://bit.ly/3KofusU. Accessed on 18 January 2022.
6. Hussain, Masood. 'Narendra Modi's knowledge of Jammu and Kashmir to be an advantage for Kashmir plan', *The Economic Times*, 3 June 2014, https://bit.ly/3nzwP8I. Accessed on 18 January 2022.
7. Tweet by Omar Abdullah, 8 December 2014, https://bit.ly/3A7AM9D. Accessed on 18 January 2022.
8. Bhatt, Anil. 'BJP fields more Muslim candidates in Jammu and Kashmir', *Mint*, 17 November 2014, https://bit.ly/3GDcVAV. Accessed on 18 January 2022.
9. 'Modi can't repeal Article 370 even if he becomes PM for 10 terms: Farooq Abdullah', *India Today Online*, 3 December 2013, https://bit.ly/3A9iJzJ. Accessed on 18 January 2022.
10. Wani, Fayaz. 'National Conference Releases Election Manifesto', *The New Indian Express*, 27 November 2014, https://bit.ly/3AaZyWA. Accessed on 18 January 2022.
11. Manifesto 2014, Jammu and Kashmir People's Democratic Party, https://bit.ly/3qECz2Z. Accessed on 18 January 2022.

12. 'Jammu & Kashmir 2008', Election Commission of India, https://bit.ly/3Kolr9h. Accessed on 18 January 2022.
13. 'Kashmiri parties in coalition bid', BBC News, 29 December 2008, https://bbc.in/3qCfON3. Accessed on 18 January 2022.
14. 'Jammu & Kashmir 2008', Election Commission of India, https://bit.ly/3Kolr9h. Accessed on 18 January 2022.
15. '2014 Lok Sabha Elections Results: PDP, BJP share J&K pie, NC-Congress combine decimated', *The Economic Times*, 16 May 2014, https://bit.ly/34Onmnh. Accessed on 18 January 2022.
16. Malhotra, Jyoti. 'Get out the vote', *India Today*, 22 November 2014, https://bit.ly/3GFS407. Accessed on 18 January 2022.
17. 'PM Narendra Modi's remarks on dynastic politics "election rhetoric": Mehbooba Mufti', *Financial Express*, 23 November 2014, https://bit.ly/3nB8yz0. Accessed on 18 January 2022.
18. Ibid.
19. 'Jammu & Kashmir 2002', Election Commission of India, https://bit.ly/3FEdedN. Accessed on 18 January 2022.
20. 'History of Cong in power in J&K', ZeeNews, 2 November 2005, https://bit.ly/3AaKAiY. Accessed on 18 January 2022.
21. 'Ghulam Nabi Azad Biography', Elections.in, https://bit.ly/3nx1WBS. Accessed on 18 January 2022.
22. Personal communication of the author with Ghulam Nabi Azad in December 2014.
23. Manhotra, Dinesh. 'Cong stretched to keep flock together', *The Tribune*, 6 November 2014, https://bit.ly/3N51UMG. Accessed on 18 January 2022.
24. 'Sonia Gandhi unhappy with coalition compulsions in Jammu and Kashmir', *India Today*, 10 December 2014, https://bit.ly/3A67Ajn. Accessed on 18 January 2022.
25. Pandit, M Saleem. 'Omar govt lethargic, failed to deliver, Rahul Gandhi says', *The Times of India*, 26 November 2014, https://bit.ly/3A78SdM. Accessed on 18 January 2022.
26. Ghosh, Deepshikha. 'Election Results: Sajjad Lone, Former Separatist With Pakistani Wife, Wins in Kashmir', NDTV, 23 December 2014, https://bit.ly/3KnByUP. Accessed on 18 January 2022.
27. Masood, Bashaarat. 'BJP's Kashmir hopes rest on Sajad Gani Lone's two seats', *The Indian Express*, 23 December 2014, https://bit.ly/3rpDumZ. Accessed on 18 January 2022.
28. 'Jammu & Kashmir 2014', Election Commission of India, https://bit.ly/3KnbAAA. Accessed on 18 January 2022.

29. Ehsan, Mir. 'Jammu and Kashmir poll results: CM Omar Abdullah loses Sonawar to PDP, wins from Beerwah', *The Indian Express*, https://bit.ly/3typji8. Accessed on 18 January 2022.
30. Sound bite of Omar Abdullah with ABP News.
31. 'Cobbling together government to take time, says PDP President Mehbooba Mufti', DNA, 23 December 2014, https://bit.ly/3KlveNj. Accessed on 18 January 2022.
32. Mukane, Prateek. 'Jammu & Kashmir: Electorate gives fractured mandate, political parties grapple for alternatives', DNA, 23 December 2014, https://bit.ly/3nA5Tpp. Accessed on 18 January 2022.
33. Ibid. Accessed on 18 January 2022.
34. 'Omar Abdullah resigns as J-K chief minister', *Hindustan Times*, 24 December 2014, https://bit.ly/3FIkgOl. Accessed on 18 January 2022.
35. Personal communication of the author with political journalists in Srinagar.
36. 'Mehbooba Mufti, Amit Shah seal Jammu and Kashmir deal', *India Today*, 24 February 2015, https://bit.ly/33nQSQG. Accessed on 18 January 2022.
37. 'Jammu and Kashmir stalemate ends, PDP to form govt with BJP', *Hindustan Times*, 24 February 2015, https://bit.ly/3qEEvsi. Accessed on 18 January 2022.
38. 'Mufti Mohammad Sayeed sworn in as chief minister of Jammu and Kashmir', *Hindustan Times*, 1 March 2015, https://bit.ly/3Ijirtb. Accessed on 18 January 2022.
39. A pracharak is a member of the RSS involved/engaged in the spreading the RSS doctrine.
40. Shah, Amita, and Iftikhar Gilani. 'Revealed: How Ram Madhav and Haseeb Drabu weaved PDP-BJP alliance', *DNA*, 3 March 2015, https://bit.ly/3AcNcNE. Accessed on 18 January 2022.
41. Anderson, Walter, and Sridhar Damle. *The RSS: A View to Inside*. Penguin, New Delhi, 2018.
42. Ibid.
43. Shrivastava, Rahul. '"Centre Not Consulted, Share the House's Anger": PM Modi Tells Parliament on Separatist Masarat Alam's Release', NDTV, 9 March 2015, https://bit.ly/33Bnruq. Accessed on 20 January 2022.
44. Das, Shaswati. 'J&K CM Mehbooba Mufti objects to torture of Kashmiri inmates in Tihar jail', *Mint*, 30 November 2017, https://bit.ly/3GDhpYv. Accessed on 18 January 2022.
45. Sharma, Neeta. '"Kashmir Ceasefire Was For Eid": National Security Advisor Drops A Hint', NDTV, 14 June 2018, https://bit.ly/3KoBynh. Accessed on 18 January 2022.
46. 'PM Modi chairs high-level meeting on Kashmir; decision on ceasefire likely',

Hindustan Times, 15 June 2018, https://bit.ly/3GH2yMF. Accessed on 20 January 2022.

47. 'J&K FM says Kashmir a social issue, sacked', *The Times of India*, 13 March 2018, https://bit.ly/3GNtBGa. Accessed on 20 January 2022.
48. Ashiq, Peerzada. 'Ram Madhav rules out rift with PDP', *The Hindu*, 17 March 2018, https://bit.ly/3qIDiQD. Accessed on 20 January 2022.
49. Sharma, Neeta. 'BJP Lists Reasons For Pullout From Alliance With Mehbooba Mufti', NDTV, 19 June 2018, https://bit.ly/3KlWxXV. Accessed on 18 January 2022.
50. Jha, Prashant, and Kumar Uttam. 'Why BJP pulled the plug on PDP: Rainbow alliances are short lived, says Ram Madhav', *Hindustan Times*, 21 June 2018, https://bit.ly/3tCIl7c. Accessed on 18 January 2022.
51. 'BJP ends alliance with PDP; Can't treat J&K as enemy territory, says Mehbooba after resigning', *The Economic Times*, 19 June 2018, https://bit.ly/327cu2S. Accessed on 18 January 2022.
52. 'BJP-PDP Alliance in J&K an 'Experiment', Ended When Mehbooba Mufti Delayed Panchayat Poll: PM Modi', News 18, 9 April 2019, https://bit.ly/3I9w91a. Accessed on 18 January 2022.
53. Alexander, P.C. *Perils of Democracy*, Somaiya Publications, Mumbai, 1995.

Chapter 2: Poster Boys

1. Geelani, Gowhar. *Kashmir: Rage and Reason*, Rupa, New Delhi, 2019.
2. Rao, Prabha. 'Online Radicalisation: The Example of Burhan Wani', Institute for Defence Studies and Analyses, 16 July 2016, https://bit.ly/3nJmCqd. Accessed on 20 January 2022.
3. Bukhari, Shujaat. *The Dirty War In Kashmir*, Leftword, New Delhi, 2018.
4. Krishnamachari, S.V. 'Kashmir tense after Hizbul Mujahideen militant Burhan Wani's killing', *International Business Times*, 9 July 2016, https://bit.ly/3qKeBmR. Accessed on 20 January 2022.
5. Jolly, Asit, and Naseer Ganai. 'A Rebellion Goes Viral', *India Today*, 13 July 2016, https://bit.ly/3tHrakJ. Accessed on 20 January 2022.
6. Geelani, Gowhar. *Kashmir: Rage and Reason*, Rupa, New Delhi, 2019.
7. Bukhari, Shujaat. *The Dirty War in Kashmir*, Leftword, New Delhi, 2018.
8. Tweet by Omar Abdullah, 9 July 2016, https://bit.ly/3GLI1Xn. Accessed on 20 January 2022.
9. Tweet by Omar Abdullah, 9 July 2016, https://bit.ly/3GLI1Xn. Accessed on 20 January 2022.
10. Ashiq, Peerzada. 'Would have saved Wani: Mehbooba', *The Hindu*, 28 July

2016, https://bit.ly/33uo6On. Accessed on 20 January 2022.

11. Ibid. Accessed on 20 January 2022.
12. Parveen, Rahiba R. 'Dumped by BJP, "desperate" Mehbooba returns to "soft separatism" to find way back to power', *The Print*, 16 January 2019, https://bit.ly/3tG6Y2C. Accessed on 20 January 2022; 'Hizbul Mujahideen slams Mehbooba Mufti, calls her visit to terrorists' kin "election drama"', *DNA*, 7 January 2019, https://bit.ly/3qBOLkK. Accessed on 20 January 2022.

Chapter 3: The Seminal Attack at Pulwama

1. Raina, Muzaffar. 'After Pulwama, panic dash by Kashmiris outside home state', *The Telegraph Online*, 20 February 2019, https://bit.ly/3rxS7oq. Accessed on 20 January 2022.
2. Bhat, Sunil. 'Pulwama terror attack: Curfew imposed in Jammu following massive protests', *India Today*, 15 February 2019. https://bit.ly/3GLbvET. Accessed on 20 January 2022.
3. Masoodi, Nazir. 'Violent Protests In Jammu Over Pulwama Attack, Curfew On, Army On Standby', NDTV, 15 February 2019, https://bit.ly/3nGWCvy. Accessed on 20 January 2022.
4. Bhat, Sunil. 'Pulwama terror attack: Curfew imposed in Jammu following massive protests', *India Today*, 15 February 2019. https://bit.ly/3GLbvET. Accessed on 20 January 2022.
5. Jammu & Kashmir Division, Department of Jammu & Kashmir Affairs, https://bit.ly/3qIbICW. Accessed on 20 January 2022.
6. 'Jammu and Kashmir Religion Census 2011', Census 2011, https://bit.ly/3nE8zCs. Accessed on 20 January 2022.
7. Zargar, Safwat. 'As Jammu erupts in violent protest against Pulwama attack, fear grips Kashmiris in the city', *Scroll.in*, 16 February 2019, https://bit.ly/3FEvKCE. Accessed on 20 January 2022.
8. Central Reserve Police Force, Official Website, https://crpf.gov.in/. Accessed on 20 January 2022.
9. PTC is a small appearance of the television reporter on camera where he narrates a part of the story or makes some observation for which visuals are not available.
10. Majid, Zulfikar. 'Security agencies fail to counter highway terror attack', *Deccan Herald*, 14 February 2019, https://bit.ly/3AfgQll. Accessed on 20 January 2022.
11. 'Major Terrorist Attacks on Security Forces and other high security targets in the Post-Kargil Period in Jammu and Kashmir', South Asia Terrorism Portal, https://bit.ly/3Il7dnP. Accessed on 20 January 2022.

12. Sethi, Nidhi. '*Bajrangi Bhaijaan* Is Mehbooba Mufti's Top Choice To Promote Tourism In Kashmir', NDTV, 18 March 2017, https://bit.ly/3AgQboa. Accessed on 20 January 2022.
13. 'Kashmir attack: Bomb kills 40 Indian paramilitary police in convoy', BBC News, 14 February 2019, https://bbc.in/3GGUOu2. Accessed on 20 February 2022.
14. 'India strongly condemns the cowardly terrorist attack on our security forces in Pulwama, Jammu & Kashmir', Ministry of External Affairs, 14 February 2019, https://bit.ly/3Igbbhw. Accessed on 20 February 2022.
15. '19 minutes, 12 jets, a big target: This is what the IAF did in Pakistan while you were asleep', *The Economic Times*, 26 February 2019, https://bit.ly/33TIPuM. Accessed on 20 February 2022.
16. 'IAF air strike Highlights: US asks Pakistan to act against terrorist groups operating on its soil', *The Indian Express*, 28 February 2019, https://bit.ly/3FK2Px5. Accessed on 20 February 2022.
17. 'Balakot: Indian air strikes target militants in Pakistan', BBC News, 26 February 2019, https://bbc.in/3nJKyJY. Accessed on 20 February 2022.
18. M.K., Nidheesh, and Sharan Poovanna. 'Indians celebrate after IAF's air strike on terror camp in Pakistan', *Mint*, 26 February 2019, https://bit.ly/3tFUqrZ. Accessed on 20 February 2022.
19. 'Balakot air strike: Pakistan shows off disputed site on eve of India election', BBC News, 10 April 2019, https://bbc.in/3KoIgd4. Accessed on 20 January 2022.
20. Sayeed, Saad. 'No access to Pakistan religious school that India says it bombed', *Reuters*, 7 March 2019, https://reut.rs/3GLM6e9. Accessed on 20 January 2022.
21. 'Pilot's return our diplomatic victory: Amit Shah', *The Economic Times*, 1 March 2019, https://bit.ly/33qKpnO. Accessed on 18 January 2022.
22. Sharma, Pragati Ratti, 'Uttar Pradesh Election Results 2017: Demonetisation + Surgical strike = 300+ seats for BJP', *India.com*, 11 March 2017, https://bit.ly/3fLUmyE. Accessed on 20 January 2022.
23. Pandit, Virendra. 'Balakot air strike brought Pakistan to its knees: Modi tells voters in Gujarat', *Business Line*, 18 April 2018, https://bit.ly/3rC9VhV. Accessed on 20 January 2022.
24. Dutta, Prabhash K. 'Narendra Modi 2.0 returns with biggest gain in vote share ever', *India Today*, 23 May 2019, https://bit.ly/3FKqu0p. Accessed on 20 January 2022.
25. Dutta, Prabhash K. 'Election results 2019: 5 reasons that got Narendra Modi another term', *India Today*, 23 May 2019, https://bit.ly/34Xcofi. Accessed on 20 January 2022.

Chapter 4: An Unforgettable August

1. Nakash, Rayan. 'Writing on the wall: In Kashmir, graffiti meets counter graffiti', *Scroll.in*, 19 September 2016, https://bit.ly/3fvZwyW. Accessed on 18 January 2022.
2. '"J&K Assembly polls likely in October-November"', *Greater Kashmir*, 29 July 2019, https://bit.ly/3fzM7Wz. Accessed on 18 January 2022.
3. Ibid. Accessed on 18 January 2022.
4. 'Fresh orders to J&K police keep Kashmir on the edge', *The Times of India*, 30 July 2019, https://bit.ly/3KlrOu8. Accessed on 18 January 2022.
5. 'Amarnath Yatra suspended citing terror threats, govt asks tourists, yatris to leave Kashmir immediately', *The Indian Express*, 5 August 2019, https://bit.ly/3FDjiDf. Accessed on 18 January 2022.
6. 'Amarnath yatra: Record 6.34 lakh visit shrine', Zee News, 12 August 2011, https://bit.ly/3fQ9J9H. Accessed on 18 January 2022.
7. Tweet by Omar Abdullah, 2 August 2019, https://bit.ly/3roYUkd. Accessed on 18 January 2022.
8. 'Kashmir turmoil: Tension may escalate with Pak in Kargil: Govt issues advisory', *India Today*, 3 August 2019, https://bit.ly/3KoH7SH. Accessed on 18 January 2022.
9. Farooq, Azhar, and Rebecca Ratcliffe. 'Heightened security and anxiety in Kashmir amid fears of unrest', *The Guardian*, https://bit.ly/33tAfmy. Accessed on 18 January 2022.
10. Dutta, Prabhash K. 'Kashmir: Why Centre is sending additional 38000 troops to J&K', *India Today*, 2 August 2019, https://bit.ly/3nC7wmf. Accessed on 18 January 2022.
11. 'Nothing to worry, rumour mongering routine in J&K: Guv Satya Pal Malik assures Valley situation normal', *India Today*, 3 August 2019, https://bit.ly/3rmTcPI. Accessed on 18 January 2022.
12. 'Don't Mix Up Security Measure With Other Issues, Guv Urges J&K Leaders as Govt Orders Trigger Panic', News18, 5 August 2019, https://bit.ly/3fvN961. Accessed on 18 January 2022.
13. 'Don't play with fire: Mehbooba Mufti warns BJP on Article 370', *The Times of India*, 8 April 2019, https://bit.ly/3tykc1v. Accessed on 18 January 2022.
14. '"On Edge": Omar Abdullah Meets J&K Governor as Uncertainty Grips the State', *The Wire*, 3 August 2019, https://bit.ly/33usjS3. Accessed on 18 January 2022.
15. 'Over 6,200 transported out of Kashmir valley after issuance of J&K security advisory', DNA, 3 August 2019, https://bit.ly/3GGBblJ. Accessed on 18 January 2022.

16. Ibid. Accessed on 18 January 2022.
17. Tweet by Anupam Kher, 5 August 2019, https://bit.ly/3qAvn7W. Accessed on 18 January 2022.
18. '"War-like situation": Separatist Syed Ali Geelani on tension in Kashmir', *Hindustan Times*, 4 August 2019, https://bit.ly/3qDPfan. Accessed on 18 January 2022.
19. 'Kashmir turmoil: Mobile internet services snapped in Jammu and Kashmir, security tightened', *India Today*, 4 August 2019, https://bit.ly/3nxuMSE. Accessed on 18 January 2022.
20. 'Kashmir unrest: PDP, NC, Congress attend all-party meet', *India Today*, 4 August 2019, https://bit.ly/3tBCY7X. Accessed on 18 January 2022.
21. 'Section 144 imposed in Srinagar: Security beefed up, Internet services suspended, many leaders "detained or arrested"', *Financial Express*, 5 August 2019, https://bit.ly/3fx9GPV. Accessed on 18 January 2022.
22. Tweet by Omar Abdullah, 4 August 2019, https://bit.ly/3IhZ0AG. Accessed on 18 January 2022.
23. Tweet by Mehbooba Mufti, 5 August 2019, https://bit.ly/3GEFyhn. Accessed on 18 January 2022.
24. Sandhu, Kamaljit Kaur. 'Home ministry lying, I am under house arrest and they want to murder us: NC Chief Farooq Abdullah', *India Today*, 6 August 2019, https://bit.ly/3A7qbeI. Accessed on 18 January 2022.
25. 'Sec 144 imposed in Srinagar; J-K leaders including Omar Abdullah, Mehbooba Mufti under house arrest', *The New Indian Express*, 5 August 2019, https://bit.ly/33EyouR. Accessed on 18 January 2022; Ashiq, Peerzada. 'Omar Abdullah, Mehbooba Mufti placed under house arrest; Section 144 imposed in Srinagar', *The Hindu*, 5 August 2019, https://bit.ly/3KlIba3. Accessed on 18 January 2022.
26. 'Supplementary List of Business', Rajya Sabha, 5 August 2019, https://bit.ly/3rrzEtA. Accessed on 18 January 2022.
27. Ibid. Accessed on 18 January 2022.
28. 'Parliament proceedings live | Rajya Sabha passes the J&K reorganisation Bill, 2019', *The Hindu*, 5 August 2019, https://bit.ly/3rvPPG8. Accessed on 18 January 2022.
29. 'Article 370, 35-A to be abrogated: Amit Shah announces in Rajya Sabha', *The Economic Times*, 5 August 2019, https://bit.ly/3KkSPxE. Accessed on 18 January 2022.
30. 'Government brings Resolution to Repeal Article 370 of the Constitution', Press Information Bureau, Ministry of Home Affairs, 5 August 2019, https://bit.ly/3tCrK3l. Accessed on 18 January 2022.

31. 'J&K underdeveloped because of Article 370, Amit Shah tells Rajya Sabha', *India Today*, 5 August 2019, https://bit.ly/3twmDBE. Accessed on 18 January 2022.
32. Ibid. Accessed on 18 January 2022.
33. 'Parliament proceedings live | Rajya Sabha passes the J&K reorganisation Bill, 2019', *The Hindu*, 5 August 2019, https://bit.ly/351KL4U. Accessed on 18 January 2022.
34. 'Centre scraps Article 370, bifurcates J&K into two Union Territories', *Business Line*, 5 August 2019, https://bit.ly/3GGHbLh. Accessed on 18 January 2022.
35. Joy, Shemin. 'Jammu and Kashmir Bill divides Opposition', *Deccan Herald*, 6 August 2019, https://bit.ly/3GEJ8bn. Accessed on 18 January 2022.
36. 'Parliament proceedings live | Rajya Sabha passes the J&K reorganisation Bill, 2019', *The Hindu*, 5 August 2019, https://bit.ly/351KL4U. Accessed on 18 January 2022.
37. Ibid. Accessed on 18 January 2022.
38. 'Parliament gives nod for removing Jammu and Kashmir's special status, splitting J&K to 2 UTs', *The Economic Times*, 6 August 2019, https://bit.ly/3KlFeq0. Accessed on 18 January 2022.
39. 'Parliament approves bill for bifurcation of J&K into two Union Territories', *Mint*, 6 August 2019, https://bit.ly/352AxRR. Accessed on 18 January 2022.
40. 'Third historic mistake: Owaisi on govt move on Article 370 in Jammu and Kashmir', *India Today*, 6 August 2019, https://bit.ly/3nBDkb0. Accessed on 18 January 2022.
41. 'Only "3 families" gained from Article 370, not Kashmiris: Amit Shah in Lok Sabha', *The Economic Times*, 6 August 2019, https://bit.ly/3tDvn9e. Accessed on 18 January 2022.
42. 'Centre scraps Article 370, bifurcates J&K into two Union Territories', *Business Line*, 5 August 2019, https://bit.ly/3GGHbLh. Accessed on 18 January 2022.
43. 'President declares abrogation of provisions of Article 370', *The Times of India*, 7 August 2019, https://bit.ly/3nAI2G0. Accessed on 18 January 2022.
44. 'Article 370: 10 facts that you need to know', *India Today*, 18 May 2014, https://bit.ly/3I9sbGa. Accessed on 18 January 2022.
55. 'Explained: When Jammu & Kashmir had its own Prime Minister and Sadr-e-Riyasat', *The Indian Express*, 15 April 2019, https://bit.ly/3nxzG20. Accessed on 18 January 2022.
46. 'Article 35A of the Constitution: A look at the provisions of the Article and what it means for Jammu and Kashmir', *Firstpost*, 5 August 2019, https://bit.ly/3AnGrIZ. Accessed on 18 January 2022.
47. Bukhari, Shujaat. *The Dirty War in Kashmir*, Leftword, New Delhi, 2018.

48. Deka, Kaushik. 'How Kashmir changed on August 5 | India Today Insight', *India Today*, 6 August 2019, https://bit.ly/3IjHUTl. Accessed on 18 January 2022.
49. Bukhari, Shujaat. *The Dirty War in Kashmir*, Leftword, New Delhi, 2018.
50. Deka, Kaushik. 'How Kashmir changed on August 5 | India Today Insight', *India Today*, 6 August 2019, https://bit.ly/3IjHUTl. Accessed on 18 January 2022.
51. Pandit, M Saleem. 'Ladakh tense over Muslim-Buddhist "love jihad" marriage', *The Times of India*, 12 September 2017, https://bit.ly/33yds90. Accessed on 19 January 2022.
52. 'Kargil District: Population 2011-2022 data', Census 2011, https://bit.ly/3FAzMfi. Accessed on 19 January 2022.
53. 'Leh District: Population 2011-2022 data', Census 2011, https://bit.ly/3tJmRW3. Accessed on 19 January 2022.
54. Crossette, Barbara. 'Buddhist-Muslim Feud Divides an Indian Territory', *The New York Times*, 13 September 1989, https://nyti.ms/3GX851X. Accessed on 19 January 2022.
55. Pandit, M Saleem. 'Ladakh tense over Muslim-Buddhist "love jihad" marriage', *The Times of India*, 12 September 2017, https://bit.ly/33yds90. Accessed on 19 January 2022.
56. 'Ladakh MP Tsering Namgyal's fiery speech on J&K bifurcation and Article 370', YouTube: *The Economic Times*, 6 August 2019, https://bit.ly/3qFQaa1. Accessed on 19 January 2022.
57. Ramesh, P.R. 'His Master's Mind', *Open*, 10 April 2014, https://bit.ly/3nzH3Ww. Accessed on 19 January 2022.
58. 'Who is Amit Shah?', NDTV, 12 June 2013, https://bit.ly/3qHUeH6. Accessed on 19 January 2022.
59. '5,116 preventive arrests in J&K since Aug 4: Home Ministry', *The Economic Times*, 21 November 2019, https://bit.ly/3fEwv3W. Accessed on 19 January 2022.
60. Bhalla, Abhishek. 'No space to hold detainees, private properties turn holding centres in Kashmir', *India Today*, 16 August 2019, https://bit.ly/3nG4U77. Accessed on 19 January 2022.
61. OB van refers to an outdoor broadcast van, which is used to uplink videos and conduct live chats with reporters or stream some event live.
62. 'NSA Ajit Doval Interacts With Locals In Shopia, Eats Lunch With Them | ABP News', YouTube: ABP News, 7 August 2019, https://bit.ly/3GHChOp. Accessed on 19 January 2022.

Chapter 5: BJP, RSS and Article 370

1. Commuri, Gitika. *Indian Identity Narratives & the Politics of Security*, Sage Publications, New Delhi, 2010.
2. 'Role of Guruji Golwalkar in the accession of Jammu and Kashmir', Organiser, 26 October 2021, https://bit.ly/3AfUzDN. Accessed on 19 January 2022.
3. Anderson, Walter K., and Shridhar Damle. *The RSS: A View to Inside*, Penguin, New Delhi, 2018.
4. Commuri, Gitika. *Indian Identity Narratives & the Politics of Security*, Sage Publications, New Delhi, 2010.
5. Raina, Badri. 'State of Siege', Sabrang India, 13 July 2016, https://bit.ly/3GJMUjx. Accessed on 19 January 2022.
6. Ibid. Accessed on 19 January 2022.
7. Kaul, Ashish. 'Rupees 500 was all it took to officially grab land of Pandits in Kashmir', *The Pioneer*, 13 July 2020, https://bit.ly/3tFefQ8. Accessed on 19 January 2022.
8. Pandey, Ashok Kumar. *Kashmirnama*, Rajpal & Sons, New Delhi, 2020.
9. Ibid.
10. Commuri, Gitika. *Indian Identity Narratives & the Politics of Security*, Sage Publications, New Delhi, 2010.
11 Shukla, Srijan. 'How erasing Article 370 became an article of faith for RSS and BJP', *The Print*, 5 August 2019, https://bit.ly/3nyIjJB. Accessed on 19 January 2022.
12. Pandey, Ashok Kumar. *Kashmirnama*, Rajpal & Sons, New Delhi, 2020.
13. Commuri, Gitika. *Indian Identity Narratives & the Politics of Security*, Sage Publications, New Delhi, 2010.
14. Anderson, Walter K., and Shridhar Damle. *The RSS: A View to Inside*, Penguin, New Delhi, 2018.
15. Ibid.
16. Rampal, Nikhil. 'Article 370: Revisiting election manifestos, BJP's push and Congress's silence', *India Today*, 5 August 2019, https://bit.ly/3KrKHLR. Accessed on 19 January 2022.
17. Ibid. Accessed on 19 January 2022.

Chapter 6: Independence Day

1. 'Protesters, security forces clash after Eid prayers in Kashmir, 1 girl shot dead', *Deccan Chronicle*, 5 June 2019, https://bit.ly/3qEbwoe. Accessed on 19 January 2022.

2. Personal communication of the author with Gyanendra Tiwari on 15 August 2019.
3. 'On I-Day, governor Malik assures J&K people their identity not tampered with', *The Times of India*, 15 August 2019, https://bit.ly/3qPpx2J. Accessed on 21 January 2022.
4. 'India PM Narendra Modi vows to "restore" Kashmir's "past glory"', BBC News, 15 August 2019, https://bbc.in/3Ijrb2g. Accessed on 19 January 2022.
5. Gupta, Swati. 'Modi praises India's actions in Kashmir on independence day', CNN, 15 August 2019, https://cnn.it/3fAlXD1. Accessed on 19 January 2022.
6. Sharma, Kritika. 'Tricolour image at Srinagar's Lal Chowk shared by BJP's Kapil Mishra is not "new J&K"', *The Print*, 15 August 2020, https://bit.ly/3nCsTnw. Accessed on 19 January 2022.
7. Insert here: Mattoo, M.K. 'Lal Chowk of Srinagar is Red Square of Russia', *Early Times*, 24 April 2015, https://bit.ly/3JfV70b. Accessed on 14 March 2022.
8. Ibid. Accessed on 19 January 2022.
9. Fazili, Ehsan. 'When BJP chief Joshi unfurled national flag at Lal Chowk', *The Tribune*, 25 January 2016, https://bit.ly/3qFPEZR. Accessed on 19 January 2022.

Chapter 7: Media in the Crossfire

1. Personal communication of author with Ashutosh Mishra on 2 February 2021.
2. Personal communication of author with Ashok Raj on 2 February 2021.
3. Pal, Alasdair, and Fayaz Bukhari. 'Attacked by both sides: journalists caught in the crossfire of Kashmir conflict', Reuters, 9 April 2019, https://reut.rs/3KlHP3b. Accessed on 19 January 2022.
4. Personal communication of the author with Jainendra Kumar on 7 February 2021.
5. Basharat, Peer. *Curfewed Night*, Penguin Random House India, New Delhi, 2008.
6. Bhat, Gulzar. 'Kashmir too has seen journalists killed in line of duty', *National Herald*, 10 September 2017, https://bit.ly/353Moz3. Accessed on 19 January 2022.
7. Report by Committee to Protect Journalists.
8. 'Editor Shujaat Bhukhari shot dead: Here's list of journalists killed by militants in Kashmir', *The Indian Express*, 14 June 2018, https://bit.ly/3GJmyOP. Accessed on 19 January 2022.
9. 'Shujaat Bukhari given tearful burial, police arrest one suspect', Moneycontrol,

15 June 2018, https://bit.ly/3FTlUNz. Accessed on 19 January 2022.

10. Bukhari, Shujaat. *The Dirty War In Kashmir*, Leftword, New Delhi, 2018.
11. Iftikhar, Aliya. 'The unsolved assassination of a journalist', CJR, 8 April 2019, https://bit.ly/3GD1nOe. Accessed on 19 January 2022.
12. 'LeT condemns Shujaat Bukhari's murder, blames "Indian agencies"', *Kashmir Life*, 15 June 2018, https://bit.ly/3qFtg2E. Accessed on 19 January 2022.
13. 'Shujaat Bukhari killing: One of four suspects arrested, J&K Police calls it "terror-related crime"', *The Indian Express*, 15 June 2018, https://bit.ly/3nEu8Tk/. Accessed on 19 January 2022.
14. Saaliq, Sheikh. 'Survival is The First Challenge for Journalism in Kashmir, Shujaat Bukhari Wrote 3 Months Ago', News18, 15 June 2018, https://bit.ly/3nDvGx0. Accessed on 19 January 2022.
15. Akhzer, Adil. 'Kashmir Press Club: Police intimidating us', *The Indian Express*, 11 February 2020, https://bit.ly/3GGvvZ9. Accessed on 19 January 2022.
16. 'India: Government must immediately stop intimidation of journalists in Jammu and Kashmir', Amnesty International, 22 April 2020, https://bit.ly/3tEryjP. Accessed on 19 January 2022.

Chapter 8: Uri: Life at the LoC

1. Hussain, Masood. 'GSI scanning Jammu border for tunnels', *The Economic Times*, 14 August 2012 https://bit.ly/3IbNVAR. Accessed on 3 March 2022.
2. Singh, Sohal Sukhdev, and Anjali Mehra. *Life on the Indo-Pak Border*, Serial Publications, New Delhi, 2016.
3. Wani, Ieshan. 'In the line of fire: Villagers in Uri face the heat of ceasefire violations', *DNA*, 2 October 2019, https://bit.ly/3nZPR8z. Accessed on 19 January 2022.
4. Naik, Raqeeb Hamid. 'On the Edge', *The Caravan*, 30 November 2019, https://bit.ly/3KrNZyH. Accessed on 19 January 2022.
5. 'Jammu and Kashmir: Suspected militant killed in Uri sector, says Army', *Scroll.in*, 19 August 2018, https://bit.ly/33PhvgV. Accessed on 19 January 2022.
6. 'Indian Army foils infiltration bid in Jammu and Kashmir's Uri sector ahead of 73rd Independence Day', Times Now, 14 August 2019, https://bit.ly/3qGPUI7. Accessed on 19 January 2022.
7. 'About the Border Area Develpment Programme', https://badp.mha.gov.in/. Accessed on 16 March 2022.
8. Singh, Sohal Sukhdev, and Anjali Mehra. *Life on the Indo-Pak Border*, Serial Publications, New Delhi, 2016.

9. 'JJ dedicates Churunda model village near LoC to locals', *One India*, 6 October 2006, https://bit.ly/3fEdJd2. Accessed on 19 January 2022.
10. 'Cross-LoC trade ban affects livelihood of 4,229 families: Study', *Business Kashmir*, 20 February 2021, https://bit.ly/3KlKSbD. Accessed on 19 January 2022.
11. 'Govt shuts down cross-LoC trade with Pak-occupied Jammu & Kashmir', *India Today*, 18 April 2019, https://bit.ly/3Kzj4AO. Accessed on 19 January 2022.
12. Raina, Anil. 'Jammu and Kashmir: Narcotic drugs seized from Pakistani truck part of cross-LoC trade', *Bangalore Mirror*, 21 July 2017, https://bit.ly/3qEfIEu. Accessed on 19 January 2022.
13. Saha, Abhishek. 'J-K police recover arms from truck engaged in cross-LoC trade', *Hindustan Times*, 1 March 2017, https://bit.ly/3qBSeQp. Accessed on 19 January 2022.

Chapter 9: Stone Age

1. Pandey, Ashok Kumar. *Kashmirnama*, Rajpal & Sons, New Delhi, 2020.
2. Singh, Vijaita. '2019 recorded most number of stone throwing incidents in Jammu and Kashmir', *The Hindu*, 5 January 2020, https://bit.ly/34TAPKA. Accessed on 19 January 2022.
3. Constable, Pamela. 'Pakistan's Kashmir Solidarity Day co-opted by supporters of detained Muslim cleric', *The Washington Post*, 6 February 2017, https://wapo.st/3IyLyZJ. Accessed on 19 January 2022.
4. 'Stone pelting tool of resistance in Kashmir: Hurriyat (G)', *Greater Kashmir*, 31 March 2017, https://bit.ly/3N64lP9. Accessed on 16 March 2022.
5. 'How 'stone pelting' is different from 'Kanni Jung', *Kashmir Observer*, 10 July 2017, https://bit.ly/3rumUCy. Accessed on 19 January 2022.
6. Bukhari, Shujaat. *The Dirty War in Kashmir*, Leftword, New Delhi, 2018.
7. Kumar, Raksha. '"They don't fear the law, they don't care for their lives": Despair over Kashmir's young offenders', *Scroll.in*, 30 April 2017, https://bit.ly/3tCKmAb. Accessed on 19 January 2022.
8. 'Newsroom : Stone Pelters Paid Money To Attack Security Forces In Kashmir', India Today: YouTube, 15 July 2016, https://bit.ly/3qK97Zk. Accessed on 21 January 2022.
9. 'How ISI funds stone-pelters via Hurriyat in Kashmir: Times Now', *The Times of India*, 6 May 2017, https://bit.ly/3FIHRhU. Accessed on 19 January 2022.
10. Mishra, Abhinandan, 'ISI's budget for Kashmir stone pelting is Rs 1,000cr', *The Sunday Guardian*, 2 April 2017, https://bit.ly/3GGJfmA. Accessed on 19 January 2022.

11. 'How Lucrative is the Stone Pelting Business in Kashmir?', *The Eurasian Times*, 5 May 2017, https://bit.ly/3tUVKrp. Accessed on 19 January 2022.
12. Personal communication of the author with Inspector Sanjay Nikam in March 2021.
13. Wani, Farooq. 'Growing Drug Addiction in Kashmir', Indian Defence Review Blog, 30 June 2020, https://bit.ly/3GHWELn. Accessed on 19 January 2022.
14. Javaid, Azaan. 'Kashmir battles drugs now — cases rise by 1,000% in 3 years at just one hospital', *The Print*, 24 July 2019, https://bit.ly/3IkYQsi. Accessed on 19 January 2022.
15. 'How Lucrative is the Stone Pelting Business in Kashmir?', *The Eurasian Times*, 5 May 2017, https://bit.ly/3tUVKrp. Accessed on 19 January 2022.
16. Shah, Khalid. 'Ideological shift, public support and social media: The "New" in Kashmir's "New Militancy"', *ORF Occasional Paper*, 10 January 2020, https://bit.ly/34TcRz4. Accessed on 19 January 2022.
17. 'Jammu and Kashmir: Stone-pelters helped 25 militants flee since last year, says army official', *Financial Express*, 23 February 2017, https://bit.ly/355yT1N. Accessed on 19 January 2022.
18. 'Stone pelters helped Naveed Jatt's aide escape Budgam encounter site – WATCH SHOCKING VIDEO', Times Now News, 28 November 2018, https://bit.ly/3qH7jQX. Accessed on 19 January 2022.
19. 'J&K: Stone pelters target security forces amid encounter, allowing militants to escape', *India Today*, 8 September 2020, https://bit.ly/3FLUiJP. Accessed on 19 January 2022.
20. Bukhari, Shujaat. *The Dirty War in Kashmir*, Leftword, New Delhi, 2018.
21. Iqbal, Sheikh Zaffar. '"We Were Shot At", Says Army After 3 Killed In Firing In Kashmir's Kulgam', NDTV, 7 July 2018, https://bit.ly/3KmUpPM. Accessed on 19 January 2022.
22. 'Army chief says stone pelters in Jammu & Kashmir must be dealt with sternly', *The Economic Times*, 27 October 2018, https://bit.ly/3qH7Jqv. Accessed on 19 January 2022.
23. 'Army chief Rawat dares stone pelters to fire weapons instead of stones', *Business Standard*, 30 December 2019, https://bit.ly/3fD6AcZ. Accessed on 19 January 2022.
24. 'By tying stone-pelter to jeep I saved many lives: Major Leetul Gogoi', ABP News, 23 May 2017, https://bit.ly/3tFwvsX. Accessed on 19 January 2022.
25. 'Major Gogoi reveals how he saved 12 lives by tying Kashmiri man to his jeep as human shield', *India Today*, 23 May 2017, https://bit.ly/3KowgIB. Accessed on 19 January 2022.
26. Sandhu, Kamaljeet Kaur. 'Farooq Ahmad Dar, who was tied to Army jeep

by Major, was a voter, confirms Kashmir police', *India Today*, 25 September 2017, https://bit.ly/3tELtz7. Accessed on 19 January 2022.

27. Maqbool, Majeed. '"I'd Given Up Hopes of Being Alive That Day": Farooq Ahmad Dar Recounts the Human-Shield Incident on Polling-Day in Kashmir', *The Caravan*, 24 April 2017, https://bit.ly/3qEWWNe. Accessed on 19 January 2022.
28. 'Justice finally done, says "human shield" Dar on Major Leetul Gogoi's indictment', *The Hindustan Times*, 27 August 2018, https://bit.ly/3Ii1WgV. Accessed on 19 January 2022.
29. Singh, Vijaita. 'What are pellet guns and why are they lethal?', *The Hindu*, 21 July 2016, https://bit.ly/3FGasES. Accessed on 19 January 2022.
30. '1.3 million pellets, 8,650 tear-smoke shells, 2,671 plastic pellets used by CRPF in a month, J&K HC told', The News Minute, 19 August 2016, https://bit.ly/3tEchQ8. Accessed on 19 January 2022.
31. 'Pellet guns have killed 24, blinded 139 in Kashmir since 2010: Report', *Business Standard*, 2 August 2019, https://bit.ly/3GP6T0w. Accessed on 19 January 2022.
32. Nagpal, Deepak. '"The soldier is not aiming for the face": Gen Bipin Rawat explains why pellets hit J&K stone-pelters in eyes', Times Now News, 16 January 2020, https://bit.ly/3fJDcBL. Accessed on 19 January 2022.
33. 'Amnesty International calls for ban on use of pellet guns in Kashmir', *The Indian Express*, 13 September 2017, https://bit.ly/3Ab1ONg. Accessed on 19 January 2022.
34. 'Try not to use pellet guns: Mehbooba Mufti to security forces', *Financial Express*, 14 December 2016, https://bit.ly/3nAt56D. Accessed on 19 January 2022.
35. '21,000 Plastic Bullets Sent To Kashmir To Reduce Usage Of Pellet Guns', NDTV, 7 October 2017, https://bit.ly/3fAM5h5. Accessed on 19 January 2022.
36. 'Pungent smelling CS shells to aid pellet guns in Kashmir', *The Economic Times*, 11 July 2018, https://bit.ly/3GXB5Xn. Accessed on 19 January 2022.
37. 'Pellet guns have killed 24, blinded 139 in Kashmir since 2010: Report', *Business Standard*, 2 August 2019, https://bit.ly/34TQRnK. Accessed on 19 January 2022.
38. Nanjappa, Vicky. 'No more pellet guns, now sound will shoo away stone pelters in Kashmir', *One India*, 24 June 2019, https://bit.ly/3ruu6yy. Accessed on 19 January 2022.
39. 'Security forces rarely use pellet guns in Kashmir Valley: CDS Bipin Rawat', *The New Indian Express*, 16 January 2020, https://bit.ly/3Ko1ejU. Accessed on 19 January 2022.

40. Zargar, Safwat. 'De-radicalisation? India's Kashmir policy pushed stone pelters to become militants, say families', *Scroll.in*, 29 January 2020, https://bit.ly/32aQDaO. Accessed on 19 January 2022.
41. Swami, Praveen. 'Slain LeT terrorist who attacked fruit-seller's family in Sopore shows how stone-pelters are turning to militancy', *Firstpost*, 11 September 2019, https://bit.ly/3fAiBzW. Accessed on 19 January 2022.
42. '5 out of 6 local militants in J&K have a history of stone pelting: Army', *India Today*, 3 August 2019, https://bit.ly/3nE6vKz. Accessed on 19 January 2022.
43. '"Stone pelters today, terrorists tomorrow": Army's grim message to J-K', *Hindustan Times*, 2 August 2019, https://bit.ly/3Ii6dRv. Accessed on 19 January 2022.
44. Tiwary, Deeptiman. 'MHA data: 88% dip in J&K stone-pelting compared to 2019', *The Indian Express*, 4 August 2021, https://bit.ly/34XADtL. Accessed on 19 January 2022.

Chapter 10: Pakistani Propaganda: Virtual War, Real Impact

1. Ojha, Ritu Kant. *Real Conversations in Digital Age*, WILYD, 2019.
2. Shah, Khalid. 'Ideological shift, public support and social media: The "New" in Kashmir's "New Militancy"', *ORF Occasional Paper*, 10 January 2020, https://bit.ly/34TcRz4. Accessed on 19 January 2022.
3. Saha, Abhishek. 'Let's talk about Kashmir: Social media has been a game changer, and militants have a head start', *Hindustan Times*, 7 July 2017, https://bit.ly/3KzSeZk. Accessed on 19 January 2022.
4. Rao, Prabha. 'Online Radicalisation: The Example of Burhan Wani', Institute for Defence Studies and Analyses, 16 July 2016, https://bit.ly/3tF2aKN. Accessed on 19 January 2022.
5. Shah, Khalid. 'Ideological shift, public support and social media: The "New" in Kashmir's "New Militancy"', *ORF Occasional Paper*, 10 January 2020, https://bit.ly/34TcRz4. Accessed on 19 January 2022.
6. Ibid. Accessed on 19 January 2022.
7. Ibid. Accessed on 19 January 2022.
8. Bukhari, Shujaat. *The Dirty War in Kashmir*, Leftword, New Delhi, 2018.
9. Sharma, Rajnish. '18,000 Pak-linked social media accounts fuel J&K unrest', *The Asian Age*, 7 April 2017, https://bit.ly/3Ksa3sY. Accessed on 19 January 2022.
10. Shah, Khalid. 'Ideological shift, public support and social media: The "New" in Kashmir's "New Militancy"', *ORF Occasional Paper*, 10 January 2020, https://bit.ly/34TcRz4. Accessed on 19 January 2022.

11. Masih, Niha, Shams Irfan and Joanna Slater. 'India's Internet shutdown in Kashmir is the longest ever in a democracy', *The Washington Post*, 16 December 2019, https://wapo.st/3fBS3hA. Accessed on 19 January 2022.
12. Saha, Abhishek. 'Let's talk about Kashmir: Social media has been a game changer, and militants have a head start', *Hindustan Times*, 7 July 2017, https://bit.ly/3KzSeZk. Accessed on 19 January 2022.
13. Bukhari, Shujaat. *The Dirty War in Kashmir*, Leftword, New Delhi, 2018.
14. Saha, Abhishek. 'Let's talk about Kashmir: Social media has been a game changer, and militants have a head start', *Hindustan Times*, 7 July 2017, https://bit.ly/3KzSeZk. Accessed on 19 January 2022.
15. Masih, Niha, Shams Irfan and Joanna Slater. 'India's Internet shutdown in Kashmir is the longest ever in a democracy', *The Washington Post*, 16 December 2019, https://wapo.st/3fBS3hA. Accessed on 19 January 2022.
16. Blog written by Afshan Anjum and her personal communication with the author in December 2020.
17. Anjum, Afshan. '*Kashmir mein keval internet nahi, Kashmirion ki zindagi ke kai darvaazein bandh the*', *The Wire Hindi*, 11 March 2020, https://bit.ly/3fDBNgf. Accessed on 19 January 2022.
18. Blog written by Afshan Anjum and her personal communication with the author in December 2020.

Chapter 11: New Colours of Politics

1. 'Gupkar gang wants foreign intervention in Jammu and Kashmir: Amit Shah', *The Wire*, 17 November 2020, https://bit.ly/32bUl42. Accessed on 19 January 2022.
2. C.G., Manoj. 'With Gupkar alliance and out of it: how Congress pushed to wall', *The Indian Express*, 18 November 2020, https://bit.ly/33xfyWP. Accessed on 19 January 2022.
3. 'J-K: Sajad Lone's People's Conference pulls out of Gupkar alliance', *Business Standard*, 20 January 2021, https://bit.ly/3tFVcFq. Accessed on 19 January 2022.
4. Iqbal, Naveed, and Arun Sharma. 'Five ex-ministers in J&K district polls: "Can't wait indefinitely"', *The Indian Express*, 3 December 2020, https://bit.ly/33LueRV. Accessed on 19 January 2022.
5. Chowdhary, Rekha. 'Turnout, Dominance, Region, Religion: The Big Takeaways of the J&K DDC Polls', *The Wire*, 29 December 2020, https://bit.ly/3tG9PZh. Accessed on 19 January 2022.
6. Ibid. Accessed on 19 January 2022.
7. 'J-K DDC polls: PAGD bags 112 seats, BJP single-largest with 75 seats', *The*

Times of India, 23 December 2020, https://bit.ly/3KmIYaP. Accessed on 19 January 2022.

8. Iqbal, Naveed, and Arun Sharma. 'Five ex-ministers in J&K district polls: "Can't wait indefinitely"', *The Indian Express*, 3 December 2020, https://bit.ly/33LueRV. Accessed on 19 January 2022.
9. Hussain, Ashiq. 'J-K administration interfering to change DDC results: Omar Abdullah', *Hindustan Times*, 26 December 2020, https://bit.ly/3rPj47h. Accessed on 19 January 2022.
10. Personal communication of the author with a journalist who wishes to remain anonymous.
11. 'Apni Party chief Altaf Bukhari demands restoration of J-K's statehood, elections', *Hindustan Times*, 8 March 2021, https://bit.ly/3AuzzJB. Accessed on 24 Janurary 2021.
12. 'Altaf Bukhari Launches New Political Party in J&K, Calls It "Apni Party"', *HW News*, 9 March 2020, https://bit.ly/3FJKb8x. Accessed on 19 January 2022.
13. 'J&K DDC poll result: PAGD wins 110 seats, BJP 75; counting deferred in 2 seats as candidates belong to PoK', Times Now News, 23 December 2020, https://bit.ly/3AfixPq. Accessed on 19 January 2022.
14. 'PM Modi assured there will be no demographic change in J&K: Altaf Bukhari', *The New Indian Express,* 14 March 2020, https://www.newindianexpress.com/nation/2020/mar/14/pm-modi-has-assured-us-there-will-be-no-demographic-change-in-j-k-altaf-bukhari-2116787.html. Accessed on 3 March 2022.
15. 'Delegation from Apni Party meets Amit Shah, discuss fears of demographic changes in J&K', *The Print*, 15 March 2020, https://bit.ly/3ibJn2X. Accessed on 3 March 2022.
16. 'Omar alleges NC candidate forced to join Apni Party, claims to have phone recording', *Hindustan Times*, 26 December 2020, https://bit.ly/3nJklLA. Accessed on 19 January 2022.
17. Mir, Shakir. 'J&K: "Laundry Politics" Sees Politicians Rush to Join "Safer" Platforms', *The Wire*, 31 March 2021, https://bit.ly/35bM5lX. Accessed on 19 January 2022.
18. Personal communication of the author with Bashir Manzar in March 2021.
19. Personal communication of the author with Haseeb Dabru in March 2021.
20. 'Roshni scheme one of "biggest land scams" in J&K history, says BJP', *Business Standard*, 13 October 2020, https://bit.ly/350CuOt. Accessed on 19 January 2022.
21. Masood, Bashaarat. 'Jammu and Kashmir Roshni Act: Who it helped own land, and why it has been scrapped', *The Indian Express*, 9 December 2020,

https://bit.ly/3rBM7ea. Accessed on 19 January 2022.

22. Dutta, Prabhash K. 'Why land grab scheme of J&K is called Roshni Act and how it happened', *India Today*, 25 November 2020, https://bit.ly/33x4jhi. Accessed on 21 January 2022.
23. Tweet by Mehbooba Mufti, 27 November 2020, https://bit.ly/3IsZmoa. Accessed on 21 January 2022.
24. Zargar, Safwat. 'What exactly is the 'land scam' in which Kashmiri parties are implicated?', *Scroll.in*, 4 December 2020, https://bit.ly/3AfDwBO. Accessed on 19 January 2022.
25. 'All Roshni scamsters to be booked: Jitendra Singh', *Mint*, 14 December 2020, https://bit.ly/3KkEIIK. Accessed on 19 January 2022.
26. Tiwary, Deeptiman. 'Explained: What is the JKCA case in which ED has questioned Farooq Abdullah?', *The Indian Express*, 22 October 2020, https://bit.ly/356U7wi. Accessed on 19 January 2022.
27. 'PDP cries of "political vendetta" after ED summons Mehbooba Mufti's mother in money laundering case', Times Now News, 9 April 2021, https://bit.ly/33A7C7d. Accessed on 20 January 2022.
28. 'Statehood restoration imperative for holistic development: Altaf Bukhari', *Greater Kashmir*, 9 April 2021, https://bit.ly/3Il6HGx. Accessed on 20 January 2022.
29. Hussain, Yawar. '"The two families would grab power if statehood is restored"', *Kashmir Life*, 22 March 2021, https://bit.ly/33s5hLK. Accessed on 20 January 2022.
30. 'Statehood will be given to J&K at an appropriate time: Amit Shah in Lok Sabha', *The Indian Express*, 13 February 2021, https://bit.ly/3nLhfa5.
31. Personal communication of the author with Nazeer in March 2021.
32. Irfan, Hakeem. 'RSS backed Muslim Rashtriya Manch on misson to change mindset of Kashmiri youth', *The Economic Times*, 1 November 2015, https://bit.ly/3Ijw9Mp. Accessed on 20 January 2022.
33. '*RSS Neta Indresh Kumar ka ye hai "Mission Kashmir"*', News18 Hindi, 19 June 2019, https://bit.ly/358N5Hp. Accessed on 20 January 2022.
34. Noorani, A.G. 'In pursuit of trifurcation', *Frontline*, 14 April 2001, https://bit.ly/3IifaKw. Accessed on 20 January 2022.
35. 'RSS reiterates trifurcation of Jammu and Kashmir', Zee News, 17 September 2002, https://bit.ly/3IijWaY. Accessed on 20 January 2022.
36. 'Advani's remarks on J&K trifurcation his own: Kishore', *The Times of India*, 8 July 2002, https://bit.ly/3qJUtRP. Accessed on 20 January 2022.
37. 'No trifurcation of J&K: Advani', *The Times of India*, 3 July 2002, https://bit.ly/3KtMgcc. Accessed on 20 January 2022.

Chapter 12: Kashmiri Pandits: Hope or Illusion of Hope?

1. Pandey, Ashok Kumar. *Kashmirnama*, Rajpal & Sons, New Delhi, 2016.
2. Ibid.
3. Ashiq, Peerzada. 'Jagmohan — political class of Kashmir disliked him but he earned people's goodwill', *The Hindu*, 4 May 2021, https://bit.ly/3IifCsc. Accessed on 20 January 2022.
4. Jagmohan, *My Frozen Turbulence in Kashmir*, Allied, New Delhi, 2017.

Chapter 13: The New Governance

1. 'Governor In J&K "Usually Drinks Wine, Plays Golf": Satya Pal Malik', NDTV, 17 March 2020, https://bit.ly/3tK23Oe. Accessed on 20 January 2022.
2. 'J&K Delimitation Based on just 2011 will be blunder in restoring Democracy', *Indica News*, 17 October 2020, https://bit.ly/32etFzB. Accessed on 20 January 2022.
3. Ahmad, Mudasir, 'J&K: IAS Officer Becomes First Bureaucrat to Be Granted Domicile Rights', *The Wire*, 26 June 2020, https://bit.ly/3u01bDI. Accessed on 3 March 2022.
4. Iqbal, Naveed. 'Explained: What land laws have changed in J&K? How have parties responded?', *The Indian Express*, 18 November 2020, https://bit.ly/33N4RPI. Accessed on 20 January 2022.
5. Rashid, Hakeem Irfan. 'Insult heaped on injury, says Omar Abdullah on new domicile law', *The Economic Times*, 2 April 2020, https://bit.ly/3FJP29G. Accessed on 20 January 2022.
6. 'J&K parties slam Centre's new domicile rules', *The Times of India*, 1 April 2020, https://bit.ly/3nHe2s3. Accessed on 20 January 2022.
7. Ehsan, Mir. 'J&K parties call new domicile rights "insult", seek suspension of "casual" order', *Hindustan Times*, 1 April 2020, https://bit.ly/3Kvkb4f. Accessed on 20 January 2022.
8. Ahmad, Mudasir. 'J&K: Hurriyat Conference Opposes New Land Law, Calls for One-Day Shutdown', *The Wire*, 29 October 2020, https://bit.ly/3nH0yg6. Accessed on 20 January 2022.
9. Masood, Bashaarat. 'Citing security, J&K sets up force to act against govt staff without probe', *The Indian Express*, 23 April 2021, https://bit.ly/33s7hUg. Accessed on 20 January 2022.
10. 'Covid-19: Jammu & Kashmir defers Darbar Move, first time in 144 years', *The Times of India*, 16 April 2021, https://bit.ly/3AeWetn. Accessed on 20 January 2022.

11. Sharma, Arun. 'Durbar Move: When J&K moves from one capital to another', *The Indian Express*, 9 April 2021, https://bit.ly/3581jZ2. Accessed on 20 January 2022.
12. 'Covid-19: Jammu & Kashmir defers Darbar Move, first time in 144 years', *The Times of India*, 16 April 2021, https://bit.ly/3rD8uA9. Accessed on 20 January 2022.

Chapter 14: Guns Don't Just Kill

1. '3 held for attack on restaurant owner's son in Srinagar', *The Tribune*, 19 February 2021, https://bit.ly/3AdQksB. Accessed on 20 January 2022.
2. Masood, Bashaarat. 'In Srinagar, jeweller killed weeks after domicile nod, militants warn of more attacks', *The Indian Express*, 2 January 2021, https://bit.ly/350NFXv. Accessed on 20 January 2022.
3. 'Slain Jeweller's Son Delinks Killing With Domicile Certificate', *Kashmir Observer*, 2 January 2021, https://bit.ly/3tIMwy0. Accessed on 20 January 2022.
4. 'The Making of a Terrorist', *India Today*, 20 November 1999, https://bit.ly/3FL0q52. Accessed on 20 January 2022.
5. Shah, Khalid. 'Ideological shift, public support and social media: The "New" in Kashmir's "New Militancy"', *ORF Occasional Paper*, 10 January 2020, https://bit.ly/34TcRz4. Accessed on 20 January 2022.
6. Bachloo, Ajay. '*Jammu-Kashmir me teen alag alag morchon par hai chunauti, dhara 370-ka hatna saabit hua gamechanger—Sena*', ABP News, 15 January 2021, https://bit.ly/3ImqBRk. Accessed on 20 January 2022.
7. 'Masked men carrying ISIS flags mark post Eid prayers on Jammu and Kashmir streets', *The New Indian Express*, 5 June 2019, https://bit.ly/3Aou9A0. Accessed on 20 January 2022.
8. 'Islamic State does not represent Islam, says Geelani', *The Hindu*, 7 January 2016, https://bit.ly/3Ae73vQ. Accessed on 20 January 2022.
9. Siyech, Mohammed Sinan. 'Why Has the Islamic State Failed to Grow in Kashmir?', *Counter Terrorist Trends and Analyses*, Vol. 10, No. 5, May 2018, 11–15, https://bit.ly/32gBchn. Accessed on 20 January 2022.
10. Azaan, Javaid. 'Zakir Musa's al Qaeda-inspired militant group "wiped out" from Kashmir', *The Print*, 23 October 2019, https://bit.ly/3qJrrBH. Accessed on 20 January 2022.
11. Javaid, Azaan. '7 militants, including chief of Al Qaeda-inspired AGH killed, Amarnath Yatra was target', *The Print*, 9 April 2021, https://bit.ly/3nDDRsP. Accessed on 20 January 2022.

12. '10,752 ceasefire violations by Pak in 3 years: Govt in Lok Sabha', *Greater Kashmir*, 3 February 2021, https://bit.ly/3AdXQUa. Accessed on 20 January 2022.
13. '150-m crossborder tunnel detected by BSF along IB in J&K', *The Times of India*, 13 January 2021, https://bit.ly/3fHPTNy. Accessed on 20 January 2022.
14. '"Time to bury the past and move forward", says Pak's General Bajwa on ties with India', *Hindustan Times*, 18 March 2021, https://bit.ly/3nGJwPb. Accessed on 20 January 2022.
15. Laskar, Rezaul H. 'Imran Khan responds to PM Modi, seeks "enabling environment" for dialogue', *Hindustan Times*, 30 March 2021, https://bit.ly/3FJSh0Q. Accessed on 20 January 2022.
16. 'A troubled Pakistan changing track to pursue peace with India', *Financial Express*, 26 March 2021, https://bit.ly/3fCLH1I. Accessed on 20 January 2022.

Chapter 15: Paradise and its Patrons

1. Hamid, Peerzada Harshad. 'Behind the names of houseboats', *Kashmir Newz*, 7 March 2006, https://bit.ly/3qKtFkz. Accessed on 20 January 2022.
2. 'Governor Manoj Sinha, actor Aamir Khan launch J&K Film Policy', *The New Indian Express*, 6 August 2021, https://bit.ly/33s1IVP. Accessed on 20 January 2022.
3. 'PM Narendra Modi inaugurates Khelo India Winter Games, says it will make J&K winter sports hub', *The Times of India*, 26 February 2021, https://bit.ly/3FEeFJ2. Accessed on 20 January 2022.
4. Ibid.

Chapter 16: The Apple: Not Just a fruit

1. Chadha, Sanjeev Kumar. 'Apple Economy In Jammu & Kashmir: Changing Paradigm', MENAFN, 22 March 2021, https://bit.ly/3GSj8cI. Accessed on 20 January 2022.
2. 'Another truck driver shot dead by militants in south Kashmir', *Daily Pioneer*, 29 October 2019, https://bit.ly/3AdSWqp. Accessed on 20 January 2022; 'Kashmir: Militants Kill Two Truck Drivers, Third Incident in 10 Days', *The Wire*, 29 October 2019, https://bit.ly/3rykumr. Accessed on 20 January 2022.
3. Bukhari, Fayaz. 'Suspected militants kill two in Indian Kashmir, set apple trucks ablaze', Reuters, 24 October 2019, https://reut.rs/33QRG0j. Accessed on 20 January 2022.

4. Bhat, Suhail. 'Amid Covid hit world markets and govt apathy, Kashmiri artisans struggle to make ends meet', *NewsClick*, 17 September 2020, https://bit.ly/3KCQ4Iq. Accessed on 20 January 2022.
5. Basharat, Peer. *Curfewed Night*, Penguin Random House India, New Delhi, 2019.
6. Bazaz, Junaid Nabi. 'Fall in exports, rise in unemployment: GoI figures reveal dismal picture of J&K economy', *Kashmir Reader*, 29 March 2021, https://bit.ly/3KtZypi. Accessed on 20 January 2022.
7. Ibid. Accessed on 20 January 2022.
8. 'J&K LG announces Rs 1,350 cr economic package: 50% discount in electricity, water bills', *The Indian Express*, 19 September 2020, https://bit.ly/3GK7KPV. Accessed on 20 January 2022.
9. 'Centre Unveils Over Rs 1Lakh Crore Budget Of J&K For 2021-22', *Kashmir Observer*, 17 March 2021, https://bit.ly/3GNkBAG. Accessed on 20 January 2022.
10. 'Highest-ever budget for J-K aims to build economy, create jobs: Manoj Sinha', *Business Standard*, 26 March 2021, https://bit.ly/3o3qByf. Accessed on 20 January 2022.
11. Ibid. Accessed on 20 January 2022.
12. Government Order No. 117–IND of 2021, 19 April 2021, https://bit.ly/33s2Tod. Accessed on 20 January 2022.
13. Tiwary, Deeptiman. 'J&K industrial policy bears fruit, investments worth Rs 23,000 cr final', *The Indian Express*, 7 August 2021, https://bit.ly/3586OHa. Accessed on 20 January 2022.

Epilogue: Kashmir in a Time Machine

1. 'We will build a "new" Kashmir for everyone, says PM Modi to Kashmiri Pandits in Houston', *The Hindu*, 22 September 2019, https://bit.ly/3qIOzQK. Accessed on 20 January 2022.
2. Faesal, Shah. 'Kashmir – A Preferable Future', Chanakya Forum, 26 March 2021, https://bit.ly/3tQDwa6. Accessed on 20 January 2022.
3. 'PM Modi meets Jammu and Kashmir leaders', *The Hindu*, 24 June 2021, https://bit.ly/3AhXITR. Accessed on 20 January 2022.
4. Tweet by PM Narendra Modi, 24 June 2021, https://bit.ly/3FIasEb. Accessed on 20 January 2022.
5. '"Why delimitation only in J&K": Who said what at all-party meeting', *The Times of India*, 24 June 2021, https://bit.ly/3fHRRxC. Accessed on 20 January 2022.

BIBLIOGRAPHY

Alexander, P.C. (1995). *Perils of Democracy*. Bombay: Somaiya Publications.

Andersen, W. & Damle, S. (2018). *The RSS: A View to the Inside*. Gurugram: Penguin Random House India.

Bukhari, Shujaat. (2020). *The Dirty War in Kashmir: Frontline Reports*. New Delhi: Leftword Books.

Chidambaram, P. (2019). *Undaunted: Saving the Idea of India*. New Delhi: Rupa Publications.

Commuri, Gitika. (2010). *Indian Identities Narratives and the Politics of Security*. New Delhi: SAGE India.

Dixit, Jitendra. (2020). *35 Days: How Politics in Maharashtra Changed Forever in 2019*. Gurugram: HarperCollins Publishers India.

Geelani, Gowhar. (2019). *Kashmir Rage and Reason*. New Delhi: Rupa Publications.

Jagmohan. (2017). *My Frozen Turbulence in Kashmir*. New Delhi: Allied Publishers Private Limited.

Kumar, Radha. (2018). *Paradise at War: A Political History of Kashmir*. New Delhi: Aleph Book Company.

Noorani, A.G. (2017). *The Kashmir dispute, 1947-2012*. New Delhi: Tulika Books.

Ojha, Ritukant. (2019). *Real Conversations*. podcast WILYD.

Pandey, Ashok Kumar. (2019). *Kaśmīranāmā: itihāsa aura samakāla*. Delhi: Rajpal & Sons.

Pandita, Rahul. (2013). *Our Moon has Blood Clots: A Memoir of a Lost Home in Kashmir*. Gurugram: Penguin Random House India.

Peer, Basharat. (2019). *Curfewed Night*. Gurugram: Penguin Random House India.

Quraishi, Humra. (2019). *Kashmir: The Unending Tragedy*. Amaryllis.

Raza, Moosa. (2019). *Kashmir: Land of Regrets*. Chennai: Context, an imprint of Westland Publications Private Limited.

Sardesai, Rajdeep. (2019). *2019: How Modi Won India*. Gurugram: HarperCollins Publishers India.

Singh, Sukhdev Sohal, and Mehra, Anjali. (2016). *Life On Indo-Pak Border: A Paradox of Security and Development*. New Delhi: Serial Publications.

Zia, A., and Bhat, J. (2019). *A Desolation Called Peace: Voices from Kashmir*. Gurugram: HarperCollins Publishers India

INDEX